MINORITIES IN THE NEW WORLD

Charles Wagley and
Marvin Harris

MINORITIES IN
THE NEW WORLD

Six Case Studies

Columbia University Press 1958
New York

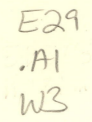

Contents

Acknowledgments

IN a book such as this one which ranges over a rather vast amount of factual data about a variety of minority groups in diverse national settings, we felt that it was important to call for assistance and criticism from those who have had firsthand experience among the groups studied. For the Indians of Brazil, this assistance was provided by Darcy Ribeiro, whose report to UNESCO is mentioned in the preface. In addition, both authors know the Brazilian scene well, and one of us has studied Brazilian Indians for many years. For the Indians of Mexico, although one author has for many years been a student of Middle American ethnology, first-hand experience was furnished admirably by Alfonso Caso and his colleagues in their report to UNESCO mentioned in the preface. We also wish to thank Miss Anne Chapman, who from her field research in Mexico was able to assist us in the preparation of the chapter on the Mexican Indians. For Martinique and Guadeloupe we wish to acknowledge the generous help of Merriam Kreiselman and Guy Dubreuil, both of whom have carried out original research in Martinique. Furthermore, we used the report prepared for UNESCO by Michel Leiris, derived from his first-hand research in the French West Indies. We particularly wish to thank Guy Dubreuil, who as a graduate student wrote a research paper which served as the basis for much of the text on the French West Indies appearing as The Negro in Martinique. The data on the Negro in the United States comes from Harry Walker's report to UNESCO and from documentary sources; several of our friends who are Negroes have read and discussed this chapter with us. For personal experience with the French Canadians we are again indebted to Guy Dubreuil who, himself a French Canadian, prepared for us a research paper for this chapter. He has further offered criticism of our version, with which he does not always agree, of the French Canadian scene. The chapter on the Jews in the United States has been read and criticized by our colleagues Josef Ben-David, Vera Rubin, and Morris Siegel. Several of the chapters have been read for criticism by Donald Young and E. K. Francis, who are specialists on minority groups in general. None of the people mentioned above are, of course, responsible for our interpretations, for often we preferred our own point of view to theirs.

In addition, we should like to acknowledge our indebtedness to the following people and organizations: to Monica Basch and Merriam Kreiselman for editorial assistance; to the graduate students in Anthropology s132 during the summer of 1956, who listened to an early attempt to analyze minority groups from an anthropological viewpoint; to the Department of Social Sciences of UNESCO and particularly to Dr. Alfred Métraux of the staff, who provided us with the opportunity and the stimulation to undertake this book; to Henry Wiggins and William Bridgwater of Columbia University Press, who encouraged us not only to make our report to UNESCO into a book but suggested some basic changes in the organization of the text; and to the Center for Advanced Study in the Behavioral Sciences for providing one of us with the time and conditions to complete the manuscript.

1957   Charles Wagley and Marvin Harris

Preface

THE problems of ethnic and other minority groups and the methods of alleviating their plight have been a central concern of UNESCO programs since the inception of this international organization. Related directly or indirectly to this subject are the UNESCO studies on international tensions, such as that carried out by Otto Klineberg, Robin Williams' study of the reduction of intergroup tensions, Gardner Murphy's inquiry into intergroup tensions in India, the studies of race relations in Brazil (Charles Wagley, Thales Azevedo, L. A. Costa Pinto, Florestan Fernandes and Roger Bastide), and two series of informative booklets, "The Race Question and Modern Science" and "The Race Question and Modern Thought." In 1952, as a continuation of this long-term plan, it was decided "to undertake, in collaboration with Member States, a critical inventory of the methods and techniques employed for facilitating the social integration of groups which do not participate fully in the life of the national community by reason of their ethnical or cultural characteristics or their recent arrival in the country" (Resolution 3/22, UNESCO General Conference, 1951).

As part of this new program, inquiries were made in six countries by outstanding scholars, individually or in groups. In these countries, various types of minority groups could be studied in their distinctive social settings, and it was hoped that, through a comparison, the various factors which have contributed to the improvement of the economic, social, educational, legal and political position of these groups might be assessed. Dr. Darcy Ribeiro, then Director of the Division of Research of the Brazilian Indian Service, was invited to carry out a historical and sociological study of the pacification and assimilation of the indigenous populations of Brazil. Michel Leiris prepared a sociological and historical study of the process of integration of the people of non-European origin into the life of the French West Indies. Dr. Gabriele Wulker, under the auspices of the UNESCO Institute for Social Sciences at Cologne, prepared a report on "Social Integration of Foreign Ethnic Groups in the German Federal Republic." A group of scholars under the direction of Dr. Alfonso Caso and under the auspices of the Instituto Nacional Indígenista cooperated on the subject of the assimilation of the Indian into Mexican society; Professor Harry J. Walker of Howard University wrote a report on recent changes in the economic, political, and educational status of the Negro in the United States. Professor Milos Radojkovic of the Faculty of Law of the University of Belgrade prepared a study on the integration of minorities in Yugoslavia. In addition, Professor Morroe Berger of Princeton University was asked by the American Jewish Committee to conduct a survey on the use of law as a means of reducing discrimination in employment, and his report was submitted as a portion of this same program.

These reports immeasurably extend our knowledge of the actual situations of minority groups in the countries selected. They provide detailed studies of the historical conditions which have affected minority groups in contrasting settings, of the varying policies and methods followed by different peoples in attempting to solve their minority problems, and of the contemporary situation of several types of minority groups. At least three of these reports have by now been published (Caso, 1954; Leiris, 1955; Berger, 1955), and it is hoped that all of them will ultimately be available to the public. Whatever their individual value, these reports as separate documents do not achieve the aim of the original UNESCO plan. Only through a comparison of the differing historical situations, the methods and techniques for dealing with minority problems, and the various results achieved can the problems of minorities be evaluated from a truly international and intercultural point of view. The Department of Social Sciences of UNESCO therefore invited the present authors to prepare a report based mainly upon the studies mentioned above. We had hoped not only to make some of the information contained in the original studies (consisting of thousands of pages) available to a larger public, but also to make at least a beginning toward applying the comparative approach of social anthropology to minority problems.

Early in the preparation of this book it was decided to use what might be called a "case study" method—that is, to make a comparative analysis of a series of specific minority groups in terms of their historical background, their degree of assimilation or integration into the society of which they form a part, the traits that differentiate them as minorities, and other aspects of the minority-majority relationship. By this means we hoped to arrive at some generalizations which might be tested more widely under different conditions.

We soon decided to limit our case studies to minority groups in the Americas. Four of the minority groups reported on for UNESCO concern the New World: the Indian in Brazil, the Indian of Mexico, the Negro in the French West Indies and the Negro in the United States. The common historical experience of the Americas provided us with a frame of reference. We have not, therefore, included among our case studies the minority groups of Germany and Yugoslavia as first envisaged by UNESCO. Instead, we felt the necessity of adding other case studies of minority groups in the New World to those made available to us by UNESCO. We have thus prepared summary accounts of the minority-group situation of the French Canadians and of the Jews in the United States. These case studies were added for two reasons: first, because we feel that our range of minority groups would be incomplete unless it included minorities of European extraction along with those of American Indian and African origin; secondly, because we believe that minorities in various stages of integration or assimilation should also be represented among our case studies.

The data included in the chapters on the French Canadians and on the Jews in the United States is derived from the work of well-known students of these particular minority groups, and thus the original sources of information on them are in every way as authoritative as the UNESCO reports mentioned above. In those chapters bearing on the countries for which UNESCO reports have been available to us (Brazil, the French West Indies, Mexico, and the United States) we have made full use of the materials prepared for UNESCO. We have not, however, limited ourselves to these reports but have often made use of other published information, and our point of view may even be at variance with those of the writers of the individual reports. It should, of course, be understood that neither UNESCO nor the authors of the reports have any responsibility for the opinions or conclusions expressed in this book.

The relation of the studies included in this book to the realization of the Universal Declaration of Human Rights and to the work of the Commission on Human Rights of the Economic and Social Council of the United Nations should be patent. The discussions of the Sub-Commission on Prevention of Discrimination and Protection of Minorities during the Sixth Session in 1953, and the reports prepared for these deliberations provide exceedingly rich materials and many seminal suggestions for the study of minority-group problems on a comparative basis. As will be seen, our definition of a "minority group" generally implies that the group does not enjoy one or more of the Universal Human Rights. Yet it must be urged that our approach to the problem is not political but, as far as is humanly possible, scientific and objective.

Something, perhaps, should be said about the various ways in which minorities have been studied and analyzed. First, the very term "minority group" came to us from Europe. All of us are aware that almost every European state contains such alien groups and that some countries, particularly those which were formed by the Treaty of Versailles after the First World War, are composed of a regrouping of minorities. National, cultural, and linguistic minorities have been very much a part of the European political scene and it is only natural, therefore, that in Europe studies and analyses of such groups have tended to be legal and political. Their aim has often been to provide legal protection for minorities, or to establish the right of a particular minority to form an independent state. On the other hand, in the United States until very recently, students of minority groups gave very little attention to the legal aspects of the problem. At least theoretically, the Constitution of the United States guaranteed equal protection before the law to all citizens regardless of race, language, or religion. But despite the United States Constitution there is considerable legal discrimination against many minority groups, and there are also discriminatory practices deriving from the economic and social institutions of American society. This reality focused the attention of American students on the dynamics of American society rather than on the legal and political aspects of minority problems.[1]

Two of the oldest minority groups in the United States, the Negroes and the Indians, differ racially from the dominant Caucasoid Europeans and the problems of these two groups, particularly of the Negro, have loomed large. Thus the study of "race relations" has become almost synonymous with the study of "minority-majority relations" in the United States. Furthermore, most of the minority groups in the United States were relatively recent European immigrants who arrived late in the nineteenth century and early in this century. Each successive wave of immigrants entered American society at the bottom of the social hierarchy as a minority group suffering from economic, social, and often legal discrimination. It was

---

[1] The situation has now changed considerably. Witness, for example, the frontal attack on the legal aspect by the National Association for the Advancement of Colored People.

to be expected, then, that the attention of students of minority problems would also be attracted to these "ethnic groups." [2] Most American studies of the immigrant ethnic groups have emphasized the
process of adaptation and assimilation to the new social and cultural
environment. With some exaggeration, one might almost say that
European scholars began with the assumption that minority groups
wish to preserve their differences while American scholars began
with the concept that everyone desires at least to adapt himself to
the dominant culture if not ultimately to be assimilated by it.

In recent years, social scientists of various disciplines have turned
to the study of minority or ethnic groups and the literature on the
subject has become massive. Scarcely a week goes by in which a new
book is not published on some aspect of the subject. It is obvious
that the problems of minorities are a subject to which each of the
social sciences may contribute. Prejudice, discrimination, and hatred
toward a group of people may be studied in terms of its individual
manifestations by psychologists. They may ask, for example: "Is there
a prejudiced personality type?" Likewise, the phenomenon may be
studied in its economic aspects: "What is the effect of prejudice and
discrimination on the livelihood of the minority group?" or "What is
the cost of prejudice and discrimination to the society as a whole?"
Likewise, the group manifestations of minorities may be examined
by sociologists: "What are the formal and informal institutions that a
society maintains between such groups, and how do they function?"
Each discipline approaches the same phenomenon in a different way.

What, then, is the approach and potential contribution of our
own discipline, which is cultural and social anthropology? Traditionally, anthropologists have contributed in two ways to the
study of ethnic or minority groups. First, anthropologists such as

[2] The term "ethnic group," used in the almost identical sense of "minority
group" in Europe, came to prevail among many American scholars. It is interesting to note that the article on "National Minorities" in the *Encyclopedia
of Social Sciences,* written by Max Hildbert Boehm, stresses the political and
legal aspects of the problem on the European scene. The article on "Ethnic
Communities," by Caroline Ware, stresses the economic and social aspects
of the problem. Their definitions of "national minorities" and "ethnic communities" differ hardly at all.

the late Franz Boas and many others have attempted to clarify and correct our views regarding human races. They have shown that the scientific facts about human racial groups contradict the commonly held ideas of inherent inferiority or superiority of any racial group. They have shown us that racial appearance is a genetically transmitted set of biological characteristics unlike one's language, nationality, religion, and other aspects of culture which are acquired by the learning process. This question hardly seems to need further elaboration in the present study. Neither of us are physical anthropologists and the biological study of physical differences is not within our field of competence. Innumerable articles and pamphlets on the subject are available, including the excellent series published by UNESCO (Dunn, 1951; Leiris, 1951). It is enough for the present study to say that to date the anthropological and genetic evidence indicates that all men are members of the same species (*homo sapiens*), and that each "variety" or "race" seems to have approximately equivalent inherent capacities. What interests us more is that most people continue to think differently and that they attribute inferior or superior capacities to physical appearance, language, nationality, and custom. This is a social fact perhaps more "true" than all that the physical anthropologists tell us, for its consequences often determine human destiny. In this study, when we deal with "race" we will be concerned with "social race," with the way members of a society classify each other by physical characteristics and not with biological concepts of race.

Secondly, cultural and social anthropologists have contributed to the study of minority groups through their studies of what is called "acculturation"—the exchange of cultural attitudes and traits between two groups which are in continuous face-to-face contact. For example, anthropologists have shown us how Navajo culture is modified under the impact of steady contact with the western European variety of United States culture. Acculturation is but one process, however, in the dynamics of minority and majority relations, and we do not intend to make it the main focus of our study. As we shall see, acculturation toward the culture of the dominant group does not always mean that the relations between the groups will be peaceful or even that assimilation will progress any faster.

In this book, we shall be primarily interested in the comparative, historical, and functional aspects of minority-majority relations. As anthropologists we tend to regard social events as influenced by their historical antecedents as well as by conditions and social forces associated with the present. Our approach to minorities thus tends to be both synchronic and diachronic. In addition, we are led by the traditions of our discipline to search for elements of similarity in apparently disparate situations, and to seek enlightenment at all stages of an analysis through comparison with other times and places. We shall have more to say about the distinctive contribution of anthropology to the study of minorities at a later point. But we should perhaps first set down some of the shortcomings of our approach.

We cannot explain the psychological nature of prejudice, the legal and political process for peaceful adjustment between groups, or any of the other facets of the phenomenon which others are better equipped to study. And, quite frankly, the social anthropologist would feel more at home approaching the study of minority groups on the local level—within the context of a small community. The traditional research methods and concepts of social anthropology were developed in work with simple primitive tribes and with relatively small communities. It is with some humility and reluctance that we apply ourselves to a subject which hardly lends itself to the traditional methods of anthropological inquiry because it involves masses of people spread out over large areas. However, we do believe that the social anthropologist brings certain advantages to this subject. Our discipline is essentially a historical science and it is above all comparative. It is natural for us to see the situation of each minority group as the result of its peculiar history in a particular setting, and to attempt to view it in terms of numerous other similar situations which have occurred in space during the long history of the development of human society. If there is any originality in this book, it derives, we believe, from the comparative point of view of our own discipline.

New York, 1957

Introduction

THE MINORITIES IN THE AMERICAS

THIS book is about a fundamental problem experienced by all the states of the world, a problem which is here examined in the perspective of the countries of the western hemisphere. Our study concerns the numerous underprivileged groups of people, ineptly called minorities, who taken together constitute a major segment of the population of the Americas. On one basis or another, these groups are singled out by the societies in which they reside and in varying degrees and proportions are subjected to economic exploitation, segregation, and discrimination. These are the people who are disliked and ridiculed because they speak a different tongue, practice a different religion; or because their skin is a different color, their hair a different texture; or simply because their ancestors emigrated from a different country.

Minority groups are especially numerous in the New World. Infinitely variegated in peoples, languages, creeds, and customs, the societies of our hemisphere are a great laboratory for the study of the origin and destiny of minority groups.

I

The people of the Americas come from many lands and are composed of three racial stocks. Perhaps no other area of the world has such a racially variegated population, and perhaps nowhere else have people of so many different origins come together to form new societies. In the highlands of Central and South America, large masses of American Indians were dominated by Europeans and welded into the population of modern states. Millions of Negro slaves, mainly from West Africa, were transported to the Americas. After a time they were liberated, and have been integrated in varying degrees into the national life of the new American nations. All the western hemisphere was once divided into colonies of European states. These European "mother countries," such as Spain, Portugal, England, France, and Holland, sent numerous people to the Americas from various stations in life—aristocrats, artisans, peasants, and indentured laborers. In the nineteenth century, additional Europeans came from Germany, Sweden, Ireland, Italy, from eastern Europe, and from other parts of that continent. In the nineteenth and twentieth centuries, emigrants came from India, southeast Asia, China, and Japan to both North and South America. Thus, over the past four hundred years our hemisphere has been the scene of the mixing and fusion of diverse peoples and cultures on a scale which is perhaps unprecedented in all of human history.

The settling of so many different people in the lands, villages, cities, and even the same apartment houses, has not been a smooth or peaceful process. Everywhere one group has tried to take advantage of the other; everywhere differences have been exaggerated, ridiculed, and used to justify exploitative economic relationships. As fast as one depressed group has thrown off its social disabilities and taken its place on an equal footing, new groups have arrived and have been subjected to the same treatment. Some groups have suffered depressed status since the period of discovery. All around us today the great pan-American "experiment in assimilation" still goes on.

Among the nations of our hemisphere there are many kinds of groups which do not share equally in the wealth, power, and prestige of the society in which they live. The poverty-stricken lower classes do not share equally in the social and material advantages of the middle and upper classes of their own society. In most lands, rural farmers live by inferior standards of health, diet, housing, and education as compared to city dwellers. Furthermore, these groups are looked down upon, discriminated against, and sometimes ridiculed just because they are poor and uneducated. Women as a group in many western nations are another downtrodden, underprivileged segment of the population. Despite centuries of feminist strivings, women are still widely discriminated against in economic and political spheres of life. There are many other groups which are set off in one way or another from the economically, politically, and socially dominant segments of a modern state. Members of political parties, especially under authoritarian regimes, frequently find themselves in the position of a depressed and persecuted group. Sexual deviants have often been described as the victims of social prejudice and even such groups as small businessmen, intellectuals, and automobile owners are frequently moved to complain about the discriminatory practices which they receive at the hands of others.

Most of the groups we have just mentioned have at one time or another been called minorities. In fact, almost any group of people who suffer some form of special social disability are likely to call themselves, or be called by others, a "minority." For many groups, everyone seems to be in agreement that minority is the appropriate label—the Negroes in the United States, the Japanese in Brazil, the Puerto Ricans in New York, and hundreds of others throughout the world. Yet we also often use "minority" in a vague and ill-defined manner, and there seems to be a considerable amount of confusion as to where to draw the line between minorities and other groups in societies who suffer disabilities for a variety of reasons.

Obviously, one of the first steps in the study of "minority groups" must be to define the term. What is it that the social groups which we commonly call "minorities" share? What distinguishes them from other groups which also are depressed and which share many of their disabilities? Most students of minority groups agree in general on a series of criteria that distinguish minority groups.[1]

First, a minority is a social group whose members are subject to disabilities in the form of prejudice, discrimination, segregation, or persecution (or a combination of these) at the hands of another kind of social group. The group which administers these disabilities is generally called the majority. *Notice that neither term, minority or majority, in this technical sense refers to a numerical minority or majority.* In fact, it is recognized that the "minority group" may actually outnumber the "majority group" of a society. This is the case, for example, in South Africa, where the native African minority is by far superior in numbers to the "majority group." Throughout

---

[1] The following are four frequently cited attempts by sociologists to define minorities:

"A subgroup within a larger group (ordinarily a society), bound together by some special ties of its own, usually race or nationality, but sometimes religion, or other cultural affiliations. Even in the common types of democracy, minority groups are precluded from expressing themselves in proportion to their numerical strength through the operation of the principle of majority rule" (Fairchild, p. 134).

"We may define a minority as a group of people who, because of their physical or cultural features are singled out from others in the society in which they live for differential or unequal treatment, and therefore consider themselves as objects of collective discrimination" (Wirth, "Minority Groups," p. 247).

"The mere fact of being generally hated because of religious, racial, or nationality background is what defines a minority group" (Rose, *America*, p. 3).

"Minorities are subgroups within a culture which are distinguishable from the dominant group by reasons of differences in physiognomy, language, customs, or culture patterns (including any combination of these factors). Such subgroups are regarded as inherently different and 'not belonging' to the dominant groups; for this reason they are consciously or unconsciously excluded from full participation in the life of the culture" (Schermerhorn, p. 5).

The terms "ethnic group" or "ethnic community" are often used by American sociologists and social anthropologists for essentially the same type of depressed social group (on this, see Warner and Srole). In the *Encyclopedia of the Social Sciences,* Caroline F. Ware writes, "Ethnic communities are groups bound together by common ties of race, nationality or culture living together within an alien civilization but remaining culturally distinct" (Vol. III, p. 607). We have chosen to use the term "minority group" because it has wider international currency.

the colonial world, native "minorities" frequently outnumber the ruling "majority." The dominant position of the "majority group" lies in its greater power over the economic, political, and social mechanism of the society; and not always in its superiority in numbers.

Minorities suffer their subordinate position as segments of complex social and cultural units which constitute political entities such as states or empires. This point needs to be stressed in order to distinguish the subordinate-superordinate relations characteristic of minority-majority groups within a political unit, from those which obtain between two independent political units—between a predatory and powerful tribe or state on one hand, and a weak and exploited tribe or state on the other. For example, among the Indian tribes of northeastern United States in pre-Columbian times, the Iroquoian tribes constantly preyed upon the neighboring Algonquian tribes. These Algonquian tribes were depressed social groups and the Iroquois disparaged their culture and moral capacities. But the Algonquian tribes did not form a distinct subordinate unit (with the exception of a few captives among the Iroquois) within Iroquoian society. They did not form, in these terms, a minority group. In fact, as we shall discuss later in greater detail, the relatively recent development in human history of politically organized states, as contrasted with tribal societies organized according to kinship, brought about the appearance of true minority groups in human society.

Second, most students of minority groups and minority problems recognize that the disabilities of minority groups are related to special characteristics which the minority shares and of which the majority (and often even the minority itself) disapproves in some degree. This disapproval ranges from ridicule or mere suspicion to hate. Such special characteristics or traits are most frequently differences from the dominant majority in physical appearance, and in language, religion, or other cultural traits. The fact that a minority is set off from the majority of a society by one of more of these special physical or cultural traits distinguishes minorities from other depressed groups within a society, such as the lower socio-economic classes, and the poorer rural groups.

The lower-class Negro in the United States, for example, shares the poverty, the lack of education, and other disadvantages of the socio-economic lower class of the nation. But in addition, the Negro carries the burden of an added and special characteristic, namely, Negroid physical appearance which is a symbol of past slave status. This added disadvantage makes him a member of a group which is the object of prejudice, discrimination, and segregation in various forms not encountered by lower-class whites. Furthermore, this same special characteristic operates to the disadvantage of the middle- and even upper-class Negroes. It is not poverty, nor lack of education, nor any other generalized low-status trait that prevents the middle-class Negro in large cities from sharing the same type of housing as the white middle class. It is his special disability trait—his physical appearance. Likewise, in Mexico or Guatemala, the rural Indian who speaks a different language, who wears a distinctive costume, and who often follows different customs from the rural Spanish-speaking peasant has added special traits which result in his being treated differently from non-Indian peasants. Thus, minority groups are distinguished from other depressed groups within a society by the presence of special traits which are associated with low status, such as differences in physical appearance, religion, language, and custom.

Third, most students of minority problems agree that minority groups are self-conscious social units. The special traits which add to the disability of members of the group are not simply shared by them; they also form the basis of an *esprit de corps,* an in-group feeling, a sense of belonging to a group distinct from the dominant majority of the society. As the late Louis Wirth so aptly put it:

Aside from these objective characteristics by which they are distinguished from the dominant group and in a large measure as a result of them, minorities tend to develop a set of attitudes, forms of behavior, and other such subjective characteristics which tend further to set them apart. One cannot long discriminate against people without generating in them a sense of isolation and of persecution and without giving them a conception of themselves as more different from others than in fact they are. ("Minority Groups," p. 348)

In addition to whatever special traits they share, their sense of isolation, of common suffering, and of a common burden makes most minorities self-conscious groups apart from all others in their society. It is often this self-consciousness, this awareness of common problems, that keeps a minority group intact. A person who no longer practices the traditional Jewish religion and who is completely acculturated to the dominant culture patterns and language of his society, often continues to identify himself as a Jew. Individuals whose physical features are mainly Caucasoid identify themselves as Negroes in the United States because of their feelings for their group. Yet, as we shall see during the course of this study, the intensity of self-consciousness of what we call minority groups varies greatly. Furthermore, within many of these groups there are marked schisms and factions. But in one sense or another, all minority groups are distinguished by an in-group feeling—a self-consciousness of themselves as a group distinct from others in their own society. Sometimes this feeling may result in a militant minority organization and the identification with those in other nations and in other societies who share the feelings of sameness but who in fact differ in important cultural and physical respects.

There are two further criteria which are seldom mentioned in most definitions but which we believe to be of great importance in distinguishing minorities from other depressed groups in a society. The first of these concerns the way in which membership in a minority is transmitted. A person does not become a member of a minority group voluntarily; he or she is born into it. One belongs to a minority because one's father and mother were members of the group. Often but one parent (father or mother) is sufficient to insure the membership of children in a minority group, and in extreme cases, a single grandparent suffices. Thus, people who belong to minorities, in addition to being set off from other groups on the basis of special physical or cultural characteristics are also considered to be different purely on the basis of a socially invented "rule of descent." By means of this rule of descent we sometimes classify persons whom we have never even seen as belonging to a particular minority if we are told his name or the name of his father, his "ancestry," or his "national origin." This method of minority identification is not used with respect to social groups whose membership procedures are not governed by a rule of descent. Membership in a minority is transmitted in a totally different way from membership in a political party or a bridge club.

The rule of membership by descent is often enforced entirely by the majority, but it is frequently re-enforced by the in-group feeling of the minority itself. In some cases, the minority group may be the primary instrument in enforcing this rule of membership by descent. A person who seeks to escape identification as a member of a minority by changing his name, adopting a new religion, and acquiring new behavioral traits may be criticized and even denounced by the minority for denying his ancestry and the heritage of his people.

Affiliation by means of a rule of descent is an ancient as well as a widely occurring method for reckoning group identity. Every society has made use of descent principles to establish at least one fundamental type of social group—the family. Other descent groups—clans, lineages, and numerous types of compound families—are found in great abundance and variety among preliterate societies. Yet it is important to bear in mind that such descent groups are essentially social fictions rather than biological realities. The classification of groups by the prevailing rule of descent can at best only vaguely approximate a classification based upon the established scientific principles of genetic descent.

Sometimes the rule of descent is the only criterion by which a majority can identify members of a minority group. A complex apparatus for tracing genealogical descent may then be developed. In such instances, the sociological rule of descent is employed to establish subjectively a supposed physical and cultural connection between two generations despite the obvious absence of any real genetic or cultural transmission.

A clear case in point is that of the Jews in Nazi Germany. The majority was often forced to consult genealogical records in order to identify members of the "hated race." It was of no avail that a "Jew" looked like thousands of German non-Jews, had been converted to Christianity, and taken a Christian spouse; he was, according to the Nazis, a "Jew." Likewise, in the United States there are people so

Caucasoid in appearance that they are physically indistinguishable from the white majority but who nonetheless live as Negroes because one of their grandparents was a Negro. There are many instances in the United States of individuals who have "passed" as whites for years, only to have someone discover that there was a Negro among their ancestors. Thus, when distinguishing characteristics such as physical appearance, language, religion, and custom grow less visible, either the majority or the minority or both tend to lean more heavily upon the rule of descent to maintain the identity of the minority.

The second criterion which we should like to add to the usual definitions of minorities is that of endogamy, or the rule of marrying within the group. As in the case of the rule of descent, the rule of endogamy is sometimes enforced by the majority, sometimes by the minority, and frequently by both. If the majority alone is responsible for prohibiting marriage between a minority and a majority member, marriage between one minority and another may be simultaneously permitted. In South Africa, for example, whites may only marry whites, but all other races are permitted to intermarry. It is seldom the majority alone which is responsible for confining the choice of marriage partner exclusively within the minority. All over the world there are minorities which consider it a disgrace for children to choose a mate who does not belong to the minority group. For many American Jews, the marriage of a son or daughter with a non-Jew is considered to be "a fate worse than death." Even the national minorities made up of immigrants from Europe to the United States urged endogamy. Italian mothers were happy only when their American-born sons married a "nice Italian girl," and Greek families in the United States still tend to place obstacles in the way of marriages with non-Greeks.

The rule of endogamy is a device which plays an extremely important role in perpetuating marked differences and inequalities of a cultural or socio-economic nature between social groups. It is employed by many minorities in order to intensify group solidarity and to increase the physical and cultural homogeneity of the group. At the same time it is used by many majorities in order to widen the cultural and physical differences from the minority so that exploitative situations may be perpetuated, and the uplift of underprivileged people may be prevented. In keeping with the great importance of the rule of endogamy, the question of intermarriage frequently provokes the most violent emotional reactions among both minority and majority members, and has been the source of numerous dramatic themes in both fiction and real life.

In résumé, we have mentioned five characteristics by which the distinctive nature of minorities may be defined: (1) minorities are subordinate segments of complex state societies; (2) minorities have special physical or cultural traits which are held in low esteem by the dominant segments of the society; (3) minorities are self-conscious units bound together by the special traits which their members share and by the special disabilities which these bring; (4) membership in a minority is transmitted by a rule of descent which is capable of affiliating succeeding generations even in the absence of readily apparent special cultural or physical traits; (5) minority peoples, by choice or necessity, tend to marry within the group.

As in any abstract model, the above definition conforms only partly to reality. Like the painting of a landscape, it selects only a few features for emphasis and leaves many undescribed. We shall not pretend that our definition is an infallible device for distinguishing minorities from other social groups. Indeed, several conspicuous examples of unresolved borderline cases come immediately to mind. Indian castes, for one, seem to contain all five of the features listed above; yet Indian castes are not usually thought of as minority groups. The Catholics in the United States present another ambiguous example. Attempting to decide whether Catholics in this country are a subordinate group is probably a matter of subjective judgment. Although it is unlikely that a Catholic would be elected President of the country, Catholic mayors, governors, senators, and cabinet members abound and have wielded vast powers. Catholics are found on the very lowest and very highest social levels. With respect to the criterion of self-consciousness, the Catholic Church is a monolithic organization which rejects as heresy the notion of a divided religious community. And yet it is difficult to maintain that Irish Catholics, Italian

Catholics, Negro Catholics, and Puerto Rican Catholics in the United States constitute a self-conscious unit that is more bound together by the fact of sharing the same religion than it is fractionated by vastly different cultural traditions and physical characteristics. As in biology, the ultimate classification of the flora and fauna of the social world may simply depend upon a conventionalized consensus of learned opinion. In the meantime, it seems to us that the best approach to these borderline cases is to classify them as minority-like social groups.

II

One of the central problems in any study of minority groups and of minority-majority relations is their great diversity. Minorities are sometimes more and sometimes less populous than majorities. Some minorities are concentrated in one region of a nation or in a colonial area, whereas others are intercalated with the majority throughout the political unit of which they form a part. Some suffer or have suffered extremes of brutal persecution; others experience only mild discrimination. Some minorities are sharply set off from majorities by culture and physical type; in other cases there are few perceptible differences between the two groups except the persistence of the self-conscious in-group feeling, a survival perhaps from a time when differences were more marked. Some minorities strive desperately to rid themselves of their distinct social identity—in short, they strive to disappear into the majority group of their society. Other minorities seek with equal determination to preserve their identity and their differences, even in the face of pressure from the majority to make them conform to the majority's way of life. Some minorities are aliens in a strange land. Some of them have migrated willingly, hoping to secure better conditions or at least to escape persecution; others have been transported by force from their homelands to new surroundings. Still other minority groups are the native peoples of the area in which they live and the majority group are the "foreigners" who came from abroad to dominate them or who became their rulers by a retracing of national boundaries.

An example of almost every "species" of minority can probably be located among the profusion of types which are found in the New World. There are minorities who display racial, linguistic, national, religious, and cultural characteristics. There are minorities who differ only slightly from the majority in race, language, or religion, and there are those who differ markedly from the majority in these ways. Many New World minorities trace their genesis to the overseas expansion of European states, or to the expansion of New World colonies or states, and before the arrival of the Europeans there were New World minorities resulting from the formation of indigenous empires and confederations. There are numerous cases of minorities arising from both voluntary immigration and forced migration into the New World. And there are minorities who seek assimilation as well as those who desperately strive to avoid it.

In 1953 and 1954, previously unknown primitive tribesmen entered into contact for the first time with white men in the wilderness of central Brazil. In doing so, they have but taken the first step toward the formation of a new minority group in Brazilian society. On the other hand, there are the Irish and the Germans who came to the United States during the nineteenth century and who have for all practical purposes taken their places as integrated members of national society and practically ceased to exist as minorities. There are large Italian minorities in Argentina, Brazil, and in the United States, and in each society they have achieved a different *modus vivendi* with the dominant majority. There are Chinese "minorities" in Peru and in the United States as well as throughout the West Indies. Like the Italians, they offer an excellent opportunity to study a minority of common origin in discrete national settings. There are Javanese and Hindus who were brought to the West Indies as indentured laborers in the nineteenth century and who there found themselves subordinate both to the Negro ex-slaves and the Europeans. And there are minorities formed by groups who migrate within the New World, such as the Puerto Ricans who are pouring into the continental United States, the "wetbacks"—Mexican laborers who each year seek higher wages in the United States—and the Jamaicans who have migrated to Venezuela and Cuba and to the plantations along the Caribbean coast of Mexico, Guatemala, and Honduras. These are but a few of the minority situations which may be studied in the Americas.

Each of the numerous minority groups that have added to the population of the New World has contributed greatly to the American scene. The study of each of them would add tremendously to our knowledge of the modern social life of the Americas and to a comparative study of minority groups. Yet in this book we must obviously limit ourselves to just a few. The six case studies which form the chapters that follow are simply intended to serve as examples of the great variety of situations found in the Americas, and our analysis of them is but an introduction to the comparative approach to a study of minority-majority relations.

However, the groups chosen for case study are not merely haphazard selections. They are representative of several important minority-group situations and types. (1) The three racial stocks—Amerind, Negroid, and Caucasoid—which make up the New World population are represented among our cases. Two of the groups studied are made up of American Indians or people of partial Indian descent; two are formed by Negroes or people who are partially of Negroid ancestry; the other two are physically Caucasoid and derivative of Europe. (2) The minority groups selected as "case studies" are set off from the dominant majority within their respective societies by a variety of special characteristics—by race or physical appearance alone (the Negro in the United States); by race and language (the Negro in Martinique); by language and culture (the Indians in Brazil and in Mexico); by language and religion (the French in Canada), or by religion (the Jew in the United States). (3) The minority groups represented are found in a variety of national settings—in societies whose mother countries were France, England, Portugal, and Spain; in modern dynamic countries such as Brazil, Mexico, and the United States; and in a small island now part of a European state society. (4) Our case studies represent almost the entire orbit of the process of integration into national life. In this sense, they vary from the almost socially independent Indian tribes of Brazil—which have been influenced by Brazilian culture in various degrees but still participate little or not at all in the life of the larger society—to the Jews in the United States and the French in Canada, both of whom have become almost completely integrated into the life of the countries in which they live despite special characteristics which set them off from the rest of the population and which act to prevent their full participation.

Our six case studies provide us with representative "sample situations" of the wide variety of minority groups and minority situations to be found in the Americas. Although each of these minority groups has its own unique history and its discrete contemporary situation in the society of which it is a subgroup, each of them is also representative of broad and general phases in the history of the New World.

These cases do not tell the whole story, to be sure, and the process of change still continues as new minority groups are formed and others disappear, absorbed into national populations. Important population elements, such as the Asiatics who came to the Americas in the nineteenth century, are omitted, as well as numerous small and rather specialized minorities such as the Dukhobors of Canada and the Amish of Ohio. Yet an analysis of these six American minority groups may give us some basis for a comparative view of the differential situation of minorities in the Americas, of the process of formation, and of integration of such groups into their respective societies. While we shall focus upon these specific minority groups in the New World, it is hoped that our conclusions will have some bearing on the problems of minority groups wherever they are found. It is our view that while there are unique features of the minority-majority relations in each society and in each culture, resulting from different historical traditions and institutions, there are similarities and common processes in minority-majority relations in all societies and in all cultures. Perhaps the comparative analysis of a small series of very different situations within the frame of reference of the New World may enable us to arrive at generalizations and hypotheses that may later be tested under different conditions in other parts of the world.

The American Indian

THE first two case studies to be presented are minorities made up of descendants of American Indians, but this does not mean that the two groups have similar backgrounds. When the Europeans arrived in the New World, they found the continent already populated by people of the Mongoloid racial stock whose cultures varied from the simple hunting and gathering tribes of southern South America and the Great Basin of the United States, to the highly complex civilizations of Mexico, Central America, and the Andes. There were perhaps as many as twenty million American Indians in the western hemisphere just before 1500, but the density of population varied markedly from one region to another.[1] In the lowlands of both North and South America, the population density was exceedingly low. There were perhaps no more than a million Indians in the whole area north of Mexico, and only two or three

[1] Rosenblat estimates only 13,385,000. The figures furnished by Cook and Simpson (pp. 38 ff.) for the Mexican plateau would add another four to five million to the total.

million in the entire lowland area of South America (Steward, p. 656). Thus by far the majority of the New World aboriginal population was found in the Andean countries of South America, in Central America, and in Mexico. There, intensive agriculture provided the basis for a population of high density and even for cities as large as those of contemporaneous Europe. There were vast differences in the social structure of the various aboriginal areas: the dense populations of the Andes, Central America, and Mexico were organized into native states, while the lowland tribes of both North and South America were generally without any socio-political unity larger than the individual band or village.

These two factors—population density and socio-political organization—were important in determining the different reactions of American Indians to conquest by Europeans and later the different processes of integration under colonial rule. Everywhere, the first contact between American Indians and Europeans was generally marked by armed violence. The Spanish conquistadors waged war in the highlands of America to subdue such highly civilized groups as the Aztecs of Mexico, the Maya states of Yucatan and highland Guatemala, and the Incas of Andean South America. In Brazil, the Dutch, French, and Portuguese penetrated deep into the interior seeking Indian slaves, laying waste the small Indian villages, and massacring whole groups in the process. In North America, not only did the English and the French make war against Indian tribes, but they used them as warriors in their own inter-European struggles for territory. New diseases such as the common cold, measles, smallpox, and whooping cough were brought to the New World by the Europeans. In both the highlands and the lowlands, as a result of war, enslavement, and disease, there was a rapid population decline among the aboriginal peoples in the years following the arrival of Europeans. By the end of the sixteenth century, for example, the Indians on the Islands of the Caribbean were reduced to a handful, living in isolated groups. The population of the Mexican plateau which may have been as great as eleven million in 1500 was reduced to 4,400,000 in 1565 and to only 2,000,000 by 1700 (Cook and Simpson, pp. 38 ff.), and the Indian population of Peru is thought to have declined 50 percent between 1531 and 1561 (Kubler, pp. 334–38).

There was a difference in outcome, however, between the highland and lowland populations. They reacted differently to the wars of conquest and to the economic exploitation which followed. In the highlands, the Spaniards were able to conquer and dominate whole native states by defeating their armies and by capturing and controlling their rulers. In Peru, in Guatemala, and in Mexico, a handful of European soldiers thus successfully conquered and set out to rule millions of American Indians. In the lowlands, on the other hand, each independent village or band had to be conquered—or destroyed. Even when "treaties of peace" were made with so-called tribes, as in North America, these treaties were seldom understood by the simple lowland Indians whose society lacked political unity. Thus wars broke out again and again, and tribes which had been conquered or with whom peace had been established had to be reconquered. Often these wars ended only with complete extermination of the aboriginal groups. Likewise, differences in social and political organization resulted in different methods of control by Europeans; the settled populations of the native states could be governed and taxed as they had been before, and they could be made to work by such systems as forced labor and encomienda—a feudalistic system by which Indians were granted to the care of a colonist. The dispersed populations of the lowlands, on the other hand, were not so easily governed. They simply faded deeper into the forest or plains as the Europeans advanced. They could be made to work only by outright slavery or by a system of trade, exchanging European articles such as firearms and steel tools for furs and other products of the forest. Thus both the wars of conquest and the later exploitation were more destructive to the lowland tribes than to the highland peoples.

Although new diseases undoubtedly killed off as many people in one region as they did in the other, there was a greater reserve of people in the more densely populated areas. By the middle of the eighteenth century, the aboriginal population of most of the American lowlands had either been exterminated or driven inland into more isolated parts of the colonies. Yet by the same date, the Indian population in the highlands had recovered from the first shocks of conquest. The people who survived had acquired immunity to the Old World diseases, and new tools, new crops, and relative peace under their new rulers made it possible for the population not only to increase rapidly but actually to exceed the number present in the highland countries in 1500. Today at least sixteen million people, most of whom inhabit the highland countries which were densely inhabited before 1500, are classified as "Indians," and if people who are genetically of American Indian ancestry were included this number would be much larger.

The large mass of Indians provided the European colonists in the highlands with a never-failing labor supply. From the sixteenth century to the present, some form of forced labor, ranging from outright slavery to "debt peonage," has been used by the dominant classes of these countries with large Indian populations to provide labor for their agricultural establishments, mines, public works, and even for their households. In all these Indian countries, Spanish culture has dominated politically, socially, and economically, although the Indian cultures have strongly influenced the way of life of the common man. Spanish is everywhere the official language, although even today literally millions of people still speak Indian tongues such as Nahuatl, Maya, Quechua, or Aymara. Catholicism is the official religion, yet in many rural communities aboriginal American Indian religious practices and beliefs persist and have been fused with Catholic dogma and ritual.

Within Indian countries—such as Mexico, Guatemala, Ecuador, Peru, and Bolivia—those people who are still identified as "Indians" have not generally been provided with educational facilities, political rights, or economic opportunity equal to those provided for non-Indians in the same country. In a sense they live outside the nation and receive few of its benefits, though they are subject to national laws and are dependent on the national economic system. But each year large numbers of people lose their identity as Indians and become incorporated into each of these countries as nationals—and each year, in most of these countries, whole communities improve their economic, educational, political, and social situation as Indians.

In several highland countries of Central and South America, the Indians and descendants of Indians form numerically important minority groups. On the other hand, the Indian population of most lowland countries is insignificant in relation to the total population of the nations in which they are found: in the United States, they form only about one third of 1 percent of the total, and in Brazil only .16 percent of its approximately sixty million people. The problems of these small Indian populations differ strikingly from those of countries where Indians and their descendants sometimes actually comprise the majority of the population. Yet the problems of these lowland Indian groups are no less real, and they illustrate another type of minority situation.

Our two case studies involving the process of assimilation of American Indians into modern American nations illustrate two distinct historical processes deriving from the contact of American Indians with Europeans in the Americas. Neither can be said to be entirely typical. Mexico, with its mass of Indians, has perhaps gone farther than any of the other Indian countries in stimulating individual assimilation and providing equal rights for those groups still identified as Indians. Among the countries with a sparse aboriginal population, Brazil has been slow in pacifying its lowland Indian tribes, and the process has been tempered by the idealism of General Candido Rondon and his associates at the Brazilian Indian Service. Each of these cases represents divergent situations and different processes of assimilation.

THE INDIANS IN BRAZIL

The Indians of Brazil never formed a single unified group. Before the coming of the Europeans, they were divided into a myriad of tribal units and they spoke a variety of tribal languages. With the exception of the fact that they shared patterns common to the aborigines of the South American tropical forest, each of the many tribes had its own distinct culture. In fact, the various tribes were often at war with each other and almost every small tribe looked upon all other tribes as "outsiders" toward whom they were suspicious and antagonistic. Many of the remaining Indian tribes of Brazil still do so. There is not, therefore, a single "Indian minority" in Brazil; there is no unity among the various tribes, no pan-Indian self-consciousness of themselves as a group. Instead, when the area of South America which they inhabited became first a colony of Portugal, then the Empire, and finally the Republic of Brazil, each Indian tribe became a cultural, linguistic, and sometimes racial enclave within a state. Each separate tribe has formed a minority group, as defined in this book. Whether the Indians are aware of the fact or not, each tribal unit, taken individually, is a depressed and subordinate group in the national scheme: each tribe is set off from the majority by special traits, namely radical differences in language and culture (in physical appearance they are often indistinguishable from the surrounding Brazilians, except for the way they dress their hair and decorate their bodies); each tribe is certainly a self-conscious "in-group"; each tribe is an endogamous unit and membership in the tribe is determined by a rule of descent; and each tribe is now a subgroup of the Brazilian nation.

The story of every one of the numerous "minorities" formed, in the past and at the present, by the Indian tribes of Brazil would provide us with rich data regarding the contact of dominant western society with simple tribal groups. But this material must be left to the detailed studies of ethnographers. Here we can only attempt to tell a more general story of the process of extermination, of disintegration of Indian groups, and of their assimilation into Brazilian national life. Despite the great variety of tribes and languages, similarities in this process appear and reappear in different places and at different epochs. The story to be told is not a pleasant one. For out of at least one million Indians who before the coming of the Europeans inhabited the area which is now Brazil, barely one hundred thousand exist today. Furthermore, this great reduction in population has not in general been the result of peaceful assimilation but of extermination by slavery, warfare, disease, and economic exploitation.

Today, innumerable Indian groups of Brazil have entirely disappeared. Their survivors, if any, are completely assimilated into the Brazilian population. There remain a few Indian "tribes" which exist as "Indians" only because they call themselves "Indians" and are recognized as such by the surrounding rural Brazilian population. In dress, language, custom, and often in physical appearance they are hardly distinguishable from rural Brazilians, and their community is integrated into the national economy. In contrast, on the expanding Brazilian frontier there still remain a few tribes which preserve many of their aboriginal customs, still speak their aboriginal tongues, still practice their aboriginal economies—although this is now tempered by new necessities and desires acquired from their contact with Brazilians. And finally, in central Brazil, especially between the Araguaia and the Manuel Teles rivers, some Indian groups are still living beyond the tentacles of the Brazilian nation, maintaining only rare and tenuous contacts with modern Brazilians. Some of these are still hostile; others are simply fearful of outsiders; but all are suffering, as did other Indian tribes in the past, from the violence of the encroacher, the disruptive effects of new disease, and the new social environment.

In a sense, various stages in the process of incorporation or decimation of Indian groups may be found in contemporary Brazil. Viewed in this way, space equals time—for one may still find in modern central Brazil a process analogous to that which took place along the coast four hundred years ago. But only as an analogy can the contact of these modern primitives with modern Brazilians—and their airplanes, trucks, and other equipment—be compared with the situation of the coastal primitives and the Portuguese adventurers and colonists of the sixteenth century. As in other cases, the process of assimilation of the Indian tribes of Brazil must be seen in historical perspective.

I

The Portuguese first arrived on the South American coast in 1500. Soon afterwards they began occupying this land which the pope had granted them in the Treaty of Tordesilla in 1494. The first Indians whom the Portuguese—and somewhat later the French and Dutch encroachers on Portuguese territory—met were the Tupi-speaking coastal peoples. Like most of the aboriginal peoples of the South American forest area, they were divided into numerous tribal groups. The coastal Tupi were known by such names as Tupinikim, Caete, Potiguara, and Tupinamba—and the latter is the generic name given them nowadays by ethnographers. Among these peoples each village of three hundred to four hundred people was generally an autonomous political unit. They were agriculturists who cultivated the soil by crude techniques of slashing and burning. They planted manioc, beans, corn, and other crops which are well-known and important in Brazil today. In addition, they were hunters and fishers. Their material equipment was simple. Both men and women were completely nude. They lived in straw-thatched long houses shared by several related families. Leadership among them was weak. Only rarely did a chieftain exercise power over more than one village; only their shamans or *pays,* as their religious leaders were called, demanded respect beyond the immediate village. Their religion, too, was loosely organized. The *pays* were not organized into a priesthood, but depended upon their personal powers to protect the people from dangerous ghosts and demons. The Tupinamba were ferocious warriors: warfare between tribes, even villages, was followed by cannibalistic feasts during which captives were dismembered, roasted, and eaten.

In short, the aboriginal culture encountered by the Portuguese along the coast of Brazil was not one likely to impress the European favorably. There was neither the mass of labor, the material riches, nor the complexity of civilization found by Europeans in Peru and Mexico. In fact, the aboriginal cultures of Brazil contained much that shocked and horrified the Europeans, such as nudity and cannibalism. Nor could the Europeans understand the lack of central authority among the natives. Time and time again the Europeans entered into "treaties" with Indian chiefs, thinking that they could thus make peace with a whole nation, only to find that their "treaties" meant nothing at all to other Indian villages. Although it is certainly true that there was a romantic tendency to see the Brazilian Indian as a "noble savage" (Melo Franco), and that the Portuguese men found the Indian women to have beautiful features, the predominant attitude of the European toward the Brazilian Indian could only have been one of disapproval. To the first Europeans, the simple tribal Indians were barbarous, savage, and brutal; and this characterization of the Indian by the Brazilian of European culture has continued for over four centuries.

Yet this attitude did not prevent the European men from taking Indian women as concubines and mistresses. In fact, from the beginning miscegenation has been one of the most important factors favoring the incorporation and assimilation of the Indian into Brazilian society. During the first century of the colonial period, Portugal sent to Brazil soldiers, government officials, traders, and other men —all without women. These men found the brown native women attractive and often hospitable to their advances. The first missions sent to form permanent settlements in Brazil found men left behind by earlier expeditions who had already fathered mestizo children. Such was the case of Diogo Alvares Correia, a Portuguese sailor who came to be known to the Indians as Caramurú. As early as 1509 or 1510, a French boat had left him in the locality which came to be Bahia. When in 1531 the Portuguese mission arrived to establish a permanent settlement there, it found him living with his numerous children and several Indian wives. And, in São Vicente (now São

Paulo), the early colonists and government officials found João Ramalho who, like Caramurú, already was the father of several mestizo children.

By the middle of the sixteenth century, there were already numerous mamelucos, as the children of European fathers and Indian women came to be known, in the Portuguese colony. Many of these mamelucos were not assimilated in colonial society but absorbed back into tribal life. Gabriel Soares de Souza, one of the most trustworthy of the early chroniclers of Brazil, mentions in a shocked tone that there were "mamelucos who were born, lived, and died as Indians," and that he saw descendants of mamelucos "who are blond, light skinned, and freckled yet taken for Tupinamba Indians and who are more barbarous than the Indians themselves" (Vol. II, p. 289). Still, a large number of these mamelucos participated in colonial life, identifying not with the Indians but with the society of their European fathers. For example, two daughters of Caramurú by an Indian wife, who herself was baptized as Catarina do Brasil, married Portuguese men. In the region of São Vicente (São Paulo), mamelucos acted as guides and interpreters for expeditions known as *bandeiras* which penetrated far into the heart of the colony looking for gold and for Indian slaves. These mamelucos who entered into, and identified with, European society during the first century in Brazil were important in bridging the gap between the Portuguese newcomers and the indigenous population.

It is not strange that the Portuguese Crown, rather than trying to prevent miscegenation, actually encouraged and recommended the marriage of Portuguese men with Indian women. Portugal, with approximately a million people, had colonies and trading posts spread over Africa, the Orient, and the Americas. The Brazilian mamelucos added to the number of loyal subjects of the Portuguese Crown. As late as the eighteenth century, laws were promulgated giving special favors in the form of public positions and land to men who married native women. In some parts of the colony, the offspring of Portuguese men and Indian women came to form the most important element in the population. This was especially true in the first century of the colony's existence.

From 1500 on, the Indian has been steadily incorporated into Brazilian society by economic exploitation. The first Portuguese to come to Brazil knew nothing about the strange new environment. They depended upon the simple Indians to teach them what foods might be planted in this strange country and what animals might be hunted; even today the names of the flora and fauna of Brazil are Indian, and reflect the dependence of the European newcomer on the aboriginal peoples to survive in the New World. At first, the Europeans sought merely to trade with the Indian tribes for food and for Brazil wood. Both the Portuguese and the French attempted to make military allies of the various Indian tribes in their struggle for control of strategic points along the Brazilian coast. Thus, at first the Europeans dealt with the Indians as tribal units; to retain trading partners and allies, it was to the advantage of the Europeans that the Indians continue their tribal life.

During the second half of the sixteenth century, however, the nature of the relationship between the European and the native changed. As Dr. Alexander Marchant has shown in his *From Barter to Slavery* (1942), the relationship between the Europeans and the natives shifted from one of barter and military alliance to one of master and slave. As stated above, the Portuguese who came to Brazil were few, probably not in excess of several thousand. And, as is well known, they did not come to the New World to perform manual labor. The colonists needed workers to supply them with food, and the planting of sugar along the northeast coast of Brazil further increased the need for agricultural labor. Africa provided an almost inexhaustible supply of labor for the Brazilian sugar plantations, but for almost a hundred years—from about 1550 to 1650—before Negro slaves were available in large numbers, the majority of laborers in the colony were Indians. Portuguese expeditions penetrated deep into the interior of the colony searching for gold and diamonds but at the same time capturing slaves to work in plantations and towns near the coast.

In the north of the colony, the famous Indian hunter, Bento Maciel Parente, led many expeditions into the interior and up the Amazon River, destroying villages and returning with slaves for the colonists.

In the south of Brazil, the famous *bandeiras* from São Vicente, which
consisted of a few Portuguese as leaders of a band of mamelucos and
Indian allies, penetrated as far westward as Paraguay and even
across the whole of Brazil into Peru (Ellis, p. 125). They returned
to São Vicente with several thousands of Indian slaves taken from
various tribal groups and from the Jesuit missions, where hundreds
of thousands of Indians had been concentrated. According to Ellis,
most of these slaves were sold to sugar planters along the northeast
coast of Brazil since the small plantations of the São Paulo plateau
could not have absorbed the large numbers of Indian slaves which
were captured (pp. 21, 200). More than thirty expeditions were sent
out by the small colony of São Vicente during the first half of the
seventeenth century. For a time, Indian slavery seems to have been
a major source of wealth to this relatively poor part of the colony.
The Indian population of Brazil was reduced drastically by these
slave raids and by slavery itself. Whole tribes were wiped out and
others fled deeper into the interior to escape the armed bands of
slave hunters.

Yet perhaps just as fatal as slavery to the Brazilian Indian in this
period were the by-products of European contact, namely, extensive
warfare between tribes, and Old World diseases which were brought
by the Europeans and which rapidly spread among the Indians. Stimulated by the struggle between the Portuguese and the French, native
warfare was exaggerated beyond the proportions of aboriginal times,
and Indian allies took part in slave raids against other Indian groups.
Many native groups were destroyed in this way. But perhaps more
deadly were the "new" diseases—such as smallpox, measles, and
respiratory infections including the common cold—to which the
native American had not acquired immunity. Just how many Indians
died of these diseases in the sixteenth and seventeenth centuries is
hard to say, but if the experience of tribes entering into contact with
Europeans in the nineteenth and twentieth century provides any
basis for an estimate, then epidemics often reduced the population
of a tribe by 50 percent or more in the first twenty years of contact.
In fact, Serafin Leite (pp. 574–76) reports that the Tupinamba

population in the vicinity of Bahia was reduced by one third in 1562, and as a result of smallpox epidemics the remainder was reduced in 1563 by about one fourth to three fifths. Imported disease, perhaps more than any other factor, seems to have been responsible for the disappearance of many Brazilian Indian tribes.

Not all Indians, of course, were killed off by slavery, warfare, and disease, for there are still Indian tribes in Brazil; and the physical appearance of innumerable Brazilians, especially in the north of the country, indicates that many were assimilated both culturally and physically into Brazilian society. In the colonial period, an important factor in this assimilation was the work of the religious missions maintained by various orders, especially that of the Jesuits. In fact, beginning early in the colonial period there was a struggle between the Jesuits and the colonists over the control of the Indians. To paraphrase Roy Nash (*The Conquest of Brazil,* p. 106), the colonists wanted the Indian's body for labor while the Jesuit wanted his soul. The missionary orders, especially the Jesuits, established *aldeiamentos* (mission villages) where they attempted to protect the resident Indians from the ravages of slave raids. Such *aldeiamentos* were formed by the missionaries who attracted or forced the Indians inhabiting the headwaters of a river system to concentrate down the river at a site more accessible to the outside and easier to control. In the Amazon Valley, *aldeiamentos* were usually situated at the mouth of a major tributary. From such a strategic spot the Jesuits attempted to control the missionized Indians and to prevent incursions of slave raiders upstream.

In these mission villages, people of several tribes speaking distinct languages were often thrown together, and the Jesuits attempted to level off cultural and linguistic differences among them. Since the coastal tribes spoke Tupi, the missionaries adopted this language— only one among many spoken by Brazilian Indians—as their lingua franca. Tupi was reduced to a European script and in a modified form known as lingua geral it was taught to mission Indians, many of whom spoke quite different languages. The Indians were taught the basic principles of Catholicism in this language; and lingua geral soon became the principal means of oral communication, throughout a vast part of the interior of Brazil, between Europeans and Indians, between Indians who spoke different native languages, and among the mixed Portuguese-Indian population. Until almost the middle of the nineteenth century perhaps as many people of this same area spoke lingua geral as Portuguese; and even today it is still spoken in isolated areas of the country, such as the upper Rio Negro region of the Amazon Valley. Thus, linguistically, the native peoples did not shift from their native tongues to Portuguese, the language of the dominant political group in the colony. Instead, they shifted from their native language to another language based upon an aboriginal tongue, and finally, as the influence of colonial rule and of the colonists was extended over the interior they came to speak Portuguese, the language of the emergent Brazilian nation.

In these Jesuit *aldeiamentos* the missionaries did not attempt to impose a change from an aboriginal tribal culture to the western culture of the time. Rather did they attempt to impose what might be called a "Jesuit culture," distinct from the culture that was taking form in the rest of the colony. It was a Utopian and well-planned society and culture, similar to that which the Jesuits maintained in Paraguay for a time. The Jesuits attempted to teach the Indians new occupations and new work habits and to control the new economy completely. They even attempted to control marriage customs; they prohibited the marriage of cousins and of a man with his sister's daughter—marriages which were formerly allowed, even preferred, in some of the tribal groups. The Jesuits set to work to wipe out "heathen belief"; the Christian God (translated as Tupan) and the saints were substituted for native culture heroes and forest spirits. Catholic rituals and medieval folk dramas took the place of native ceremonials.

The missionaries were not altogether successful in their efforts. First, Indian culture influenced and entered into this new Jesuit culture. Along with the Tupi language, and through this language, the Indians taught the padres much of their customs and beliefs. Not only did the padres, like the colonists, have to accept the Indians' knowledge of the environment and how to deal with it, but many native religious beliefs and superstitions were accepted as well. The culture of sixteenth-century Portugal retained many medieval folk beliefs—such as the concept of werewolves—in which the padres either partly or fully shared. It was not surprising that the missionaries accepted many Indian concepts, since often these differed only in detail from those in which they themselves believed. From the Indians the padres learned of Curupira and other forest demons, while the Indians learned from the Jesuits not only of the Christian pantheon, but also of witches and werewolves. Thus, the culture created by the Jesuits in their missions was a mixed culture containing much of the old Indian heritage.

Second, the Jesuits failed to create their ideal society because their efforts were counter to the economic interests of the colonists and thus of the colonial government itself. The colonists needed Indian labor. The Jesuits fought for complete control over the Indian groups. From time to time the colonists raided the mission villages for slaves—or for temporary forced labor. And civil authorities drafted Indian labor from mission villages despite the protests of the Jesuits. On occasions the civil authorities, incensed with the activities of the missionaries, went to the extreme of arresting the Jesuits on the pretext that they were working against the best interests of the Crown and seeking to overthrow civil power. Finally, in 1759, during the regime of the Marquis de Pombal who was a veritable dictator of Portugal and its colonies from 1750 to 1777, the Jesuits were expelled from Brazil. At the same time, their mission villages were by decree transformed into colonial towns and villages and given legal charters. The descendants of those mission Indians, who no longer belonged to a tribe, were now legally considered colonials of Brazil. In this way, a large mass of people who biologically speaking were primarily American Indian, but who were carriers of a mixed Indian-Iberian culture, were assimilated into colonial life. Without the protection of the missionaries, they soon became peasants in Brazilian society just as did the mestizos and Indians brought into the orbit of colonial society by slavery and commercial relations.

At the beginning of the nineteenth century, therefore, a large mass of people inhabiting the vast interior of Brazil had a culture which was a mixture of American Indian and Iberian traits, but had lost their identity as Indians. They were rural peasants or *caboclos,* as they were called in north Brazil, and they were inhabitants of small towns and even of cities. They were Brazilians—descendants of Indians but assimilated into Brazilian life. However, the process of assimilation of tribal Indians in Brazil had not come to an end. During the nineteenth century, Indian tribes continued to enter into contact with western civilization as Brazilians slowly began to penetrate the uninhabited interior of their country. As before, disease, armed warfare, and economic exploitation—even slavery which, as late as the second half of the nineteenth century, persisted illegally—led to the disintegration and extermination of numerous tribes.

Where products in demand on the international market might be found, Indian tribes were soon driven out, decimated, or brought into peonage or outright slavery. This was particularly true, for example, in the Amazon Valley, where the increasing demand for rubber during the late nineteenth century attracted Brazilians into the headwaters of Amazon tributaries still inhabited by tribal groups. In the rubber forests, the process of detribalization and assimilation which took place along the coast of Brazil was again enacted. But in the Amazon Valley and elsewhere in Brazil during the nineteenth century, the Jesuits, the protectors of the Indians during the colonial period, were absent. Perhaps the only reason that any Brazilian Indian tribes persisted into the twentieth century was the indolent expansion of Brazilian civilization into the interior of the country; poor communications allowed many Indian tribes to survive in distant and isolated parts of the country.

II

The year 1910 marked the beginning of a new era in the process of assimilation of the tribal Indians of Brazil. It was the year that the *Serviço de Proteção aos Indios* (Indian Protection Service) was founded. Less exactly, this date also marks the increased expansion of the economic life of Brazil into the interior. Only a few years before

Indian wars had broken out, not deep in central Brazil, but just inland from the coastal strip which had been occupied during the first wave of colonization in the colonial period. Now in this second surge of occupation, Brazilian civilization again encountered tribal groups. The Kaingang tribe spread terror along three hundred kilometers of the Northeast Railroad which was being constructed inland from the city of São Paulo. In the Rio Doce Valley in the states of Minas Geraes and Espirito Santo, where the rich iron deposits of Itabira are located, the Aimore resisted with arms as the Brazilians penetrated their tribal domain. The Italian colony which had been established at Santa Matheus was in danger of being abandoned because of Indian attacks. And, in the pine forest of Paraná and Santa Catarina states, the Xokleng Indians were being hunted by professional Indian hunters who were paid by public funds to drive the Indians out of lands destined to be colonized by Italian and German immigrants.

Newspapers in Rio de Janeiro, São Paulo and other principal cities were filled with stories of these Indian wars, which were interrupting the economic expansion of the country. The problem was discussed in the Legislative Assembly, and the president of the Republic called meetings of his ministers to study the possibility of sending federal troops to end these attacks. All were eager to complete the railroads (the construction of which was suspended by Indian hostility), to guarantee the lives of the Brazilian farmers who were clearing forests to plant coffee, and to provide land for the new European immigrants. Only a few philanthropic and scientific organizations and a few idealists raised their voices in defense of the Indians and against the horrors of the Indian hunts and massacres.

In this atmosphere the Indian Protection Service was established in 1910. The service was the creation of a group of Brazilian army officers, the so-called Rondon Commission, led by Candido Mariano da Silva Rondon, who has by now become a Brazilian national hero for his humanitarian and scientific achievements. By 1910, Rondon had already acquired considerable experience with the problems of the interior of Brazil and with Brazilian Indians. As early as 1890, soon after he graduated from a military academy, he was sent to serve in his home state of Mato Grosso as a member of an expedition which was stringing a telegraph line from the state capital at Cuiabá to the more eastern state of Goiás. The line crossed the territory of the Bororo Indians, who were then hostile to the Brazilian settlers in the area. Rondon's commanding officer, General Gomes Carneiro, issued an order stating that any act of hostility on the part of civilian or military personnel and directed toward the Indians would be punished. Later, when Rondon assumed command of the expedition, he placed the Indians under the protection of his troops. When the telegraph line was completed, the Bororo tribe was living in peace with settlers and soldiers. Rondon had established, at least for his military mission, an Indian policy which he was later called upon to establish for the nation.

Rondon was afterwards charged with extending the telegraph line to the borders of Paraguay and Bolivia. During these activities, Rondon met with Indians already in contact, and living at peace, with Brazilian settlers. Such tribes as the Terena, the Kadiweu, the Guato, and the Guarani were settled in this zone. They had already been despoiled of their land; many of them lived as peons on ranches. Rondon could see the results of economic exploitation of tribal groups. Then, in 1906, he was charged with his most difficult task; namely, not only to extend the telegraph line across a thousand miles of arid semi-desert and almost one thousand two hundred miles of Amazon jungle between Cuiabá and the newly acquired District of Acre, but also to carry out scientific studies of this unknown region. Over a period of about eight years Rondon and his associates made important contributions to knowledge in the fields of zoology, botany, geography, ethnography, and other natural sciences, for which it is justly famous. But it is just as important that during these years Rondon began to put into practice his Indian policy.

During the latter expedition innumerable tribes came into contact for the first time with western man. Rondon made every effort to "avoid the calamity and cruelty suffered by the inhabitants of other regions where railroads, roads, navigation systems, even simple geographical expeditions, and commissions to establish political frontiers have penetrated" ("Mission Rondon," in Ribeiro, "Assimilação"). Furthermore, he attempted to protect the Indians' rights to their lands; he wrote of "backwoods of Brazil where no civilized man ever trod which already appeared on the books of the public registries as belonging to such and such citizens; sooner or later, according to the convenience of their personal interest, these proprietors [*cara deum soboles*] will expel the Indians who, in a monstrous inversion of facts, reason and morality will be then considered and treated as intruders and thieves" (Rondon, quoted in Ribeiro, "Assimilação"). Out of such thinking came Rondon's famous motto which he set forth for his mission and later for the Brazilian Indian Protection Service: "Die if you must; kill never."

It was during this expedition that Rondon and his associates developed their techniques for the pacification of warring Indians. The territory between Cuiabá and the District of Acre was inhabited by several tribes who were in a state of constant war with Brazilians. In this same area there were other Indian groups totally unknown to civilization. Among the known tribes were the Nambikuara, who were famous for their ferocity. The telegraph line had to pass directly through their territory, but Rondon was determined that somehow it should be done peacefully. He recognized that the men of his Commission constituted encroachers into the land of the Nambikuara and that inevitably the Indians would attack. But he knew also that any reprisal against the Indians would mean that the telegraph line could only be completed at the cost of many human lives, both among the Indians and the Brazilians. And it was not long before the Nambikuara did attack the expedition. Rondon, rather than order armed reprisal, had his soldiers leave presents of iron tools and other articles much sought-after by the Indians in places where they would find them. Such behavior was hardly comprehensible to either the Indians or to the soldiers and the guides of the expedition. From the Nambikuara point of view, here was a curious group of enemies who rather than counterattack left valued presents. This was also certainly against the accepted code of conduct of the Brazilian soldiers who thought of the Nambikuara as terrible savages. Furthermore,

among the guides of the expedition were Paresi Indians, traditional
enemies of the Nambikuara. Perhaps Rondon's most difficult task
was to restrain his men from reprisal.

Finally, in 1910, his methods proved successful. After numerous
Indian attacks, a small group of Nambikuara confronted members
of Rondon's expedition on peaceful terms. They left burdened with
presents which had been saved for the occasion. Then, just a few
months later, hundreds of Nambikuara Indians—men, women, children, young and old—came to see the strange men who had entered
their territory and had sought peace. During the years that followed,
other tribes such as the Kepkiruwat, the Rama-Rama, the Tupi
groups on the Gy-Paraná River were pacified by the Rondon Commission by similar means. These same peaceful methods are being
used today in the heart of central Brazil. In recent years, the Service
has been able to pacify the Chavante living along the Rio das Mortes
between the Araguaia and the Xingú river basins; although the lives
of one entire "pacification team" were lost, never did the Indian
Service men resort to arms against the Chavante when their own
lives were in danger. Since 1950, "pacification teams" have entered
into contact with tribes such as the Xikri and Kubenkrankegn (both
Kayapo hordes), the Parakana, the Asurini, and the Gavioes—tribes
which were constantly at war with Brazilians. And now, expeditions
led by Claudio and Orlando Vilas Boas, famed Indian officers of the
Brazilian Indian Protection Service, are in tenuous contact (which
will ultimately lead to pacification) with several hitherto entirely unknown tribes of the upper Xingú River and the valley of the Rio Teles
Pires.

During the early part of the telegraph line mission, Rondon had
his first experience with what might be called "controlled acculturation." The first Indian tribe to be encountered by the Rondon Commission between Cuiabá and the District of Acre were the Paresi.
For centuries, the Paresi had been exploited by Brazilians: first by the
bandeirante expeditions, then by miners who found their women attractive, and finally by rubber gatherers. Those who lived close to
frontier settlements were fully involved in regional extractive indus-

tries. As he had done before, Rondon placed the Paresi under the protection of his Commission. He made every attempt to see to it that they were no longer removed from their villages by force, robbed of their land, or introduced to *cachaça* (an alcoholic beverage) by frontiersmen and rubber gatherers. He was able to convince the Paresi chiefs to move their people to better village sites where the Commission might guarantee their lands and where the men might work as line keepers for the telegraph line. Schools were established among the Paresi and many of them were taught to read and write Portuguese. Many Paresi men became artisans of one kind or another and a few became telegraph operators, taking charge of the telegraph stations in their area. Rondon was able to reanimate the Paresi by showing regard for them as people, by respecting their institutions and authorities.

Rondon's early experience provided him with the basis for framing the idealistic and humanitarian policies of the Brazilian Indian Service. From the time of its foundation in 1910, these policies have been the protection of tribal lands, the respect of tribal cultures, and the gradual assimilation of Indian groups into Brazilian society. Throughout the vast hinterland of Brazil the service maintains ninety-seven posts of contact with Indian groups of the most varied degrees of acculturation and also eighteen "attraction teams," as the groups involved in pacifying warlike groups are called. Today, as in 1910, the individuals and forces which would guarantee the Indians' rights to their traditional lands and some measure of protection during the shock of contact with western society, are found in the Indian Service. Rondon became a Brazilian national hero and is now known around the world for his continued efforts on behalf of the Brazilian Indian.

III

Unfortunately, the idealistic and humanitarian policies of the Indian Protection Service formulated by Rondon and his followers were difficult to put into practice, for various reasons. First was the difficulty implicit in the great variety of tribal cultures and languages with which the Service must deal. Second was the great difference in contact situations, since the Brazilians involved varied from rubber gatherers eager for Indian labor to the cattle ranchers anxious to remove the Indian from the lands. Whatever the protective policy adopted, whether it tried to guarantee an honest wage or attempted to set aside lands for the Indian, it always seemed to run counter to the economic interests of the Brazilian frontiersmen—just as Jesuit activities were against the economic interests of the colonists. And third, contact with modern Brazilians has continued, as European contact did in the past, to bring new disease to the Indians, with the same deadly result.

Thus, despite the humanitarian and idealistic efforts and policies of the Indian Service, the process of acculturation and assimilation of the Indian groups in Brazil has continued to be disastrous to them. In fact, it might be said that after forty years of activity the protective work of the Brazilian Indian Protection Service and the pacification of warring tribes has been of more value to the expansion of modern Brazilian society than to the Indians themselves. The Indian Service has been successful in many cases in bringing whole Indian groups into the orbit of Brazilian society, but it has not been successful in integrating them into this nation. It has been able to pacify tribes but it has not been able to protect them from disease, exploitation, and social and cultural disorganization resulting from the clash of values and conflicting economic interests between simple tribal societies and complex national interests.

Perhaps this story may be best told in the dramatic example of the Kaingang of São Paulo state, one of the tribal groups which in 1910 caused so much trouble to Brazilian frontiersmen. The Kaingang were semi-nomads inhabiting the São Paulo forests, which later became some of the world's richest coffee lands. In 1910 they were at war with the Brazilians. They not only attacked the railroad as it was being built but they also impeded the settlement of European immigrants eager to clear the forests and to plant coffee. The pacification of the Kaingang became of national interest to Brazil. It was clear that either they must be pacified by the newly created Indian Service or troops would ultimately be ordered to wipe them out in a one-sided war between bows and arrows and machine guns. In 1912, Dr. Bueno

Horta Barbosa and his associates of the Indian Service established peaceful contact with a band of the Kaingang comprised of about two hundred people and led by the Indian Vauhim. But this was only one of six wandering Kaingang bands, and was itself at war with the other five. The other bands, certain that Vauhim had made peace with the Brazilians in order to secure allies in his battles with them, fled deeper into the forest and continued their running battles with Brazilians and with other Kaingang. Only in 1915 was the Indian Service able to establish peace with them and by then the hostile groups had been reduced to but one remaining band.

By the time peaceful relations were fully established with the Kaingang, the ravages attending contact with the western world had already taken their toll. In 1912, according to Dr. Barbosa, the six bands numbered at least seven hundred people in total. In 1916, just one year after the last band was pacified, less than two hundred Kaingang were left. Influenza and measles wiped out not only the pacified band but were transmitted by casual contact between Indians to the bands still at war. On one occasion Dr. Barbosa received news that a hostile band of Kaingang were starving because so many had fallen ill from the new diseases. But when the men of the Indian Service arrived to give them aid, there was nothing but "bones" at the camp site (Barbosa). In 1916 influenza and measles again attacked the remaining Kaingang and at present there are only eighty-seven members of this tribe. Thus, foreign disease continued to devastate the Brazilian Indian population just as it had in the colonial period, wiping out entire tribes and reducing others to mere handfuls of people despite the presence of the Brazilian Indian Protection Service.

This rapid depopulation of the Brazilian Indian groups has been repeated time and time again throughout Brazil, and it continues into the present. For example, the Tapirape Indians of central Brazil numbered at least one thousand when first contacted by missionaries in 1914. Although they maintained only very sporadic but always peaceful relations with Brazilians, they were reduced to one hundred and forty-seven people in 1940. And, with more frequent contact since then, their numbers have been reduced to less than fifty. Perhaps more than anything else it was the common cold that caused this tremendous death rate among the Tapirape.

In 1950 Dr. Darcy Ribeiro witnessed what must have been the first epidemic of measles among the Urubu Indians of northeastern Brazil (Ribeiro, "Assimilação"). In a matter of a few weeks, measles spread from village to village among these relatively untouched aboriginal people. Of the total of some seven hundred and fifty Urubu Indians, one hundred and sixty died of this first epidemic. Not all died of measles; many succumbed to hunger, thirst, and exposure. Ribeiro describes the scene dramatically:

The epidemic had begun before our arrival and it was spreading fast. The first village we encountered was deserted. All of the inhabitants had fled believing that the sickness was caused by a supernatural being which had attacked the village and might be avoided if they moved far away. We found them camped in the forest fleeing the disease [measles] yet already attacked by it. Some of the Indians still had the strength after they arrived at the camp to build themselves a shelter made of banana leaves over their hammocks; but the majority prostrated by the disease were without shelter in the steady rain and they were burning with fever. Attacked by measles and the complications from it . . . they became so pauperized that they did not have the strength to reach their gardens where they might have got some food. Neither could they go for water. They were already dying of hunger and thirst as well as from disease. Sick children crawled about on the ground attempting to keep the fires going in spite of the rain in order to keep warm. Their parents, burning with fever, were not able to do anything. Mothers, unconscious, repelled their infants when they tried to nurse. (Ribeiro, "Convivio," pp. 7–8)

That some aid can be given to Indian groups faced with foreign diseases, despite their almost complete lack of "natural" immunity during the first years of contact with the western world, is indicated by the events during the recent measles epidemic among the Indians of the Xingú River headwaters in 1954. When the Indian Service was informed of the epidemic over short-wave radio by their representatives, an airplane was sent to this distant and relatively unexplored part of Brazil. It was able to land on the airstrip near the Indian post. The doctor and the Indian officers attempted to isolate all of the exposed Indians but several escaped and carried the disease to their various villages. It is estimated that six hundred ninety-eight

Indians suffered from measles, and that of these a total of one hundred eight died before the epidemic subsided. But of four hundred Indians with the disease who were under the care of the doctor, only twenty-eight died, while among the two hundred ninety-eight who remained in their villages, eighty died. Although the medical officer administered the most modern medicines, it is his conclusion that the most important factor in saving his patients was not the medicine so much as the regular diet furnished the Indians at the Indian post while they were ill (Ribeiro, "Convivio," p. 10). Because during at least their first years of contact with Brazilians the Indian groups live isolated and distant from lines of transportation, it is difficult for the Indian Service to provide them with the aid that might allow them to survive the first epidemics and acquire some sort of immunity to these new diseases.

Yet by some means a few Indian tribes have weathered the shock of new diseases and have apparently achieved a stable population. This seems to be the case of the Terena in southern Mato Grosso whose population was approximately three thousand in 1845 and who have more or less the same number today. It would seem that the Tenetehara of the state of Maranhão have also recuperated from the shock of new diseases. Although exact figures on Tenetehara population during the seventeenth century, when they first entered into contact with western man, are not available, these Indians now number about two thousand and have maintained a population of that number for several generations. Most groups, however, lack a large population reservoir which would allow them to withstand the tremendous devastation from disease over a long enough period to acquire some immunization.

One of the most important policies of the Indian Service has been the preservation of Indian lands. Rondon was very early impressed by the fact that the Indian was being pushed off his land and thus reduced to peonage and semi-slavery by the new Brazilian landowners. With stimulation from the Indian Service, both federal and state laws have been passed to provide reservations for Indian tribes. The Indian Service continues to fight hard to provide adequate areas for tribes now coming into contact with the expanding frontier. But

in reality, neither the laws nor the constant efforts of the Indian
Service have met with any but indifferent success. The pressure of
frontier expansion has in general been too great. A few tribes such
as the Kadiweu and the Terena of southern Mato Grosso have title
to their lands; in these cases the titles are held by the Brazilian government but the use is reserved to the Indians alone. Several northeastern tribes such as the Fulnio are situated on reservations, but
numerous other tribes have been left without any patrimony at all or
have retained but a small parcel of the territory which they once
inhabited. Other tribes, such as the Karaja and the Tapirape along
the Araguaia River in central Brazil, occupy lands which have been
officially requested for them as reservations but on which they have
only a precarious tenure, since Brazilians continually encroach upon
them.

The Kaingang of São Paulo offer a dramatic instance of the process
by which the tribal groups have been deprived of their land, and
thereby of their basis of economic support. When the Kaingang were
still at war with Brazilians, the land they occupied was already the
legal property of one man, Sr. Luis Piza. While the Indians remained
at war, the land was almost worthless. As soon as the first band of
Kaingang was pacified, however, the land became worth 100 milreis
(the Brazilian currency unit at that time) an *alqueire* (24,000 square
meters), then 150 milreis; soon afterwards it was bringing as much
as 1,000 milreis per *alqueire*. Sr. Piza became a rich man and a sen-
ator. The Kaingang, who once inhabited an enormous area, were left
with about one thousand *alqueires*. Settled upon this relatively small
patrimony, they were introduced with difficulty to agriculture (they
had practiced only some shifting cultivation before). In 1917, their
pacifier thus described their economic condition: "They have clothes
which they absolutely do not use; houses which are better constructed
and protective than their primitive huts; platforms as beds in substitute for those which they made out of palm leaves on the floor next
to their fires; food with salt and fat; and they use food unknown
before, such as rice, sugar, and beans" (Barbosa, p. 73). Yet despite
these advantages of a settled reservation life, the Kaingang were indifferent agriculturists. The economic life they had known was ended,

for great stretches of their former territory were converted into coffee plantations.

Other tribes are now going through the same experience. The Chavante, who occupied a vast territory west of the Araguaia River, were finally pacified in 1946. Already much of the land over which they still wander and perhaps even upon which their villages are built has been sold to Brazilians from São Paulo or Rio de Janeiro. In but a few years, the Chavante will find themselves ousted from much of their territory and settled upon a small reservation, or they will be forced to live on the lands of the new owners. As in the colonial period and in the early nineteenth century, the expansion of the frontier of modern Brazil is once again forcing Indian tribes off their traditional lands—but this push into central Brazil will be the last. Only a small handful of tribes have yet to feel the impact of the explosive growth of the Brazilian population.

In addition to the problems of new disease and loss of land, the Brazilian Indian Service has been faced with the disorganization of tribal societies and a clash between the social values and customs of the numerous tribal groups and of the Brazilians themselves. As in the colonial period, Brazilians continue to regard the Indians as "savages" and to be suspicious and afraid of them. The Kaingang of São Paulo provide an example of the conflict of values between the tribal and the national cultures. The Kaingang were famous warriors but they saw early that they were outnumbered and that they would have to make peace with the new "white tribe" which was penetrating their territory. From their point of view, it was the Brazilians who had to be "pacified." On one occasion, before they came into contact with the Indian Service, the leader of a Kaingang band decided to "pacify" a group of Brazilian railroad workers. This warrior, leaving his arms behind and taking his son with him, approached the "band of men in the new tribe." But the railway workers, frightened by the sudden appearance of the "savage," received him with a volley of bullets. The Indian child was killed and the warrior escaped wounded.

In 1910 the same Kaingang leader again tried to pacify the hostile "tribe," this time with greater success, for he had discovered a party sent out by the Indian Service. Until 1914, the Kaingang believed that it was they who had pacified the whites; or to put it another way, the Kaingang and the Brazilians each believed that they had pacified the other. But in 1914 a group of Kaingang was taken by Indian Service officers to the city of São Paulo by railway. At each station they became more and more amazed at the number of Brazilians, and upon reaching the city they realized that this new tribe so vastly outnumbered them that it was they, not the whites, who had been pacified. After returning to their reservation they seemed disheartened, and their pride in their dances, songs, and customs was diminished. They saw now that they had been conquered. Previously, they had been proud before the Brazilians; now they were humble. As Dr. Barbosa wrote, "From the moral point of view, it seems unquestionable that they [the Kaingang] have received a great shock" (cited in Ribeiro, "Assimilação"). Numerous other Indian tribes have received similar "moral shocks" during the first years of contact with Brazilians.[1] It has led them rapidly to abandon their own culture patterns for others which they have not fully understood.

The new situation with which these tribal peoples have been faced has called for difficult adjustments in tribal values, customs, and institutions. The Kaingang rules of marriage are a case in point. In aboriginal times, the Kaingang of São Paulo were divided into two hereditary groups, or moieties. Each individual of the tribe belonged to the moiety of his or her father and had to seek a spouse in the other moiety. Each of these moieties was further subdivided into clans, and a person of one subdivision or clan of one moiety might

---

[1] An example is given in a recent news article (*Diário de Notícias,* July 27, 1955):

"The director of the Indian Protection Service, Sr. Mota Cabral, introduced the Minister of Agriculture to the Indian Okét, chief of the Kubenkrankegn group of the Kayapó who inhabit a zone along the middle Xingú River . . . in the state of Pará. This is the first time that Okét has ever seen a large center of civilization [i.e., Rio de Janeiro] and during the days he has stayed at this capital, he has shown himself to be quite astute. . . . He explained that he had come here in a 'large noisy bird' . . . to buy pots and iron tools. . . . The forest dweller invited the Minister to visit his people in their villages and the Minister promised to do so, if an opportunity offered itself. According to the Director of the Indian Service, Okét became very reserved and quiet just after he arrived in Rio although he was normally quite vivacious. Then, suddenly, he blurted out this question, which shows his power of observation: 'And the gardens? Where are the gardens to provide food for so many people?' "

only seek a spouse in certain clans of the other moiety. Marriage, or even extramarital sexual relations, with a fellow moiety member—or with a member of the wrong clans in the opposite moiety—was considered incest. The offending pair were severely punished in aboriginal times, and sometimes were even killed. The number of potential marital or sexual partners was very limited, but in the days when the Kaingang had several bands, spouses of proper clans of the opposite moiety might with little difficulty be found. By 1916, however, when the entire Kaingang tribe had been reduced to a mere two hundred people, some of the clans were represented by only a few individuals and several clans had died out altogether. Under these circumstances, some people were denied all rights to marriage since there were no unmarried individuals of the opposite sex belonging to the moiety and clans into which they were allowed to marry. Faced with this situation, a few couples broke the incest taboos, of course; they did not do so publicly by open marriage but by occasional and furtive sexual relations. The first couples to do so were executed when apprehended, according to tribal rule. Dr. Barbosa, the Indian officer, learning of the marriage regulations and the tradition of enforcing them, had to intervene. Whenever he noticed a young couple who seemed to be attracted to one another, he inquired of their moiety and clan. If it was not of the proper moiety and clan, he tried to persuade them to run away to live on the reservation of a group of Guarani Indians whose ideas of the proper marriage were different. Several couples thus ran away and only after many months did they dare return to their people.

It took almost a generation for the Indian officers to persuade the Kaingang to modify their strict marriage regulations. This seems to have been accomplished finally by Sr. Erico Sampaio, who was in charge of the Kaingang Post for more than twenty years. Sr. Sampaio, in whom the Kaingang had great confidence, married a woman whom he introduced as his father's brother's daughter and thus of his own moiety and his own clan, from the Kaingang point of view. Only after they saw the Brazilian fly in the face of danger by marrying a woman of his own moiety and clan were the elders convinced that it was not wrong for "kin" to marry and have children. But it was already too late. By clinging so long to their old marriage rules, the Kaingang had accelerated the rate of depopulation, thus hastening their own demise. Adherence to the old marriage regulations evidently contributed to a sharp drop in the birth rate; in fact, Dr. Barbosa reported that from 1912 to 1916 there were only three live births among the Kaingang. These three infants died during the first year of life.

Even after the Kaingang had accepted the modification in their rules of marriage, old values persisted and still continue to trouble them. For many years couples who lived in a state of "incestuous marriage" would not admit they had sexual relations. They claimed to live as brother and sister for convenience. If the woman became pregnant, she went with her husband to the forest on a "hunting trip" when the time to give birth grew near. Some days later they would arrive back in the settlement without a child—she had resorted to infanticide. Even in 1953, one such couple explained to Dr. Ribeiro that they were not really married: "We simply live together," they said (Ribeiro, "Assimilação"). Old values and concepts die slowly, and they have added to the task which the Brazilian Indian Service has assumed in attempting to bring the numerous tribal groups into national life. Like the Kaingang, many other Indian groups have not been assimilated by Brazilian society because their native concepts and institutions have hindered adjustment to the new situation.

IV

It is a strange paradox that Brazil, a country known throughout the world for its democratic policy and practice in race relations, has not been successful in providing equal rights and conditions for its tribal Indians. The fact is that most Brazilian Indian tribes suffer serious disabilities. Contact with Brazilian civilization continues to be highly disastrous to most groups. Many tribes have lost, or are in the process of losing, their land. Their aboriginal culture provides them with little basis for adaptation to the complex modern civilization of Brazil, and the Indian Service has seldom been able to protect them from exploitation or to introduce change rapidly enough to prevent social disorganization in their tribal life. Despite the idealistic and humanitarian official policy of the Brazilian government, the segment of the dominant majority which these tribesmen encounter, namely the Brazilian frontiersmen, look down upon the Indians for their "inferior" culture. The realities of the economic structure of Brazil's expanding frontier and the great cultural gulf between the tribesmen and even the simple Brazilian peasant work against idealistic and humanitarian legal provisions intended to protect the Brazilian Indian minorities.

As in the past, some Brazilian Indians are being assimilated into Brazilian society each year. Theoretically this is not unexpected. There are no strong barriers against the assimilation of Indians. An Indian who separates himself from his tribal group, speaks Portuguese, wears European clothes, learns Brazilian custom, and practices Catholicism soon loses himself in the Brazilian population. Only the memory that he was once a *bugre* (a term of disparagement for the Indian) remains as a mild stigma. But in reality, it is doubtful that assimilation is ever very frequent in modern Brazil. Only Indians who are torn from their tribal groups as children, to be educated by missionaries or others, ever learn the language and culture of Brazilians well enough to "pass" as Brazilians. And only such individuals are sufficiently free from the memory of their tribal cultures not to think of returning when they feel the pressures of an alien world. Many instances are known of Indians who have lived for years in Brazilian society, only to return to their tribes rather than live on as "marginal men." [2]

Intermarriage does not nowadays seem to have the same impor-

[2] The most famous instance is that of the Bororo Indian, Aipobureu, known in the Brazilian world as Tiago Marques. Educated by Salesian missionaries, he received a secondary school certificate. He spoke Portuguese well and learned several other European languages. In 1913 he traveled in Europe and in 1915, after his return to Brazil, he went back to his tribe and married an Indian woman. At first, urged by the padres, he served as a schoolteacher for his tribesmen but soon gave up, saying that children could not learn in the mere two hours that the school functioned. He preferred to work in the fields and to hunt like any Bororo man. Finally, he moved his residence far from the mission station to the most isolated Bororo village where aboriginal life and custom continued relatively unchanged. There he lived out his life a "marginal man" in both cultures. (Baldus)

tance as a mechanism leading to assimilation which it had in the early colonial period. Although casual sexual encounters between Brazilian men and Indian women are frequent, stable Brazilian-Indian unions are exceedingly rare. Brazilian men look with disapproval upon Indian women as wives. Unless they have had long experience in Brazilian society, these women do not know how to perform the normal household duties expected of a wife in Brazilian frontier families. But resistance to intermarriage also frequently comes from the Indians themselves. The reaction of many Brazilian Indian tribes to their minority status is a strengthening of their in-group consciousness and a strict insistence upon tribal endogamy. They become aware, as one Tapirape Indian man stated, that "It is all right for Tapirape men to marry *tori* [i.e., Brazilians] and Karaya [the neighboring tribe] but Tapirape women must marry Tapirape. If this is not so, then the Tapirape will end" (Wagley, unpublished field notes). Such tribesmen consciously and sometimes militantly try to enforce tribal endogamy.

Even the adoption of Brazilian culture in part or quasi-totally by an Indian group does not lead to assimilation. For example, in the northeastern backlands of Brazil:

After several hundred years of Brazilian cultural domination, there are a series of Indian groups which still regard themselves as distinct ethnic and cultural entities. That these aboriginal descendants usually present evidence of long time and continuing racial intermixture with Negroes and Caucasians and that they are culturally indistinguishable from the local neo-Brazilian populace does not prevent them from considering themselves to be "true Indians." (Hohenthal and McCorkle, p. 288)

One of these groups, namely the Fulnio of Aguas Belas, in the state of Pernambuco, has been able to retain its tribal identity, its language, and a surprising amount of aboriginal culture by the strength of its "in-group" consciousness. Their insistence on a closed society is so strong that "no non-Indian and hardly even any non-Fulnio may be permitted to enter through adoption or marriage; if a tribal member does marry a non-Fulnio the latter is excluded from the *urikuri* [i.e., tribal rites symbolic of tribal unity] although the children of the union are permitted to attend" (Hohenthal and McCorkle, p. 293). Not all Brazilian tribal groups have been acculturated toward the dominant majority culture to the degree of the northeastern tribes, nor have all maintained a closed society to the extent of the Fulnio, but it is clear that a high degree of acculturation will not necessarily lead to assimilation.

If it is true that the present rate of assimilation is slow, and that even when a tribe becomes acculturated to the majority culture patterns it can maintain its identity as a distinct social group—then it would seem that some Brazilian tribal groups may have a long career ahead of them as minorities. Especially if they are somehow able to hold on to their land through a system of reservations, a few tribal groups may survive for many years to come. But, despite the best efforts of the Indian Service, disease, economic exploitation, and social disorganization, brought about by the loss of old aboriginal cultural values, will continue to chip away at their numbers, affecting the birth and mortality rates until all but a handful of the hundreds of tribes which formerly existed within the area that is now Brazil will have disappeared.

RECOMMENDED ADDITIONAL READINGS

Baldus, Herbert. Ensaios de Etnologia Brasileira. São Paulo, 1937.
Marchant, Alexander. From Barter to Slavery. Baltimore: Johns Hopkins Press, 1942.
Nash, Roy. The Conquest of Brazil, New York: Harcourt Brace, 1926.
Ribeiro, Darcy. "Assimilação dos Indios do Brasil" (forthcoming). Brasiliana, Editora Nacional, Rio and São Paulo.
Schaden, Egon. Aspectos Fundamentais da Cultura Guaraní. Faculdade de Filosofia, Ciencias, e Letras da Universidade de São Paulo, Bulletin No. 188. São Paulo, 1954.
Steward, Julian, ed. Handbook of South American Indians, Vol. III. Washington, D.C.: Bureau of American Ethnology, 1948.
Wagley, Charles. "The Indian Heritage of Brazil," in T. Lynn Smith and Alexander Marchant, eds., Brazil: Portrait of a Half Continent. New York, 1951.
Wagley, Charles, and Eduardo Galvão. The Tenetehara Indians of Brazil. New York: Columbia University Press, 1949.
Watson, James. Cayua Culture Change. Memoir of The American Anthropological Association, No. 73. Menasha, Wisconsin, 1952.

THE INDIANS IN MEXICO

About 15 percent of the total population of Mexico consists of people who are regarded as Indians. Like the Indians of Brazil, these Mexican Indians do not form a single minority group. There is no self-conscious group feeling among them. They speak 46 different native languages, although by now almost half of them also speak Spanish. Even those who speak the same language or dialect seldom have any feeling of unity. The only self-conscious social unit among them is their own local community: to the Indians of one community, the Indians of other communities are generally as much strangers as Mexican nationals. They are "not conscious of being a fragment of an ethnic group larger than the simple nuclear society . . . Much less do they think of themselves as members of a nation . . ." (Aguirre and Pozas, p. 177). Thus, in Mexico there are almost as many Indian minority groups as there are Indian communities.

Mexico assumes special importance for us because of its energetic, humanitarian, and scientifically oriented Indian policy. Led by a group of enlightened and idealistic leaders dedicated to the cause of Indian welfare, the Mexican government since the agrarian revolution in 1910 has attempted to raise the standard of living of the Indians, to improve their educational and health conditions, to protect them from economic exploitation, and to return to them their community lands lost during previous centuries. To a large extent, the policy of the Mexican government toward these Indian minorities since 1910 has attempted to respect traditional Indian customs, institutions, and languages. On the other hand, the policy has frankly sought to integrate them into national life and to "convert in fact this Indian minority into Mexicans" (Aguirre and Pozas, p. 178). In short, there has been an attempt to bring these Indian groups the benefits of Western civilization and equality within Mexican society and at the same time to avoid the disruptive and disorganizing influences which so often accompany rapid change. Many of the policies and programs initiated in Mexico have now been adopted by other governments with large aboriginal minority groups and are used today by international organizations working in underdeveloped areas. The Mexican experiment with the Indian minorities should be of great interest to the world.

I

At the time of the Spanish conquest, the area of the New World which is now Mexico was inhabited in the main by American Indians who had achieved the cultural level of a great civilization. Only in the northern part of the country were there simple hunting and gathering tribesmen. In the central and southern parts of the country lived the Aztecs, the Tlaxcaltecans, the Culhuas, the Huastecs, the Tarascans, the Zapotecans, and other highly civilized peoples. These peoples were divided into a series of native states often at war with each other, and at least one hundred twenty-five different languages were spoken throughout the area. There was considerable cultural diversity from one native state to another but everywhere their complex cultures were based upon a system of hoe agriculture which produced maize, beans, squash, and other aboriginal American crops. Trade was highly developed. A system of writing and an efficient numerical system were widely used. These peoples had a calendric system based in part on the solar year. They had an organized government and a priesthood which administered their elaborate religion. They constructed pyramids, temples, fortresses, and palaces. Their stone and metal work was marked by a high degree of artistic refinement. Their society was divided into classes of nobility, commoners, and slaves. While the majority of the people in these native states were rural farmers, there existed great cities such as Tenochitlan and Texcoco, both in the Valley of Mexico, which together had populations of al-

most a half million. In these cities there were busy markets that ri-
valed anything in Spain at the time. The central and southern areas
of Mexico had an aboriginal population that numbered at least four
million people, and perhaps as many as nine million, in 1521.

In 1519, 600 Spaniards landed on the Mexican coast. Within a few
years they had dominated these millions of native peoples. How this
was accomplished is a fascinating story, too complex to be related
here. Briefly, the Spanish conquistadors were quickly able to capture
and crush the ruling classes of native society, and they were aided in
their conquest by conflicts between the various native states. The first
conquistadors were, of course, soon joined by other Spanish colonists,
but during the whole colonial period (1521 to 1810) not more than
200,000 Europeans emigrated to New Spain, as the colony came to
be called. In addition, perhaps as many as 250,000 Negroes were
brought into the colony as slaves. The wars of conquest, the new
diseases brought to New Spain by the European and the African, and
the disorganization of the native economic system rapidly and drastically reduced the Indian population by more than 50 percent during
the sixteenth century (see Zavala and Miranda, p. 37). Yet "at no
time, did [the white and the Negro] represent more than 1 to 2 percent of the total population of the country" (Aguirre and Pozas, p.
176).

During the colonial period, however, other important population
elements began to develop. Almost immediately after the conquest,
the process known as *mestizaje* (miscegenation or race mixture) began. Only 10 percent of the European immigrants and approximately
35 percent of the African slaves were women. Caucasoid and African
men sought unions with Indian women and the variety of groups of
mixed descent came to form a series of social strata (*castas*) who
were intermediate in social position between the dominant Spaniards
and the subordinate Indians. Since this mixed population generally
identified with their European ancestors and acquired European culture patterns early in the colonial period, the Indian was faced not
only by a dominant Spanish group but also by a large group of non-

Indians of mixed descent. These mestizos [1] were shopkeepers, lesser merchants, small landowners, and even lowly agricultural and mine workers, but they developed a new culture, mainly derived from Spain but retaining many traits from the aboriginal cultures of Mexico, which became in time the dominant way of life of the colony and later of the Republic of Mexico.

The greatest problem facing the Spanish after the conquest was how to administer the vast Indian population with its numerous languages, cultures, and political divisions. At first, the Spanish were forced to make use of the remnants of the native aristocracy, the so-called *pillis,* as auxiliaries in administering and controlling this large mass of Indians. The *pillis* were able, through their traditional powers over the common people, to maintain control over the local communities and to exact tribute for themselves and for their Spanish masters. But, as Spanish power was stabilized throughout the colony, and particularly as Spanish numbers were increased by immigration and by their mixed offspring, this indigenous aristocracy was gradually deprived of power. Thus, the Spaniards and their descendants came to substitute for the ruling class of the native states. The common people among the Indians now paid tribute and provided labor to the Spanish as they had done for their own ruling class in the past. But they had not simply changed one group of masters for another. They had, in fact, ceased to be a lower class in their own society and had become a series of minority groups in another society. This change in status resulted in profound changes in their way of life—in their economy, their community organization, their religion, and in their customs. Every effort was made by the Spanish authorities and by the religious missionaries to weld them into colonial society as vassals of the Spanish Crown and as Christians. So effective were these efforts that the way of life of numerous Indian communities in Mexico which have resisted incorporation into national life contains

[1] Biologically the term "mestizo" is used to mean a person of mixed Indian and Caucasoid descent, but here it must also have a cultural meaning and will be used for people who, although of American Indian descent, have abandoned the culture of Indians and live as non-Indians.

more of Spanish colonial heritage than of aboriginal patterns and institutions.

The tremendous modification in Indian life in Mexico during the colonial period was the result of a consciously planned policy of the Spanish Crown but was tempered, and even distorted, by the realities of the colonial scene. The policy of the Crown in regard to the administration of the Indians was humanistic, protective, and idealistic. These objectives, however, often clashed with economic and political interests in New Spain. Furthermore, even the laws often reflected this clash of interests by their ambivalence. The Indian was granted liberty by the law, but other laws limited this liberty in order to supply labor to the mines, the new cities, the workshops, and agricultural enterprises. While the Crown declared itself the protector of the Indians, both the Crown and the colonial administration passed laws that usurped the lands of the Indian. Thus, despite the declared idealistic policy of making the Indians subjects of the Crown with rights equal to those of other subjects, a series of laws set them off from other members of colonial society. Before the law they were considered minors or rustics (*personas miserables*), subject to special legal statutes. Many of these statutes theoretically were issued to protect the Indians, but they actually often worked to their disadvantage. Spaniards, Negroes, and mestizos, for example, were prohibited to live in Indian villages or in the Indian quarters in cities. All Indians who came to the city to work or to trade were obliged to return home at night or retire to the Indian quarters at the end of the day. Indians were prohibited to have horses and saddles, to own firearms, and even to dress like Spaniards. These special laws for Indians, limiting their movements and their economic participation, contributed to maintaining the Indian as a separate group in the colonial society in Mexico.

In their new status as a minority (or better, as a series of minorities) in the Spanish colony, the Indians were exploited as a source of cheap labor. In aboriginal times, the common man in the native states had often paid a labor tribute to his rulers or to conquering groups. Now they had to work in mines, and in industry; they had to build churches and other edifices, and to raise food for the new Spanish "majority." At first, the Spanish resorted to outright slavery, but strong voices of idealists such as Bishop Vasco de Quiroga and Bartolomeu de las Casas against slavery were raised in Spain. By the middle of the sixteenth century Indian slavery was decreed out of existence.[2] Likewise, the system of feudal servitude known in the New World as *encomienda* was quite early limited in scope, although it continued throughout most of the colonial period to be an important system of exacting tribute. By this system a Spanish colonist was granted the right by the Crown to collect tribute from the Indians of a given area. This right was limited to one or two generations and it did not include ownership of the land on which the Indians lived. The *encomendero* might collect tribute in food or in personal services. Thus many mines were operated by workers paying off tribute and, for a time, the *encomendero* could hire out his "serfs" to work for others. But by the middle of the sixteenth century it was decreed that tribute might not be paid in personal labor but only in goods or in money. The Spanish colonists then turned to another system, that of forced labor or *repartimiento,* for their labor supply. Although "forced labor" had been specifically prohibited by law, it was decreed that Indians must fulfill their obligations as citizens by working in tasks of "public interest." Production of foodstuffs, operation of the mines, and construction of public buildings, churches, and convents were all interpreted for a time as being in the "public interest." Under this system 4 percent of the males of an Indian community could be called upon to work for wages for one week in a mine, on a hacienda, or in constructing church or town hall.

The Spanish Crown, sometimes sensitive to humanistic ideas but often conceding to economic pressure, abolished this forced labor

---

[2] In a minor way, Indian slavery continued in New Spain to almost the end of the colonial period. Although it was generally prohibited, exception was made of warlike Indians hostile to the Spanish. The Indians of northern Mexico incessantly attacked the Spanish colonists and captives often appeared in Mexico City bound in wooden collars and ropes to be shipped off to Cuba.

system in 1632, with the exception of labor in the mines. But by this time the owners of mines, of haciendas, and even of industries had found debt bondage to be a much more efficient system of securing Indian labor. Sometimes, this took the form of offering Indian families a piece of land on a hacienda in payment for which they worked for the owner. More often it involved an advance of wages, either in money or in goods. Once the Indian had accepted an advance, he generally found it very difficult to free himself of debt to his employer. Debt bondage was enormously extended in the eighteenth century, and the Crown attempted to control it by limiting the legal amount that might be advanced, fixing wage levels, and establishing better working conditions. But in the small sweatshop textile mills called *obrajes,* debt-bound workers were locked in behind double doors. Recruiters traveled great distances to secure debt-bound labor for the mines. Isolated on the great estates, debt-bound peons were without recourse to law and were subject to corporal punishment by their employers. Debt peonage seems to have been the most effective and the most lasting system for securing Indian labor and in Mexico it lasted into the twentieth century. By this means, innumerable Indians were torn from their communities to become in time culturally identified with the growing mestizo class.

Throughout the colonial period, however, the majority of the Indians remained in their own communities. These Indian communities were partly autonomous under the Crown-appointed viceroy, who was the central authority in New Spain. Yet provincial magistrates collected tribute and held criminal and civil jurisdiction over their districts. The Indians were often badly exploited by the lesser Spanish functionaries who were in direct contact with them. In fact, some of these advanced credit to the Indians, charging interest rates as high as 30 percent to be repaid in produce which they sold for an additional high profit. Indian villagers were, as indicated above, sometimes subject to forced labor and they sometimes paid tribute to a Spanish overlord or *encomendero.* They had heavy burdens in taxes to pay both to Crown and Church, and their community organization, their religion, and much of their whole way of life was radically modified from what it had been in aboriginal times. Yet in their communities they were able to maintain their group spirit, their own languages, and enough of their distinctive cultural traditions to persist as distinctive social units in colonial society.

For a time, the Spanish rulers attempted to reorganize and relocate these Indian villages. At first they merely attempted to persuade the Indians who lived in scattered hamlets and homesteads to move into Spanish-type villages and towns, but toward the end of the sixteenth century, *congregaciones,* or concentrated villages, were established by force. Numerous Indian villages were formed with a Spanish-style central plaza and regular streets radiating out from it. Indians were organized in work squadrons to build the new towns and villages. Once the new pueblo was ready, the old homes on scattered farms were burned so people would not return to them. Those who tried to leave the new village were returned to it by force. These forced relocations had devastating effects on many Indian groups, particularly such groups as the Otomi of northern Mexico who were not sedentary agriculturalists. The Otomi are reported to have burned the new villages and fled. When recaptured, many of them committed suicide rather than return. The clergy protested the inhumanity of forced relocation and even the colonists pointed out the grave economic disturbances which it caused among the agricultural Indians. By 1607 the Crown saw its mistake and the project was abandoned, but not before it had modified the settlement pattern of many Indian communities in Mexico.

The Spanish Crown continued to be interested in the Indian communities. As early as 1569 the viceroy ordered that all Indian pueblos were to be granted land for the building of homes and for their agricultural pursuits. This land granted to the Indian pueblos was to be held in common but to be used in individual usufruct. Further, no land was to be granted to Spanish colonists near the Indian communities so as not to jeopardize the Indians' rights. The Crown also undertook to establish a community government for these Indians based upon the Spanish municipal pattern; each was to have a series of elected officials such as *alcaldes* (mayors) and *regidores* (town councilmen). Even the internal economic life of these communities was modified. Maize continued to be the Indians' principal crop but the Spanish introduced new crops such as bananas, citrus fruits, wheat, and other Old World domesticated plants. The Indians were obliged to raise a certain number of "birds of Castile" (chickens) as well as "birds of the land" (turkeys). Although the Indians could raise European livestock, the raising of cattle, sheep, and horses became by tradition a Spanish occupation. The Indians were encouraged to maintain their old crafts but new techniques were introduced by the Spanish. The aboriginal markets were retained, particularly because of the serious subsistence problems of the colony, but the Spanish system of weights and measures was introduced and there was an attempt to regulate prices and the actions of middlemen in these Indian markets.

In addition to the pressures exerted by the civil authorities, the Indians in their communities were also subjected to the influence of the Catholic Church. The Indians were not only to be made into loyal subjects of the Crown; they were to be Christian subjects as well. At first, the Catholic missionaries resorted to mass conversion and baptism and in the first decades after the conquest several millions of Indians were baptized in the first flush of missionary zeal. Later the missionaries settled down to the slow job of teaching the ideology of Christianity. Eventually, the teaching of Christianity came to be seen as the best method by which the mass of Indians would become "civilized" Spanish subjects. At first the missionaries attempted to use Nahautl, the language of the Aztecs, as a lingua franca in religious teaching, but they soon gave it up for the Spanish language. In fact Archbishop Lorenzana, in the latter half of the eighteenth century, came to see the teaching of Spanish as a "cure-all"; once the Indians had learned Spanish, he reasoned, they would accept Christianity and also accept the superiority of Spanish civilization. So the padres became teachers; they introduced schools and they trained Indian assistants to go into the villages to aid them in their work. It cannot be said that the padres were very successful in teaching Spanish to the Indians, for even today the aboriginal tongues of Mexico still persist in many Indian communities. But the Indians did become Catholics. Catholic baptism, marriage, and burial, Catholic rites and festivals and Saints' days, and Catholic associations and brotherhoods are today a traditional and integral part of "Indian" community culture. These Catholic rites and ceremonials, often replacing or fusing with old aboriginal custom, provided the Indian communities with a new basis for community participation and solidarity. Along with the communal land system established by the Crown, the dedication of the Indian to the patron saint of his community and his obligations and duties to the local religious brotherhoods helped to preserve the community intact, and to maintain the Indian as a distinct social and cultural unit.

Thus, by the end of the colonial period Spanish rule had made profound changes in the social structure of Mexico. A large number of Indians had already been assimilated into colonial life through incorporation into the labor force of the colony, through miscegenation with the Spanish and their African slaves, and through acculturation to the emerging Spanish American culture patterns. At the end of the eighteenth century, it is estimated that of a total population of somewhat over six million people in Mexico, some 30.9 percent were mestizos, only 0.5 percent were Europeans and Negroes, and approximately 60 percent were Indians. The way of life of this large mass of Indians, however, was considerably modified from what it had been in aboriginal times. Although they continued to speak their native languages and retained much of their aboriginal belief and custom, by the end of the colonial period they were Catholics, had a Spanish community organization, and had acquired many Spanish customs and beliefs.

Equality before the law for all citizens—Indians, Negroes, mestizos, or natives born of Spanish parents—was the basic theme of the Mexican struggle for independence and was reflected in the constitution of the Republic which was formed in 1823. In keeping with this point of view, the special legislation, both protective and dis-

criminatory, which concerned the Indians during the colonial period
was abolished. Like all citizens, the Indians had theoretical legal
equality, so why should they be the subject of special legislation?
Furthermore, during the political confusion of the first decades of the
Republic, the government could hardly concern itself with the rural
areas of the country, much less with the special problems of the Indians. Only when there were Indian insurrections and rebellions did
the government take notice of the Indian groups, in the form of military action to maintain law and order.

During the early years of the Republic, left alone in their communities, the Indians lived out the round of life from birth to death
according to the Spanish-Indian culture which they had acquired
during the colonial period. But no matter how isolated, they were a
part of Mexico and the influence of the larger society continued to be
felt. Indians left the villages to work "temporarily" on large Spanish-
owned estates (haciendas) from which some of them never returned.
From time to time there were visitors from the outside to the Indian
villages, and steady economic intercourse with rural mestizos was
maintained. In a diminished form, the influence of the Church continued to have an important effect on Indian life. The Indians constituted the lowest and most impoverished of the rural classes. They
were but marginal to the new state and they were viewed increasingly
with disdain by the rural mestizos and the middle and upper urban
classes. The epithet "Indio" came to refer to an uncouth, barbarous
person.

While the laws of the new republic were not aimed at either protecting or discriminating against the Indian, the total effect was discriminatory and some of the laws challenged the very existence of
the Indians. As a citizen, the Indian had the right to vote, but most
states denied this right to illiterates and domestic servants. Thus,
without being singled out, the Indians were excluded from the electorate. Far more important to the Indian communities were the laws
regarding land tenure. It was the aim of the liberal leaders of the
Republic to make Mexico a country of small landholders. They also
proposed to divide up among the peasantry the enormous estates that

had been accumulated by the Church. It was the natural right of all men, they reasoned, to hold and accumulate property individually. So in 1856 and 1857, laws were passed which prohibited both civil and ecclesiastical corporations from owning or acquiring any category of real estate, except that upon which buildings were to be constructed. This was a blow to the Church, but it was equally a blow to the landholding Indian communities throughout the country whose *ejidos* and *fundos legales* (common lands) were thrown into jeopardy.

The intent of these laws may not have been to dispossess the Indians of their lands but rather to establish them as landowning peasants. The government did urge repeatedly that the Indians legalize their individual titles for the land which they had formerly held in common. But the effect of the laws was to strengthen the position of the large estates or haciendas. The *haciendados,* as the class of owners of the large estates were called, gave their full support to the new laws. They were anxious to extend their holdings at the expense of the Church. They knew from experience that small Indian landholders were more apt to be a source of seasonal labor for them than the Indians living in a landowning community with the resources of inalienable agricultural gardens and communal wood and pasture lands. The *haciendados* knew that individual ownership meant the right of sale and that it would be easy to increase their holdings further at the expense of the Indian. Finally, they knew that it was communal landholdings which held the Indian to his community and kept him from contributing to the labor force of the nation.

The Indians resisted subdivision of their community lands and a wave of armed uprising spread throughout the country. Often their lands were declared *baldío* (unappropriated or wasteland) and taken over by the neighboring haciendas. Complex cases of land litigation filled the courts as a result of which many Indian groups found that they had lost their lands. As the communities lost their lands to the haciendas, many Indians were forced to leave their communities and to work permanently as peons in debt bondage. The loss of communal lands often led to the disintegration of the Indian community.

The individualization of landholdings and subsequent sale resulted in
the penetration of the Indian community by outsiders. The result was
a rapid assimilation of Indians into the gowing mestizo population.
By 1910, the mestizo had already become the predominant element
in the Mexican population; it was estimated that 43 percent of the
total population was "mestizo" while 20 percent was "white" and
37 percent was Indian (Aguirre and Pozas, p. 176).

But despite the legal pressures on their communal landholdings,
many Indian communities persisted. In fact, it is estimated that 41
percent of the Indian communities were able in one way or another
to retain, against the law, some of their traditional lands in common
holdings (Navarro, p. 129). In some communities, the land was subdivided into individual holdings, but community *esprit de corps* prevented the owners from selling to outsiders. Sometimes, communities
resorted to the subterfuge of registering their lands in the name of an
individual representative. Other Indian communities retained some
of their lands simply by default—they were so isolated or situated so
high in the mountains that their lands were considered "worthless"
by the *haciendados*. Furthermore, one student of Mexican society has
suggested that the haciendas often allowed the continuation of corporate, organized Indian communities and sometimes even acted in
their defense. He points out that the *haciendados* lacked capital and
that beyond a point they could not develop their holdings nor control
the large population of peons under their power: "At this point,
haciendas ceased to grow, allowing Indian communities like Tepoztlan
or Sierra and Lake Tarascan villages to survive on their fringes."
These "free" Indian villages provided seasonal labor to the *hacien-
dado* who sometimes resented interference with "his Indians" and
even acted in their defense (Wolfe, pp. 1069 ff). Thus, in one way
or another many Indian communities were able to live on to the end
of the nineteenth century; yet by the time of the revolution of 1910,
the majority of the villages, particularly in the highly populated central plateau, had lost their lands, and perhaps one half of the total
rural population of Mexico was bound in debt peonage to the
haciendas (Whetten, p. 89). "Land, Liberty, and Death to the Ha-

ciendados" was the call to arms of the revolution which set off a new epoch in Mexican history.

II

In the period of the Republic immediately preceding the revolution of 1910, the ruling class of Mexico had looked abroad for its inspiration and guidance. The government under Porfirio Díaz had invited foreign capital and hoped to make Mexico a European type of state. Under the influence of the "Social Darwinism" of the nineteenth century, it was believed that the Indian was destined to adapt or to disappear in the competition of the "survival of the fittest." The poverty and illiteracy of the Indians was taken as proof of their racial inferiority and they were considered a burden to society.

The Revolution reversed this trend and sought to build a national future using native materials. While an important segment of the reformers looked abroad for cultural guidance . . . it did not deny the ability of native peoples to change for the better . . . . in contradiction to the aristocracy of Porfirian Mexico, the reformers of the Revolution denied the validity of Spenser's Social Darwinism. They believed that the environment, an environment made by individuals and subject to change by individuals, and not heredity determined the success or failure of peoples and races. . . . To transform the environment . . . the reformers gave the peasants land and schools. In them, the idealists of the Revolution saw the key to the future of the rural scene, for both gave the peasants the means for survival and, equally important, . . . they said to them, as the old regime did not, you are an integral part of Mexico. (Ruiz, p. 475)

Thus, the revolution of 1910 marked the beginning of a new and different policy toward the Indian minorities. It brought with it an idealization of the Indian and of the Indian heritage as a symbol of nationalism and as a reaction against the foreign orientation of the old regime. Yet it also set off a basic disagreement among the leaders of the revolution concerning action to be taken in regard to the Indians. Some of the leaders argued that the purpose of the revolution was to improve the lot of all rural Mexicans by means of land reform, education, extended communications, and other reforms. They denied that the existence of the Indian groups called for special programs and agencies distinct from those that would serve the mass of rural peasants. On the other hand, the so-called "Indianists" (*Indigenistas*) "insisted that there were Indians with individual needs other than those of the general rural population, whose heritage merited a cherished notch in the Mexico of the future" (Ruiz, p. 475). Both groups (except the most extreme among the Indianists) seemed to agree upon ultimate integration of the Indian minorities into Mexican society, but they also seemed to disagree as to how this was to be brought about and as to what "integration" meant. Indianist leaders stoutly maintained the value of preserving and teaching the aboriginal languages. The other side promoted linguistic unity and the spread of Spanish. The Indianists have advocated the preservation of the "best of . . . pre-hispanic and colonial legacy" among the Indian communities (Gamio, cited in Ruiz, p. 481), whereas the other group has argued for unity in Mexican culture and total assimilation of the Indian groups.

Each of these opposing ideologies regarding the Indian minorities has achieved acceptance at different times since 1910. In the early years of the revolutionary movement the anti-Indianists, or assimilationists, seemed to have set the policy of the government. Between 1934 and 1940, during the regime of pro-Indianist Lázaro Cárdenas, president of Mexico, the Indianist policy seemed to gain the upper hand. But at all times the influence of both schools of thought has been present in Mexico and continues into the present. Thus, at times, Indian communities have been the object of special agencies and programs aimed at their distinctive problems. At other times, they have been treated as part of the larger depressed rural population of the country. Always, the result has been in one way or another increased contact with, and greater accommodation to, Mexican society and culture. For even the special agencies and programs of the Indianist have tended to break down the isolation of the Indian villages and eliminate the differences between the Indian and non-Indian segments of the rural population.

Perhaps the most important program of the revolution was agrarian reform, which intended to return the lands of the villages that had been usurped by the haciendas. Although it was the aim of the reformers to help the Indians, it is doubtful whether this gigantic program has actually benefited the Indian minorities as much as it has hastened them along the road to becoming mestizos. One of the first acts of the revolution, the "San Luis Plan," was to proclaim the right of the villages "in their majority Indian" to regain the lands taken from them by the haciendas. In the new Mexican constitution of 1917 this right was carefully formulated, and later a detailed agrarian code was established governing the distribution and system of land tenure. Lands which a community could prove to have been illegally appropriated by individuals or groups could be repossessed. The system of land tenure was modeled on the corporate and collective holdings of the Indian communities in pre-hispanic and colonial times. Collective holding of land was known as *ejido:* in colonial times, this referred only to the pasture lands of a community, but now it came to include cultivated lands, pastures, woodlands, public buildings, house sites, and water rights. *Ejidos* were now granted both to communities as well as to cooperatives and other groups. The government withheld rights of eminent domain over the land which could not be sold, rented, or mortgaged by the holders of the individual plots. Between 1916 and 1945, the total amount of land distributed in the rural zones as part of this program amounted to 30,619,321 hectares (75,660,317 acres), over 15 percent of the total area of the Republic.

As one segment of the rural mass of Mexico, the Indian communities obviously did benefit from this program. Yet in the first years of the period the program was slow in getting under way. The first to receive land were the peons and peasants who had fought in the revolution. Later, land was given to the members of communities who had lost their lands and who, therefore, were already highly dependent upon the haciendas. Such groups were more apt to be culturally mestizos than Indians. The Indian communities which had escaped absorption by the hacienda system were also often aided by

the *ejido* program; the titles to lands they already held were confirmed and given a legal basis, and frequently they were able to
expand their holdings. But their participation in the program was
"more formal than real" (Aguirre and Pozas, p. 208). In fact, one
observer has stated: "The subdivision of the *latifundio* in the regions
of dense indigenous population has not changed the situation of these
peoples in any serious way. . . . A specific analysis of this problem
shows that the simple and unadorned granting of *ejidos* to indigenous
population is almost ineffectual in solving their economic necessities
and promoting their incorporation into a superior culture" (Noble,
cited in Aguirre and Pozas, p. 208).

Yet the *ejido* system seems to have brought about the incorporation
and assimilation of a considerable number of Indians into national
life. By 1940, 48,000 "heads of families" speaking only aboriginal
languages had benefited from *ejido* grants. Pushed by the demographic pressure, Indians have requested *ejido* land grants and thus
have been forced to adopt a form of social structure determined by
the agrarian code. As a result, they are split from their parent Indian
communities and rendered highly vulnerable to government-sponsored
programs of social, educational, and economic change aimed at all
ejido cooperatives, whether they be Indian or mestizo. From the
point of view of total assimilationists, this process is all to the good.
But the Indianist group feels that the rupture with traditional Indian
culture and community should not be so abrupt and complete. They
would like to see *ejido* grants made to Indians in the near vicinity
of their parent Indian communities so that there will not be a "brusk
break, during the period of organization and consolidation, of the
umbilical cord that maintains these colonies tenuously united with
the communities of Indians from which they derive" (Aguirre and
Pozas, p. 208). The question still seems to be whether such peoples
should be incorporated into Mexican society as Indians or as rural
Spanish-speaking peasants.

Education was second to land as a program announced by the
revolution of 1910. "Tierra y Libros" (land and books) was one of
the calls to arms for the peons and the Indians. Prior to the revolu-

tion, education in Mexico was to a large extent in the hands of the Catholic Church. Most of the schools that did exist were located in the cities and the mass of Indians and mestizos in the rural areas were considered hardly capable of profiting from education. On the eve of the revolution, 70 percent of the entire Mexican population over ten years of age was illiterate and an overwhelming proportion of the literate population was in the cities. The revolution enthusiastically began a gigantic effort to bring educational facilities to the rural masses and particularly to the Indian who was at once a symbol of the new movement and the most depressed segment of the rural population. Since 1910, Mexico has become well known for its intensive program of rural education. Rural schools, each known as the *Casa del Pueblo* (Home of the People), were established and were dedicated to educating the whole community, children and adults alike, and to promoting community projects. Rural schoolteachers were trained in a system of normal schools where they learned not only the techniques of formal pedigogy but also practical agriculture, animal husbandry, and crafts. "Cultural Missions," consisting of groups of specialists, were stationed for a period of six to eight weeks in rural schools where they gave instruction to rural teachers and worked to promote community projects in the locality.[3] In the campaign to reduce illiteracy, literate citizens were obliged to teach the illiterate, and by 1946 over seven hundred thousand people had passed literacy tests as a result of this campaign (Whetten, p. 422).

Although the various governments of Mexico since 1910 have made a sincere and heroic effort to fulfill the promise of the revolution to the Mexican masses, it would seem that in spite of the rural educational program, the urban population has benefited more than the rural population. And although it is difficult to cite statistics, it is certain that in the rural areas the Spanish-speaking mestizos have benefited more than the Indians. The reasons for this relative lack of success in the predominantly Indian areas seem to flow from the dif-

[3] After 1942, the Cultural Missions took a new form. They were aimed at adult education and community improvement and were stationed three to four years in a locality.

ficulties of language (inability of pupil to speak Spanish and of teacher to speak aboriginal tongue); from the inadequate adaptation of pedagogical methods to the Indian cultures; from the scattered settlement pattern of the Indian; and from the necessity for the whole family, including small children, to cooperate in Indian agriculture (Aguirre and Pozas, p. 251). Even in Indian towns such as Cherán, in the Tarascan-speaking area of the state of Michoacan, studied by Ralph Beals in 1940–41, ". . . the Cherán schools do not train children in any sense for life in Cherán." Instead, the Indian in Cherán who secured some local education was equipped to "cope with the mestizo world that impinges upon Cherán to some extent" (cited in Whetten, p. 423). The conclusion seems inescapable that the Mexican rural school which was aimed at rehabilitating the rural masses was better adapted to the mestizo or Ladino communities and not to the traditional Indian communities. Likewise, the Cultural Missions, even in their new form, have not been successful in their efforts "in the communities which are one hundred percent Indian and which are in an inferior stage of acculturation, because their methods are not derived from the ethos of the indigenous culture but rather from Western culture" (Aguirre and Pozas, p. 250).

It is in the policies and the programs of Mexican education since the 1910 revolution that one sees most clearly the battle between the Indianists and the assimilationists. On the whole, it is the assimilationists who have had the strongest voice in regard to rural education since 1910, although such Indianist leaders as Moisés Sáenz, Manuel Gamio, and Alfonso Caso have all held important posts in the Secretariat of Education during these years. In the first years after the revolution, the main aim of education among the Indian groups was to teach them to speak, read, and write Spanish. The formula was "Give all Mexico one language." The Spanish language was seen as the "necessary vehicle" by which all knowledge was to be transmitted and the *sine qua non* of the process of incorporation of the Indian into Mexican society. The process of *castellanización* (teaching Spanish) in the rural schools proved to be slow and ineffectual. Indian children did learn some Spanish during the years they attended school, but in their homes and in their daily lives, they continued to speak their native language. A few years after they left school, their meager knowledge of Spanish faded into the background.

The lack of success of the rural school in the Indian communities fed the old doubt among the Mexican aristocracy and urbanites that the Indian was innately unable to learn and to adapt to modern civilization. In 1925, the Indianist group of educators, anxious to disprove this theory of the racial incapacity of the Indian, were able to persuade their government to carry out an educational experiment. In the very heart of Mexico City, the House of the Indian Student (La Casa de Estudiante Indígena) was established. Youths from such Indian groups as the Otomis and Yaguis in the north and from communities speaking Zapotec and Tzeltal in the south came to live in this establishment and to study in Mexico City schools. In all, 26 linguistic groups were represented among the students. This experiment was, like so many others, both a success and a failure. On the positive side of the ledger it proved to Mexico once and for all that the Indian had the same capacity to learn as did non-Indian Mexicans. The Indian students were tested and observed, and in time they learned as quickly and as thoroughly as other students in the same schools. Furthermore, the experiment proved that the Indian could adapt easily to civilization. The Indian youths quickly learned to wear shoes, Western clothes, to take part in sports, and generally to live as urban Mexicans. Even the scoffers and skeptics were satisfied.

On the other side of the ledger, the experiment of the House of the Indian Student also proved that the Indians, once accustomed to urban life, preferred that life to that of their native villages. They remained in the cities as scholars, mechanics, bartenders, and clerks. They did not want to return to their Indian communities upon which they, like other urban Mexicans, had now learned to look with disdain. Few of them could be persuaded to return to their villages to serve as rural schoolteachers. Later, the House of the Indian Student was given a new and specific purpose, that of training rural schoolteachers, but again the newly trained teachers refused to return to their rural areas. In 1932 it was abandoned entirely, and as one well-known observer of the Mexican scene has stated, "The problem of converting a static rural population into a creative one was no further advanced than before" (Tannenbaum, *Mexico,* p. 166). Yet again and again governments have repeated the mistake of the House of the Indian Student by educating technicians and specialists from the rural zone in the city and expecting them to return home.

This failure, however, convinced many Mexican educators that a special program for the Indian was worthwhile and necessary. Thus, in 1932 ten centers for Indian students were established in different parts of the country, making use of the funds which had formerly been allotted to the House of the Indian Student. In the program of these centers, which took the form of boarding schools, an attempt was made to adapt the educational process more closely to rural life. But it was not until 1934, when Lázaro Cárdenas, who has been called "the first president of Indian Mexico," took office, that the Indianist policies were fully applied. In 1936 an autonomous Department of Indian Affairs was created to deal with Indian problems, and one of the first statements of this Department pointed out the shortcomings of the rural school insofar as it concerned the Indian. Therefore, in 1937, a special Department of Indian Education was formed in the Secretariat of Education. The number of Indian boarding schools (*Centros de Educación Indígena*) grew to 33. In these schools, young Indians from diverse linguistic groups came for three or four years during which they not only learned Spanish and the elementary academic subjects, but also were taught practical agriculture, animal husbandry, hygiene, and other applied subjects. It was hoped that the graduates would return to their native villages, taking with them the knowledge they had gained, and that they might even be instrumental in the creation of new centers in other parts of the country.

Again, this very idealistic and, in many ways, very practical program erred on the human side. Few of the graduates wanted to return to their villages and those who did return were ill at ease. Many of them sought positions with new government agencies, or, in their eagerness to become incorporated into national life, sought positions in mestizo communities. In a sense, they had learned their lessons too well; they no longer wanted to think of themselves as Indians but as Mexicans. "Unfortunately," admits one contemporary Indianist leader, "these experiments, one after the other, made it clear that these boarding schools had only produced maladjusted individuals discontent with the environment of their village" (Aguirre and Pozas, p. 254). But much had been learned; it was clear that if Indian schoolteachers and leaders were to be trained and to be useful in their own communities, they must not be torn from their communities in the process and must retain their identity with their people.

It was also during the regime of President Cárdenas that the movement to teach Indians in their own native language was first initiated, although this was actually only put into practice in 1944, after Cárdenas had been succeeded by Manuel Avila Comacho as President of Mexico. In 1939 in Mexico City, the first Assembly of Philologists and Linguists, convened by the Department of Indian Affairs, proposed that Indians be taught first how to read and write in their native languages before being taught in Spanish. Their argument, briefly, is that the Indian makes use of Spanish only for his relations with the non-Spanish world, which are in the main mercantile. In his daily life he uses his native tongue. His native language is closely tied up with his way of thinking, his emotions, and his aspirations. The acquisition of a second language (i.e., Spanish) is a process of super-imposition of concepts. The bilingual continues to think in his native tongue and makes use of the second language by translation. Thus, the difficult process of learning to read and write should begin with the native language in which the individual feels and thinks. Once a concept of reading and writing is learned, these skills would be more easily acquired in a second language. To do this, the linguists proposed to reduce the previously unwritten aboriginal language to the phonetic alphabet, and to prepare primers in both the native languages and Spanish.

These proposals were not accepted with enthusiasm by many Mexican educational authorities, who pointed out that much time would be lost in first teaching reading and writing in the native language. Even today the debate continues in Mexico—and in other countries with large populations of speakers of native languages—between two schools of thought, those who would teach the Indians directly in Spanish and those who believe that it is more efficient and more thorough to teach them first in their native languages. Despite considerable opposition, the Indianist group has been able to make use of the method in several programs. Teaching in the native language was first used in the Tarascan areas with considerable success. Then in 1944, during the campaign against illiteracy in Mexico mentioned above, the authorities were convinced that initial teaching in the native language might be necessary to extend literacy among the Indian groups. In 1945 the Institute of Literacy in Indian Languages (Instituto de Alfabetización en Lenguas Indígenas) was established. This institute brought together bilingual schoolteachers from five districts where important native languages were spoken. Linguists set to work with them preparing primers in the native languages and in Spanish. The schoolteachers were given intensive training in teaching methods especially devised for this program, and they were taught some of the essentials of physical and cultural anthropology and the science of linguistics. Each of these teachers then returned to his district, where he was to instruct thirty additional bilingual teachers in the methods he had learned.

In spite of continued opposition, this program in the five native language areas has been maintained on an experimental basis. In terms of the number of people that have become literate in Spanish (or the native language) it can hardly be called a success. It is said to have had magnificent results in the Tarascan-speaking areas of Michoacan, but to have had little effect among Otomi and Nahuatl speakers among whom the teaching groups have by now been disbanded (Aguirre and Pozas, p. 255). Still, even with its limited success in terms of numbers, the program has definitely shown that in a very short time a monolingual Indian can be converted into a bilingual Indian. Furthermore, it has shown that such bilinguals are able to learn to read and write both their own languages and the second language which they have acquired.

With the retirement of Lázaro Cárdenas from political life, the Indianists lost considerable support in the government and the tide turned against them. In the crucial field of education, there was a swing back to the concept of unity of education for all Mexicans. Special educational programs for Indians were even compared with segregated schools for Negroes in the United States and were criticized as undemocratic. Since 1940 the Mexican government has put great emphasis upon the total economic development of the country and upon industrialization, and the special problems of the Indians have tended to be overlooked. The Indianists were accused of "making the Indian more Indian" and "of turning out charity cases, unable to think for themselves" (cited in Ruiz, p. 490). In 1946, the Department of Indian Affairs was abolished and its functions turned over to the Secretariat of Education. For a time, it seemed as if the cause of the Indianist was lost and that the Indian minority groups would be treated as any rural Mexican citizens, to become incorporated into Mexico as best they could.

In recent years, the Indianists, rather than admit defeat, have devoted their efforts to profiting from past mistakes and to developing a new scientific approach to the Mexican Indian. During the last two decades, an outstanding, active group of social anthropologists have come to the fore in Mexico. Some of them were trained abroad, but most of them received training from the National School for Anthropology (Escuela Nacional de Antropología) in Mexico City. These scientists have carried out numerous field investigations among the Indian groups of the country, and in their studies they have focused upon problems of cultural change. Today social action programs concerned with the Indians in Mexico are being based upon a sound scientific knowledge of the various Indian groups.

Since 1940, Mexico has actually been the leader of a hemisphere-wide Indianist movement. In that year, under the auspices of the government of President Cárdenas, Mexico was host at Patzcuarro, in the heart of the Tarascan-speaking region of Michoacan, to the First International Indianist Congress. At this congress, in which Mexico's Manuel Gamio and Alfonso Caso and others played a prominent role, it was decided that each participating country in the Americas would establish a specialized agency concerned with Indian affairs. In 1948, the Indianists were able to persuade the government to replace the abolished Department of Indian Affairs with the National Indian Institute of Mexico (Instituto Nacional Indígenista de Mexico) in order that Mexico might continue to live up to its international commitment. The National Indian Institute is today the most important single organization working with the Mexican Indian minorities. This institute was empowered to study and survey the Indian groups of the country and to recommend and undertake concrete projects in the Indian communities. Cultural anthropologists are the directors, policy makers, administrators, and field officers of this new institute. Its studies of Mexican life and its programs for improvement of the conditions of Mexican Indian groups and their ultimate integration into Mexican society have become justly famous throughout the world, and are closely watched by other governments with large aboriginal populations.

The basic principle underlying the policies and programs of the National Indian Institute is that of a multiple, coordinated approach to the problems of the Indian minorities. In the words of two writers who are closely associated with the Institute:

The assimilation of the indigenous nuclei into the national community can only be realized by means of an integral effort, that is to say, by means of constructing roads, the teaching of new methods of cultivation, the introduction of new techniques in the workshops, the improvement of the industries, the diffusion of the most modern concepts of hygiene, and providing the experience of the benefits of medicine; finally, by establishing communication between the indigenous nuclei and the rest of the country, raising their standards of living, improving their health and hygiene, and giving them the elementary education necessary for the life of a modern man. (Aguirre and Pozas, p. 256)

In order to carry out this many-sided attack on the problems of the Indian communities, the Institute has established a series of coordination centers (centros de coordinación) in Indian regions. Under agreement with the appropriate government agencies, a committee is established for each center which, under the director of the center, attempts to coordinate programs in education, agriculture, health, communications, and the preservation of natural resources of the Indian group concerned. To date, the Institute has founded coordinating centers for the Tzeltal-Tzotzil in the state of Chiapas, the Tarahumara of Chihuahua, the Papoloapan of Vera Cruz and Oaxaca; and the Mixtecas of Oaxaca.

The first of the centers was established in 1950 in the town of Las Casas, high in the mountains of Chiapas. The formation of this early center and its activities will give us a picture of an important Mexican experiment in assimilation. Las Casas is not an Indian city, but it is the center of attraction of a large and dense Indian population, the Tzeltal- and Tzotzil-speaking peoples who are widely known for their conservatism and their resistance to outside influence. Each of the Indian communities in the region had its own system of traditional community organization derived from the colonial period. Each of the communities retained the old cultural patterns representing a fusion of Spanish and aboriginal traits. By far the majority of the Indians spoke only Tzeltal and Tzotzil languages. In the region, the relations between the non-Indians (known locally as "Ladinos," or Latins) and Indians were marked with bitterness and tension. The Chiapas highlands was a difficult place for the Institute to experiment with its new program. It was greatly to the Institute's advantage, however, that the area had previously been surveyed and studied from both the anthropological and medical points of view.

One of the first problems of the Las Casas Center was to break the isolation of the region. The center therefore focused upon creating a system of neighborhood roads connecting Las Casas with the main Indian villages of the region. The construction of these roads, however, has sometimes caused great alarm among the Indians whom they were meant to benefit. The penetration of the road into the municipality of Chamula, for example, caused such tension between the Indians and the Ladinos that the physician, the nurse, and the nurse's assistants at the health post which had been established at Chamula by the Center were forced to flee the community. Even the Indian municipal president of Chamula fled to Las Casas, his life threatened because, with the road building, he had brought Ladinos into the community. Despite such incidents, as communications were improved in the region, the center was better able to carry out its other activities.

In 1950, when the Las Casas Center began its activities, there were few schools in the surrounding Indian communities, and those that existed functioned in a fashion totally inadequate for the needs of the region and its people. Most of the teachers were Ladinos and had little interest in Indian problems. In the municipality of Chamula— to use this very conservative community again as an example—there was but one school for a total population of over twenty-one thousand people. This school was taught by a Ladino teacher and his wife and the average attendance on any day was about fifty students. The situation was somewhat better in other Indian communities; yet the Ladino schoolteachers had only been able to teach a few hundred Indians to read and write in several decades of activity. Even those who had finished the rural elementary schools soon forgot what they knew, as was evident when an attempt was made to use the "graduates" as census takers for the 1950 census.

Despite this unfavorable situation, the Center decided from the start to put the educational program into the hands of the Indians themselves. A group of bilingual and literate (more often semiliterate) Indians were recruited. With considerable difficulty, 45 individuals were found who were willing to be trained for positions as promoters or "instigators" of culture change (*promotores del cambio cultural*). As far as possible, the men selected enjoyed positions of prestige in their communities—some of them had been clerks of their villages and some of the older men had even been municipal presidents. At the Center in Las Casas, these *promotores* were given intensive training in agriculture, hygiene, arts and crafts, and other practical matters important to Indian life. They were then sent back to their communities as schoolteachers and as assistants to agronomists and public health specialists working in the region. From time to time, these *promotores* were asked to return to the Center for further studies; in turn, educational and other specialists visited them in their communities. In many cases, their ability to explain the advantages of the Center's programs to fellow villagers, in their own terms, has been of crucial importance.

The procedure of the Las Casas Center for establishing schools in the Indian communities of the Chiapas highlands has always begun with an intensive use of these *promotores* to secure local support and cooperation. Furthermore, in each community an educational committee has been formed, composed of leaders among the Indians themselves. The community has been asked to provide the land for the schoolhouse, for a sports field, and for a school garden. Schools have sometimes had their beginnings in temporary buildings rented for the purpose or in clearings under trees. Later a schoolhouse would be built by the Indians with the financial and technical assistance of the Center. The school calendar in these Indian communities is adapted to the local agricultural cycles and work patterns. Pupils do not attend school when they are needed by their parents for work in the fields. In one community, at least, the elders insisted that school sessions be held only in the afternoons after the boys had returned from work in the fields with their fathers. These schools also do not follow the regular curriculum of Mexican rural schools. Their programs are geared to local life. Regular academic subjects receive less emphasis than hygiene, gardening, carpentry, and other subjects which have practical value in terms of local life. Often the schoolhouse has a sewing room where the women of the community can learn to sew, and it may have an oven where bread-making is taught. There is an intensive effort to teach reading and writing—first in the native language and then, if possible, in Spanish. Attractive primers have been prepared by the Center in Tzeltal and Tzotzil—and in Spanish. Visual aids such as slide projections and movies are used extensively. By 1953, the Las Casas Center had put 45 new schools into operation, with a total enrollment of 1,541 students (1,398 boys and only 143 girls). The average attendance in April of that year was 1,122 students.

The health program of the Las Casas Center is also well underway. Intensive vaccination campaigns against smallpox, typhoid, whooping cough, and diphtheria have been carried out. Houses, clothing, and the people themselves have been treated with DDT to rid them of disease-carrying insects. Four clinics and five medical posts had been established by January of 1954 in the Indian communities of the region. In these clinics and medical posts, more than eighteen thousand people were given treatment from 1952 until the end of January in 1953 (see *Acción Indígenista,* January, 1954). Small-scale public works have been undertaken for public health purposes, such as the building of safe water-supply systems and the construction of sanitary privies, thus reducing the prevalance of intestinal parasites. These measures have been supplemented by educational campaigns conducted in the schools, by visual aids carrying legends in both the native languages and Spanish, and by *promotores* especially trained in public health. As a result, modern concepts of the cause and prevention of disease have been introduced into the Indian communities.

A number of agricultural experimental stations are also maintained by the Las Casas Center. All of these serve to demonstrate modern methods of cultivation. Fruit trees and vegetable gardens are planted in these stations and improved seeds of maize and other traditional crops, as well as of crops new to the region, are distributed to the Indians. Through *promotores* trained in agriculture and by means of instruction in the schools, modern techniques of agriculture and the proper use of modern tools are being introduced.

Programs similar to that being carried out in Las Casas are underway in the other three centers maintained by the National Indian Institute. Such programs are, in a sense, the culmination of the experience which enlightened Mexican leaders have acquired since the revolution of 1910. Yet these programs are frankly "experimental," in that the science of anthropology is for the first time being directly applied to problems of cultural and social change. Anthropologists are not simply acting as advisors to those responsible for the programs, but they are directly in charge and are administering every phase of the work. Furthermore, the programs of these centers are committed to the concept of the interrelatedness of the many aspects of a society and they thus seek to stimulate change in the society as a whole and not by partial measures. These are frankly long-term programs making it clear that the integration of the Indian into national life is a slow and complex task.

III

It has now been over four and one-half decades since the beginning of the social process which Mexicans speak of as the revolution of 1910. In this time, Mexico has made many positive attempts to improve the economic and social position of its Indian minorities and to integrate or assimilate them into modern Mexico. Just how successful these often idealistic and humanitarian programs have been is difficult to judge. Undoubtedly, the Indian minorities have a higher standard of living, better health, and better educational facilities than they did in 1910. Yet the fact remains that a large number of Indian minorities persist in Mexico at the most marginal level of integration. What is the present situation of the Indian minorities of Mexico and what does the future hold for them?

To answer this question, one must first define what is meant by "Indian" in Mexican terms. This will give us several clues as to how the process of assimilation is proceeding. First, it should be emphasized that "Indian" cannot be used in Mexico in a biological sense. A very large proportion of all Mexicans are, at least in part, descendants of American Indians. As described earlier, in comparison to the great mass of Indian population the European and Negro newcomers to Mexico were few in number. Thus the Indian made the greatest genetic contribution to the Mexican population. Rather than biological, the term "Indian" then has a *cultural* meaning. It means those people who are "Indian" in their cultural traditions rather than Mexican in the modern sense. But even this cultural definition is loose and much in need of qualification. Modern Mexicans, whether they be of Spanish, Indian, or mixed descent, share many cultural traits with those who are classified as Indians. Likewise, the "Indian cultures" of present-day Mexico are more properly "colonial-Indian cultures"—fusions of aboriginal and colonial Spanish culture traits. Both Indians and non-Indians in Mexico are Catholics, although much aboriginal belief certainly persists within the Catholic framework of the religion of the Indian groups. Both Indians and non-Indians share many other culture elements of colonial Spanish origin, such as the traditional system of ritual co-parenthood (*compadrazgo*) and even many ingredients of their cuisine.

Yet there are a series of cultural criteria which set off the Indian from the Mexican. First, the Indian generally speaks an aboriginal tongue. Second, the Indian often wears a "native" costume and generally goes barefooted or wears *huaraches* (a type of sandal). Third, he eats "Indian foods" such as *tortillas* made of maize, rather than wheat bread. Fourth, he lives in an endogamous community which has retained traditional forms of organization such as the religious brotherhoods (*cofradías*) and the colonial system of municipal officers. In certain parts of the country where there are numerically large enclaves of Indians, such as in the north and in Chiapas, cultural criteria clearly do mark off Indian groups from Mexican. The majority of the Tarahumara, for example, are easily distinguished from the neighboring rural Mexicans. Most of them speak their native language; they live in scattered hamlets apart from the rural Mexicans; and some of the more conservative Tarahumara men still wear loin cloths and allow their hair to grow long. In the state of Chiapas, the majority of the Tzeltal and Tzotzil speak their own language, wear a distinctive and colorful native costume, and live by a body of colonial-Indian tradition strikingly different from that of the Mexicans of the region. This does not hold for all Tarahumara or Tzeltal-Tzotzil Indians, for there are many individuals among them who are able to speak Spanish with ease, dress as do Mexicans, and live by cultural standards similar to the Mexicans of the region. Yet in these regions, and in others where the Indian has retained his colonial-Indian way of life, the distinction between the Indians as a group and the Mexicans can usually be made on the basis of objective cultural criteria.

But this is not so throughout the country. In many regions of Mexico, the Indian no longer wears his distinctive costume, and Indians and rural Mexicans dress alike. Sometimes, as in the Tarascan-speaking region of Michoacan, Indians differ from Mexicans only in the language they habitually speak and hardly at all in dress and custom. In various localities, both groups may speak Spanish, wear similar clothes, and follow essentially the same customs. An "Indian" in these areas is one who performs the most menial jobs and has the lowest standard of living.

Perhaps the only criterion that may be safely used in all parts of the country to define the Indian is a subjective one. After considering the many criteria that have been used, Alfonso Caso states: "An Indian is an individual who considers himself to be an Indian and who considers himself a member of an Indian community" (cited in Aguirre and Pozas, p. 115). And perhaps one should add to this definition that an Indian may also be an individual who is considered by non-Indians to be an Indian. Now what does this subjective definition imply? It means that whether or not he adopts the language, dress, and behavioral patterns of the non-Indian, as long as he continues to identify and be identified with his Indian group, he remains an Indian. As long as he does so identify and is identified, he will tend to associate with members of his own Indian minority group, tend to marry an Indian, and his children will continue to be Indians. Theoretically, then, it would be possible for whole communities to become thoroughly acculturated to modern Mexican culture, to forget their native tongue and adopt Spanish, yet remain as an "Indian" minority enclave within the national society.

In reality, this has seldom, if ever, taken place in Mexico. The whole history of Mexican society from the colonial period to the present shows a steady process during which individuals and whole groups have ceased to identify themselves as Indians and have become Mexicans. There are no rigid barriers to prevent this process of assimilation of Indians into Mexican society. Although light skin color and Caucasoid features are often preferred, the Indian is physically similar enough to Mexicans of mixed ancestry that physical appearance alone is no barrier. But everywhere in Mexico the Indian is placed at the bottom of the social scale, is in one way or another looked down upon, and is the object of prejudice. The intensity of the prejudice which the local Mexicans hold for the Indian varies in different regions from a mild form deriving mainly from the Indian's poverty and ignorance to a strong quasi-racist belief, "attributing to Indians a lack of intelligence or rationality, retarded or infantile mind, incapacity to progress or to engage in certain occupations, possession of animal qualities or other degrading characteristics supposed congenital" (Fuente, pp. 81–82). Thus, in some areas, transfer from the Indian group into the Mexican group is often only a matter of changing one's language, educational level, dress, and standard of living—or even just one or two of these overt cultural criteria. Although one's Indian ancestry may be remembered and act as a mild drawback, the individual functions for all practical purposes as a Mexican and the chances are that his (or her) children will be so considered. Sometimes, intermarriage between Indians and Mexicans is the method of assimilation. In Michoacan, if a mestizo man marries an Indian woman, both she and her children are said to acquire his status. And, in the district of Villa Alta in Oaxaca, Julio de la Fuente speaks even of a few marriages of non-Indian girls with Indian men who "are hispanized in language and culture and perhaps rich" (Fuente, p. 395). In many areas of Mexico, as individuals acquire Spanish as their primary language, as they improve their material situation, and as they learn to live as modern Mexicans, they tend no longer to identify themselves with their Indian community and either they or their children come to be Mexicans.

In certain areas of the country, however, such as highland Chiapas and some parts of Oaxaca and Vera Cruz, the relations between the two groups assume caste-like proportions (Fuente, pp. 76–96). In these regions there is greater prejudice against the Indian and stronger barriers to assimilation. The Indian communities generally are more conservative, and, in a sense, look down upon people who do not share their way of life. Among these conservative groups there are strong pressures against marrying Mexicans and, to a lesser extent, even against marrying "foreign" Indians. Such Indians look down upon any of their contemporaries who would attempt to "pass" into the Mexican group. Thus, the minority group itself strongly resists assimilation. Furthermore, in these areas the viewpoint of the Mexicans is that formal marriage with Indians is socially taboo, and the offspring of informal unions between Mexicans and Indians generally are given the status of Indians. Neither the children of mixed unions nor Indians who have become completely acculturated both linguistically and culturally are accepted as Mexicans. Local society remembers the Indian origin of these people, and by a rule of descent places them in the lowly Indian category. Only by moving to another region and into a town where one's genealogy is not known may such people "pass" as Mexicans. In these conservative parts of the country, the process of the assimilation of the Indian minorities into national life will be slow and painful. Although Indians may become bilingual, improve their standard of living, acquire education, and learn to live by Mexican cultural patterns, a rule of descent will continue to set them off as Indians. And as long as they are able to maintain separate communities with their strong self-consciousness as distinct groups, they will remain minority enclaves.

Assimilation continues, but it can be seen from the difficulty of defining "Indian" that no real statistical index of the rapidity of the process of assimilation can be compiled. The best available indications are the statistics on those who speak aboriginal languages. Although the use of an aboriginal language does not always mean that a person is an "Indian," nor the use of Spanish that a person is Mexican, "whoever uses an indigenous language exclusively or principally, has to be a man who feels himself to be an Indian" (Parra, p. 13). It is through one's language that the cultural characteristics and the attitudes that set off a person as an Indian are transmitted. Using language as a rough criterion, it is possible to estimate the present number of Indians in Mexico and to trace roughly the process of assimilation of the Indian into national society over the last few decades.

In 1940, 2,490,909 people over 5 years of age, roughly 15 percent of the total population of this age in the country, spoke indigenous languages. It is interesting to note that from the time of the Spanish conquest to the present, the number of Indians in Mexico has not diminished appreciably, although they are today a numerical minority in a society of almost thirty million people.[4] Since immigration does not account for the rapid growth of the non-Indian population of Mexico, this provides proof of the steady and continuing process whereby descendants of Indian minorities have lost their Indian identity.[5] Actually, the number of people who speak Indian languages has increased since 1910, but they have steadily decreased in terms of the total population of the country. In other words, Indian language speakers have multiplied at a much slower rate than that of the Spanish-speaking element of the population. Particularly since 1930 has there been a sharp decrease in the proportion of Indian language speakers to Spanish speakers.

It could be argued, of course, that the Indians with their generally low standard of living have not benefited equally from improved health conditions in Mexico and that a higher rate of infant mortality and shorter life expectancy have prevented them from multiplying as rapidly as other segments of the Mexican population. This in part is probably true, yet there seems to be little likelihood that the disparity in the rates of increase can be attributed to differential mortality rates alone.

Furthermore, looked at in another way, the figures on language support the proposition that assimilation has taken place with greater velocity in the last twenty years. In 1930, of all of those who spoke Indian languages, 53 percent were monolingual (i.e., spoke only the Indian tongue). In 1940, slightly over 49 percent of the Indian speakers were monolingual and by 1950, only 33 percent were monolingual. At least one authority on Mexico predicts that if this process continues at the same rate, within fifty years the monolingual population in Mexico will have disappeared (Lewis, "Change"). At once the question arises of whether the disappearance of monolingual In-

[4] Cook and Simpson have estimated the pre-conquest population of Mexico as high as nine million, but other authorities would bring this down to as low as three or four and a half million people (see Aguirre and Pozas, p. 175).

[5] Mexico has not experienced waves of European immigration on any large scale. Population growth has been mainly in excess of birth over deaths. (See Whetten, pp. 22 ff.)

dians would mean the assimilation of all Indians by Mexican society. Certainly it would not, for many individuals and whole groups who are bilingual, and even some monolingual Spanish speakers, are identified and identify themselves as "Indians."

Yet bilingualism for most individuals usually does bring assimilation a step closer. Using language as a criterion of assimilation, it would seem that we might discern four stages along the road to becoming Mexicans: (1) monolingual Indians, (2) bilingual Indians, (3) monolingual Spanish-speaking Indians, and finally (4) Mexican rural peasants. The increase of bilingualism among the Indian population in the last twenty years is, then, a strong indication that the Indian is being prepared for assimilation into Mexican national society faster than ever before. Although some of the Indian groups may continue to resist assimilation and even increase in numbers, they will represent a progressively smaller percentage of the total population of Mexico.

Today the portion of the Mexican population which is Indian occupies the lowest rung on the social and economic ladder. A large mass of people representing some 37 percent of the total population of the country lives, on the whole, only little better than the Indians. At the top of the socio-economic hierarchy in Mexico are some nine and one half million people or about 48 percent of the population as of 1940, who are divided by sharp class lines and economic differences, but who may be said truly to participate in modern Mexican life. Howard Cline, in his excellent book *The United States and Mexico,* speaks of these broad categories or segments of the Mexican population as three distinctive Mexican worlds: the Indian World, the Transitional World, and the Modern World. Not all the people of the Indian World live in abject poverty. In fact, "more than 100,000 . . . live better than the great majority of more culturally modern" people (Cline, pp. 78–79). But most of those in the Indian World lead a poor and miserable existence. As Cline describes their situation, "Plagued by diseases, exploited by their fellows and more modernized Mexicans, they exist but do not live" (p. 78). He estimates that these people approach two million in number, and that just above them but still in the Indian World are a half million who

often have ranchos of their own or subsist in village communities that are generally inadequately supplied with elemental cultural equipment. More changed, and sometimes happier, are still another group of nearly equal size who have given up their native costumes for the characteristic peasant dress of rural workers—white pajama-like pants and blouses and straw hats. Many even now wear overalls like the unskilled workers of towns and cities. Except for their ignorance of Spanish, they are Mexicans; they are Indian only in language, and even that sometimes is shared. (p. 78)

Thus, to be an Indian in Mexico, despite the romantic attachment which Mexico holds for its Indian past,[6] is still to be a member of the most depressed segment of Mexican society.

IV

The Indian minorities of Mexico are in many ways representative of the Indians of the other highland sections of Central and South America. They are descendants of a people who possessed an advanced civilization and they are numerically an important segment of the national population. Their way of life was drastically modified after the Spanish conquest by the colonial regime, but through isolation and resistance they have maintained a "mixed" Spanish and Indian culture and their own languages into the twentieth century. Like other minority groups, they are subject to prejudices and they are economically depressed. And they lack the necessary linguistic and cultural equipment to participate fully on an equal basis with other nationals of Mexico. Yet they live in a society in which the majority of the population constitutes, at least in part, descendants of Indians and in which the Indian civilizations of the past have become a symbol of Mexican pride. In skin color and in general physical features, they differ little or not at all from a large non-Indian body of the population. Unlike the Indians of Brazil, they do not face a

[6] A law of October 10, 1949, establishes that the Indian hero of the conquest, Cuauhtemoc, "is the symbol of our nationality and therefore deserves the sincere devotion of the Mexican people" (cited in Lewis, "Change").

totally unfamiliar cultural world. The Mexican people have borrowed much from their Indian cultural heritage and the way of life
of the contemporary Indian minorities is as much European (representing Spain of the sixteenth and seventeenth centuries, and modern
Mexico) as it is aboriginal.

For centuries the policy of the dominant social and cultural group
in Mexico has been divided between that of protective isolation, and
that of aggressive incorporation, of the Indian communities into the
larger society. But often incorporation of the community and assimilation of the people into Mexican life has not been so much a question
of the policy of the superordinate group as the reaction of individual
Indian communities to the contact situation. Many Indian communities have consciously been, and still are, able to resist incorporation
and assimilation. These, however, grow fewer every year. Except for
relatively rare enclaves, the Indian minorities of Mexico will undoubtedly ultimately be fully acculturated and assimilated by the
mass of the Mexican population. Many idealists in Mexico and abroad
look upon this outcome with some distaste. Quite rightly, they argue
for the right of the Indian groups to maintain their own culture and
their own language. They see that Mexico, and the world at large,
would be the poorer for the loss of the many positive values embodied
in these Spanish-Indian cultures. But with the efforts of the government to extend education, modern concepts of health, scientific farming, and other aspects of the contemporary Mexican culture to the
Indian, and with the rapid extension of transportation and communication facilities and the encroachment of a modern commercial
system, the isolation of these Indian communities has been broken.
In one way or another, the people of such communities will be drawn
into the web of modern Mexican social life. With few caste-like barriers around him, the Indian will continue with ever-increasing speed
to be assimilated by the Mexican majority.

RECOMMENDED ADDITIONAL READINGS

Caso, Alfonso, and others. Métodos y Resultados de la Política Indígenista
    en México. Memórias del Instituto Nacional Indígenista, Vol. VI.
    Mexico, 1954.

Cline, Howard. The United States and Mexico. Cambridge: Harvard University Press, 1953.

Lewis, Oscar. Life in a Mexican Village, Tepotzlan Restudied. Urbana: University of Illinois Press, 1951.

Redfield, Robert. The Folkculture of Yucatan. Chicago: University of Chicago Press, 1941.

Tannenbaum, Frank. Mexico: The Struggle for Peace and Bread. New York: Knopf, 1951.

Tax, Sol, and others. The Heritage of Conquest. Glencoe, Ill.: Free Press, 1952.

Whetten, Nathan. Rural Mexico. Chicago: University of Chicago Press, 1948.

II

The Negro in the Americas

TWO of our case studies involve people who are Negroes, or at least in part descendants of Negroes, in the French West Indies and in the United States. In both instances their ancestors came to the New World as slaves. The story of the American slave trade is well known and need not be discussed in any detail here. As we have seen, the European newcomers to the lowland areas of the New World soon exterminated or drove back the sparse American Indian population as they occupied the land. In the tropical lowlands of the Antilles, the Guianas, and Brazil, the land and climate were soon found appropriate for sugar cane, and sugar was a much-sought luxury in Europe. Sugar production brought wealth, comparable to that which might be derived from gold and silver in the highlands, but a steady labor supply was needed. Lacking a large Indian population, the Europeans looked to Africa. The densely populated area of West Africa provided a never-ending supply of labor, and slave trading with the New World planters became another source of wealth for the Portuguese, the Spanish, the English, the Dutch, and later for the New England Puritans. It is estimated that more than fifteen million Africans were brought to the New World during approximately three hundred years of the slave trade. During the colonial period, there were more Africans than Europeans in the tropical and semi-tropical lowlands of the southern United States, the Antilles, and eastern South America. Even today, people of African descent predominate in certain areas.

Throughout those areas of the Americas in which the Negro once was, or still is, the predominant element in the population, the processes of assimilation had certain features in common. As the outstanding student of the Negro in the New World, Melville Herskovits, has shown, most of the slaves came to the Americas from a single African culture area (Herskovits, pp. 33 ff.). They came from West Africa—Sierra Leona, Liberia, the Gold Coast, Nigeria, and the Congo. In this area, although there were numerous cultural differences from one tribe or kingdom to another, there were also many features of economic, social, political, and religious life which were shared by all the groups. Furthermore, although the languages of West Africa are diverse and not mutually understandable, most of them are of a common ancestral stock and thus share many aspects of syntax and structure, which facilitated the development of mixed patois languages in the New World. Perhaps because of this shared West African cultural tradition, a large body of African culture has persisted—in different degrees in various localities, to be sure—in the New World. African influence is apparent in the music, the folklore, the cuisine, the family organization, the work habits, and the religion of most of the areas into which Negroes were imported.

Moreover, the areas of the Americas with large Negro populations were all characterized by plantations, which produced cash crops on a large scale and which were once all manned with slave labor. Throughout the West Indies and northern South America, sugar cane was the principal crop, and the exigencies of organization demanded by this crop created striking similarities in social life throughout the area. Even in the United States, where cotton rather than sugar cane was the basis of the economy, plantation life greatly resembled its

South American and Caribbean counterparts (Freyre, p. xx). Throughout the Americas, plantations produced a "caste society" based upon the dependence of a relatively small group of white landed gentry on the labor of a large group of Negro slaves. But the barriers between the two "castes" were not sufficient to avoid miscegenation. Throughout the Americas, including the United States, white men took Negro (and later mulatto) women as mistresses and concubines. Throughout these areas, Negro slaves were the nurses, cooks, chambermaids, and playmates of the dominant white "caste." Such intimacy meant that each "caste" learned from the other, yet it was the dominant white group that enforced most its ways of thinking, its customs and rules of behavior upon the helpless slaves. It is not by chance that Brazilians and people from the West Indies found Margaret Mitchell's *Gone With the Wind* understandable and interesting.

As a result of these basic similarities, the process of assimilation of the Negro has also been similar in many respects throughout the plantation areas irrespective of the specific locale. Whereas the Indians of Mexico and Peru continued to live in their villages and to inhabit their accustomed environment, the Negro, in contrast, was torn from his homeland, his social group, and those who spoke his language. Negro slaves came to the New World not as families, kin groups, or tribal units, but as individuals (Hughes, *Peoples,* p. 27). Furthermore, they came to a strange environment in which they had to learn to eat new foods, speak new languages, adopt new rules of behavior imposed by slavery, change their tribal religions, and worship new gods. Unlike the mass of Indians of the highland countries, the Negro did not have the force of his own social group to support him in the process of adjustment to the new social situation. And unlike the Indian who was exploited by such devious means as *encomienda* and "debt peonage," the Negro was throughout the Americas treated as chattel to be bought and sold by his owner.

In the nineteenth century, under the impact of growing humanitarianism and the realization that slave labor was in the long run costly, slavery was abolished in all American nations and colonies. Abolition took place in 1834 in English colonies, in 1848 in French

colonies, in 1863 in Dutch colonies, in 1867 in the United States, and
finally in 1888 in Brazil. Thus, but a few generations have gone by
since the majority of the Negroes of the Americas were emancipated,
and everywhere they still feel the effects of slavery. In general, they
are still poor, uneducated, and relegated to manual labor; and their
physical features—the color of their skin, their hair and facial features—everywhere remain as symbols of their former slave status.
In all American nations, the Negroes and descendants of Negroes
suffer from color prejudice which varies in degree from the mild
Brazilian variety to the intense form it takes in the southern United
States. Yet everywhere in the Americas (even in the United States)
miscegenation early in the slave period produced a large group of
people of mixed descent—the *mulatos* of Brazil and the *mulâtres* of
the French colonies—who were often granted freedom by their white
fathers and early came to form a middle group between the Negro
slaves and the white masters. Even before the end of slavery, a class
of freed Negroes everywhere appeared to join the mulattos in a status
between the white upper class and the slaves. Since emancipation, a
few Negroes and people of color have achieved high economic and
social status in all American countries. And, despite many barriers to
assimilation, these Negro minorities have everywhere made considerable progress in achieving full participation in their respective
societies.

But the assimilation of Negroes and people of color has not been
a uniform process in the various countries and colonies of the Americas. The barriers to assimilation, while often similar, have differed
in intensity in the different nations. In general, it may be said that
whereas in certain British islands of the West Indies and in the
southern United States "color" prejudice has been more intensely
felt as a barrier to the assimilation of Negro minorities, class prejudice has been a stronger barrier in countries colonized by the Spanish,
Portuguese, and French. This is a result of differences already formed
in the mother countries before expansion to the New World, as well
as differences in historical events in the New World. As many writers
before us have stated, the Portuguese, and perhaps to a lesser extent
the Spaniards, were already accustomed to people of color before

1500. Unlike northern Europeans they did not acquire "color preju- dice" so readily.

Perhaps more important were differences between northern and southern Europe in economic development and ideology in the cen- turies just following the discovery of the Americas. Southern Europe in the sixteenth and seventeenth centuries continued to be semi- feudalistic in its class alignments and predominantly Catholic in re- ligion. The highly organized hierarchy of the Catholic Church insisted upon granting equal spiritual status to people of color, both freed and slave. On the other hand, the mores of northern Europe in the seventeenth and eighteenth centuries were dominated by the rapid growth of capitalism and the rise of a new socio-economic class, the bourgeoisie, with its own personal, material, and moral values. These values, expressed through the doctrines of Protestantism, tended to encourage the spiritual as well as the physical segregation of masters and slaves.

In the New World other differences developed. The Spanish, French, English, and Portuguese colonists in the West Indies were sugar planters and sugar brought them great wealth in the seven- teenth and eighteenth centuries. By the nineteenth century, sugar production was no longer as lucrative and the sugar planters were no longer as eager to hold on to their slaves. Slaves represented a large capital investment. They had to be fed, even though poorly, during times of serious losses as well as during times of high profits. A sys- tem of share-cropping by which the laborer shared in the risk, or a system of wage labor by which the worker might be dismissed when no longer needed, seemed preferable to slave labor. But in the South of the United States the plantations developed later, and in the nine- teenth century they grew cotton, which was a highly profitable crop at the time when sugar declined. Thus, in the nineteenth century, when the planters of the North American South were hungry for slaves, the Latin American planters were hard put to make a living from slave labor. Hence, although the abolition of slavery came peacefully and even advantageously to the West Indies and South America, it came as a real blow to North American cotton planters and was accompanied by a cataclysmic war and the trials of the so-called Reconstruction. Furthermore, following emancipation, the North American economy reached its great period of expansion; in the West Indies and South America, on the other hand, a colonial economy continued which was essentially agrarian and furnished raw materials to more industrial areas. In many cases, the economic life of these sugar-producing areas became stagnant, offering little opportunity for the mass of people to improve their lot, regardless of their color.

These differences between North America and Latin America—some inherited from Europe and some resulting from different historical factors in the New World—contributed greatly to the barriers which each country emphasized in the assimilation of ex-slaves and their descendants. Therefore, one of our cases is taken from the French West Indies; and the other concerns the Negro in the United States. Although the case of the Negro in the French West Indies does not portray the extreme of Latin American ease in race relations (Brazil would be better suited for this purpose), it furnishes us with a situation which contrasts strongly with that of the contemporary North American South. It illustrates the process of assimilation of a Negro and colored minority in a predominantly Catholic country with an agrarian economy and a rigid system of socio-economic classes persisting out of its semi-feudal past. The southern United States, on the other hand, gives us a picture of a rapidly changing society with an expanding economy, especially when compared to almost any Latin American area, where a Negro minority group has been able to improve its material situation in the face of rigid color prejudice, discrimination, and segregation.

THE NEGRO IN MARTINIQUE [1]

Sailing north from Venezuela toward the Atlantic, one encounters a group of small volcanic islands known as the Lesser Antilles, which form a long archipelago gradually bending north and west from Trinidad to Puerto Rico. At various times and to different extents during the seventeenth and eighteenth centuries, these islands were important in the economic life of the great European powers. So important were they, in fact, that France in 1763 ceded Canada, the Ohio and Mississippi valleys and Grenada (one of the Windward Islands) to the British, but held firmly to the two small islands of Guadeloupe and Martinique. The Lesser Antilles were valued for their wealth in sugar, eagerly sought in Europe and abundantly produced in their volcanic soil and tropical climate. Sugar and the rum produced from it furnished the basis for a vast mercantilist network, first developed by Holland and Britain.[2] The growth of trade and manufacturing made this mercantile system possible. But with an increase of production costs due to soil depletion, the domination of Britain over the triangular trade began to wane, and the French islands, where cane cultivation started at a later date, began to thrive.

At one time France held most of the islands of the Lesser Antilles from Hispaniola to Tobago, and French planters were for a time

[1] The authors gratefully acknowledge the assistance rendered by Mr. Guy Dubreuil of the University of Montreal in the preparation of the research draft of this chapter. Mr. Dubreuil is not responsible, however, for errors of fact or interpretation.

[2] Britain developed a triangular trade carried on with her islands, the North American colonies, and Africa. North America supplied the islands with food, the importation of which was necessary since all available land and labor were devoted to the sugar fields. North America in return received molasses to make rum, which in turn went to Africa in exchange for slaves, who went to the plantation areas to produce sugar. This is a simplified picture of the situation which enabled Britain to expand her merchant fleet and to develop a great manufacturing industry at home. The market for the manufactured goods was the colonies, which in the mercantilist system were prevented from producing anything but raw materials.

virtually in control of Trinidad. Now all that is left of these island possessions is Martinique and Guadeloupe and its five small dependencies. Both Martinique and Guadeloupe now have the status of overseas departments of the Republic of France. The department of Guadeloupe consists of Guadeloupe itself (actually two islands, Grande-Terre and Basse-Terre, divided by a narrow tidal channel) and a group of smaller islands, namely Les Saintes, Marie-Galante, Désirade, Saint-Barthélemy, and the French portion of Saint Martin (part of Saint Martin is Dutch). The total area of Guadeloupe is but 583 square miles and the smaller islands add another 105 square miles to the total area of the department. The population of the department is about 240,000 people. On the other hand, the department of Martinique consists of but one island with an area of 385 square miles and with some 239,130 people (1954). With French Guiana, this is the remnant of France's once vast empire in the New World.

The principal products of both these French departments in the New World is still sugar and rum, but sugar-cane production is no longer such a prosperous enterprise. In fact, it is said that Guadeloupe and Martinique are now a financial liability to the mother country. Much of Basse-Terre (Guadeloupe) and a large portion of Martinique are too high and broken for sugar-cane cultivation. Both have high mountainous regions capped with volcanic cones: Mont Soufrière in Basse-Terre is the highest peak in the Lesser Antilles (4,869 feet above sea level); Mont Pelée in northern Martinique erupted in 1902 with such violence that it destroyed Saint Pierre, then the capital city of Martinique, and laid waste a whole section of the island. Most of the sugar cane is thus grown on a relatively limited area of Grande-Terre in Guadeloupe and on the Lamentin Plain inland from Fort-de-France, the new capital of Martinique. Other crops such as bananas, cacao, coffee, vanilla, and pineapples are grown but sugar cane is still of major importance in the economic system.

Reliable statistics as to the racial origin of the people of Martinique [3] are impossible to secure, but it is probably safe to say that

---

[3] In this chapter, for purposes of simplification and because better data are available, we shall stress the situation of people of color in Martinique; only from time to time will comparative data from Guadeloupe be presented.

at least 97 percent of the population is, in part, of African descent. There is a small group of European whites, probably not exceeding four thousand people, and there is a small group of descendants of East Indian laborers who were imported in the nineteenth century. Among the mass of people of African descent—or "people of color," as we shall refer to them—there is every degree of African ancestry, varying from people of seemingly "pure" West African physical type to individuals who are phenotypically Europeans but who have a mulatto or Negro ancestor. As we shall see, these people of color do not form a unified group facing the small white elite, for they are split into many categories of color and socio-economic classes. Nor do these people suffer legal disabilities. As members of a department of France, they have officially the same rights as any continental citizen and they are represented in the French National Assembly, in the Council of the Republic, and in the Council of the French Union. Moreover, there are people of color in nearly all strata of Martinique society—in the professions, in the bureaucracy, and in political life. It would seem doubtful then that we could consider the people of color in Martinique as a minority group. Yet, not only are they, as a group, depressed economically, but their Negroid physical characteristics (or the memory of a Negroid ancestor) remain as a symbol of slave status and as a barrier to their complete assimilation into French national society. They are subject, as we shall see, in varying degrees to prejudice deriving from a highly visible special stigma, namely Negroid appearances. Taken as a group, however, the people of color of Martinique, like many minorities throughout the world, form a majority in numerical terms.

Furthermore, most of the people of color in Martinique are set off both culturally and linguistically from other nationals of France and even from the upper-class whites of the island. The way of life of the people of color, particularly of the rural and urban lower class, is a blend of African, French, and local traits acquired under slavery. As in Mexico, the culture of the peasants in Martinique resembles the contemporary culture of the national society, yet has many of its own distinctive traits. The language of the mass of people of color in Martinique is not French but a creole language which is essentially

French in vocabulary and African in structure, with many words borrowed from English, Spanish, and the aboriginal Cariban language. Although French is taught widely in schools and is the official language of Martinique, many people do not speak French at all and others are bilingual. Thus, along with physical characteristics, language and culture also set off the majority of the people of color in Martinique from the dominant group of their society. These people lack an *esprit de corps* as a group but they share many other characteristics that mark them as a distinct minority. Their situation is made especially difficult by the unfavorable economic conditions on the crowded island, and the persistence of a social structure that took form during slavery.

I

Martinique, discovered by Columbus on his fourth voyage, was a Spanish possession until 1635. Over three hundred years of continuous French rule have now gone by and little trace of the early Spanish presence remains. The influence of the first settlers of Martinique—the warlike Carib Indians—may likewise be discounted. Although some of the local islanders claim that they are directly descended from the "brave" Caribs, by 1692 there were only 160 Indians left on Martinique. The rest had been decimated by war and disease.

The French had at first no intention of entering the African slave trade. The first policy for the islands was to settle the land with a self-supporting French peasantry as in Canada, and it was not until late in the seventeenth century that conversion of the suitable part of the island to sugar-cane plantations worked by Negro labor began to take place. Sugar cane was introduced as a cash crop in 1654, evidently by a group of Jewish refugees from the Dutch settlements on the northeastern coast of Brazil. By the beginning of the eighteenth century, this little colony had become a wealthy sugar island.

The sugar plantations, known as *habitations,* were almost self-contained communities, each with its own lodgings for the laborers and its own *usine,* or sugar mill. At the center was the big stone house of the *habitant,* as the owner was called. Many *habitants* were ruined noblemen. Others were commoners who were permitted to buy titles from a company set up for the purpose. Fields cultivated for the commercial crop extended in every direction. In addition, small plots were allotted for subsistence crops to feed the people. Thus, in the seventeenth century the importation of food was not a problem, for sugar had not yet demanded every available bit of good land.

At first the *habitants* tried to solve the labor problem by using indentured workers, called *engagés*. The remuneration was three hundred pounds of tobacco payable at the end of three years of service, at which time the workers were free to remain on the island if they wished. Unlike the Iberian countries, France had had no tradition of slavery and the French government, as opposed to the planter class, consistently objected to bringing Africans to the islands. The government preferred *engagés* who, as French nationals, could be called on for defense. Another reason for this policy was the belief that peasants, not *habitants* and slaves, were the best consumers and the ideal citizens for colonial outposts.

Indentured labor, however, did not fit the needs of the island. Knowing that the *engagés* would cease to work at the end of their contract period, the *habitants* dealt with them more harshly than with slaves whose continued good health was an advantage. Not enough *engagés* were willing to subject themselves to this treatment. An effort was made to ship criminals, Protestants, and other "undesirables" from France as *engagés forcés* (literally, forced endentured laborers) but the demand was still not filled. In a further attempt to lure voluntary labor, the contract period was reduced to eighteen months, but even as early as 1737 the stream was running dry. By the time that the *engagé* system was officially abandoned in 1774 as fruitless and costly, slavery had already become the chief source of labor.

It had always been apparent to the *habitants,* as it had to sugar planters elsewhere in America, that Negroes were the most secure source of slave labor. In 1671, there were about three thousand Europeans in Martinique and already some four thousand Africans. Insisting that it was too expensive to buy slaves from other countries, the planters forced France to go into the slave trade. By 1713, there were about 14,500 Negroes in Martinique, and just twenty years later the slave population had increased to as much as 72,000. The number seems never to have gone beyond about 80,000 (Philémon, p. 77).

Because the death rate was extremely high in the New World, and because under slavery the Negroes did not reproduce fast enough to replenish the population, the increase can only be accounted for by a constantly renewed flow from Africa. Among slaves, those in Martinique seem to have had a comparatively favorable birthrate. In 1699, among 13,292 Negroes, some 32 percent were children. Yet this was still not enough for replacement. The pattern for the population composition of Martinique was set by the influx of Africans during the eighteenth century, at the end of which there were at least eight times as many Negroes as whites on the island. During the first half of the next century, few Europeans came; and the Negroes, after adjusting to the new environment and gaining some freedom of family life, increased rapidly. In the last one hundred years the total population (which is largely of Negro descent) has doubled; the excess of births over deaths in 1951 was 5,276 (Leiris, *Contacts*, p. 17).

In terms of numbers alone, one might expect this mass of people of color gradually to have absorbed the small number of Europeans. To some degree this has been true biologically, but cultural assimilation has been toward the economically, socially, and politically dominant heritage of France. Acculturation of all subjects to French patterns of living has long been a French ideal, and it was officially encouraged in the Antilles whenever possible. This trend was also an involuntary result of slavery. Africans came to the islands not as families, kin groups, or villages, but as individuals who had been abruptly cut off from their former life. They were people with different languages and from different cultures who were mixed together and grouped in ways determined only by the requirements of plantation organization. They had, therefore, little opportunity to perpetuate their old ways of living.

Despite these unfavorable conditions, a number of culture elements of African origin—or betraying African influence—have survived into the present. Some of these, such as certain foods and seasonings, musical rhythms, and folktales, are now a part of the culture of whites and Negroes alike. Others are found only among the people of African descent. The creole language is the most striking example. In addition, some items of women's dress, especially the immense handkerchief called a *madras,* are probably Africanisms. Cooperative work parties called *coups-de-main* have also been traced to Africa, but models for such behavior might well have been furnished by similar institutions found in France. Of undoubted African origin is a mock fight in the form of a dance performed to the rhythm of African-type drums. On the whole however, the African influence in Martinique seems less marked than in such centers of Afro-American culture as Haiti, and Bahia, in Brazil. There is no doubt that most of the formal institutions as well as the dominant value system that finally prevailed were those imposed by the Europeans.

The relative lack of African survivals in the culture of Martinique can be accounted for to some extent by several rather obvious factors. Chief among them is that Martinique is a small island. Escaped slaves were not able to form communities—as in Jamaica, Surinam, Brazil, and Haiti—which could perpetuate African traditions. Supervision of slaves was strict and close contact with the whites has been the rule ever since the time when the first slaves found themselves working side by side with the French *engagés.* Furthermore, unlike the population of Haiti, for whom independence severed contact with France, the people of African origin in Martinique have had continuous relations with the metropolitan French.

Some believe that one of the strongest forces working toward acculturation in Martinique has been religion. Today, except for a few recently converted Protestants, everyone is Catholic. Under Catholicism, slave owners were morally obligated to teach their slaves Christianity, to have them baptized, and whenever possible to grant them the privileges of the other sacraments. Priests seem to have been relatively numerous even during the early colonial period. Many *habitations* had their own chapel or church and a resident priest, who was able to exert pressure on the masters to enforce religious instruc-

tion. Father Labat, who visited the island at the end of the eighteenth
century, says that on most *habitations* there were morning and eve-
ning prayers attended by both the slaves and the French owner and
his family. This same observer was impressed with the slaves' faith
in the efficacy of Christian prayers and especially of the mass
(Labat).

Yet on many plantations, religious training was limited to a few
prayers and the most elementary catechism. Frequently, when there
was no priest, a French indentured laborer or even a Christian Negro
slave led the services. It was also the custom to have a recently arrived slave share the hut of a Christian slave who was entrusted to
help the newcomer adapt to his environment and to the labor. It was
assumed that the neophyte would be readily convinced of the superiority of Catholicism and that he would of his own accord seek
baptism. For all formal purposes such practices welded people into
one religious body.

The religion learned by such methods was gradually transformed
into a hybrid type of Catholicism containing vestiges of various
African beliefs. There is even today a large body of practice and
belief in no way derived from Catholicism, though whether it derived
more from Africa than from medieval French folklore is doubtful.
Belief in supernatural beings such as *volants* (werewolves) and
sukuyans (female vampires) is widespread. The world is populated
also by *anticris* (antichrists), who are a kind of homunculus, and the
ubiquitous *zombis* that seem to be any object associated with fear.
The capricious wandering souls called *mouno-mo* may well be derived from Africa, but such fear of the dead is also an old European
belief. There is a wide belief in protective charms, which is also extended to Catholic objects. Among the peasants of Martinique it is
possible that the respect for prayer is as much magical as religious
behavior, since it appears to differ in no way from attitudes toward
the definitely magical folk beliefs.

A man's funeral, the peak of his career, at which there is a *veillée*,
or wake, is accompanied by group singing and stories, as in Africa.
And perhaps of African derivation, too, are the *quimboiseurs* and

guérisseurs (sorcerers or medicine men) who cure by magical and herbal methods, and who can cast spells and remove the evil effects of magic. Many plantations are said to have their official *quimboiseurs*. However, there is no religious organization of *quimboiseurs*, nor are there elements of religious belief associated directly with African deities, such as are the Haitian *vodun* or the Brazilian *condomblé*.

Though many cases of supposed possession may be pointed out in Martinique and Guadeloupe, and although the *quimboiseurs*, especially, often go into trance in the manner of shamans, this behavior seems to possess neither the religious character nor the appearance of collectively organized manifestations which would permit a comparison with possession as it is found in cults of which the Haitian vodou is a typical example. (Leiris, *Contacts*, p. 53*n*)

The conversion of slaves in the French West Indies occurred with greater regularity than in the South of the United States or in the British West Indies. It was not until 1793, for example, that the Consolidated Slave Act of Jamaica stipulated that owners were to instruct their slaves in religion and facilitate the baptism of Negroes. This law had little effect, for the English planters resisted any movement to Christianize their slaves and were antagonistic to the missionaries. They feared that conversion would interfere with the master's rights and that Christian slaves might be more ready to throw off the yoke of slavery. When the Negro slaves finally became Christians in British colonies, they usually belonged to a different denomination and church from those of their master.

Judging the slave to have a soul did not, as the British feared, interfere with slavery; for the French in Martinique proved that a chattel can have a soul. As Frank Tannenbaum points out, the French system of slavery seemed to fall between the Spanish and Portuguese system at one extreme and the British, American, Dutch, and Danish systems at the other. While the latter group had no previous slave tradition and slave laws, and their religious institutions were little concerned with the Negro, the Portuguese and Spanish possessed, prior to their experience in the New World:

both a slave law and a belief that the spiritual personality of the slave transcended his slave status. In between them the French suffered from the lack of a slave tradition and slave law, but did have the same religious principles as the Spanish and Portuguese. If one were forced to arrange these systems of slavery in order of severity, the Dutch would seem to stand as the hardest, the Portuguese as the mildest, and the French, in between, as having elements of both. (Tannenbaum, *Slave*, p. 65)

It seems that at first the slave in the French West Indies was not considered as an outright chattel, but very soon the Code Noir, which will be discussed below, made him one. The Catholic French planters opposed laws which limited their outright control over their slaves no less than the Protestant planters of the British colonies. Yet the fact that Martinique was colonized by a Catholic nation certainly seems to have tempered slavery and the attitude of the whites toward the Negro.

This attitude toward the Negroes is reflected in the frequence of miscegenation between Negroes and whites (and later mulattoes) in Martinique. Everywhere in the New World European men formed mixed alliances with Negro and Indian women and miscegenation was not infrequent in the British colonies and later in the United States, but all contemporary observers constantly emphasize its occurrence in Martinique and its consequences for both the mother and her offspring. By the end of the seventeenth century the proportion of Negroes to whites was about three to one, and the number of slaves rapidly increased. As elsewhere, the number of European men was vastly superior to their women. French men took concubines from among their slaves. At first these mixed unions were not considered degrading, but they were never wholly acceptable in plantation society. Soon the unions and the resulting offspring came to clash with the economic interest of the planter class. Mixed unions led to frequent manumission. Usually the child went with the free father. The slave mother of a mulatto (*mulâtre*) child, whether married to the father or not, might be freed along with her child. In such a case, the mother might migrate to the mountains where she would cultivate land given her by the father of her child. Or she might move to Saint-Pierre. Sometimes she would remain on the plantation and enjoy special privileges while the child was educated by his father. It was not infrequent for mulatto sons to inherit the material possessions of their French fathers.

Along with miscegenation went other ways to achieve manumission, such as the right of a slave to purchase his freedom or to earn it by performing special services for his master. Soon there was a large group of freedmen, most of whom were mulattoes. On the other hand, in Guadeloupe, where there was always a labor shortage, the whites resisted manumission, expressing the attitude usually associated with Protestant countries: "Once an African, always an African." The freedmen of Guadeloupe, as in the United States and in contrast to those in Martinique and the possessions of the Iberian countries, could not remain where they had once been slaves, but had to move to another area.

On Martinique the freed *mulâtres*—many of whom had received some education and some of whom had the support of their rich French fathers—soon emerged as competitors of the *petits blancs,* the white indentured laborers and their descendants who held minor bureaucratic positions or worked as craftsmen and small farmers. Since the island was small and control by the *grands blancs* (as the rich *habitants* were also called) was virtually complete, there was little economic opportunity for the *petits blancs*. Their already insecure position was further challenged by the rapid growth of the free *mulâtres* group. The *petits blancs* were largely responsible for the clamor which arose against miscegenation during the seventeenth century. But the small group of white women on the island were equally opposed to mixed matings; their men, both of the *petit* and *grand blanc* class, were too easily tempted by the mulatto women (*les belles mulâtresses*) who used their charms and beauty as a way of social climbing. The plantation owners demanded that more white women be brought to Martinique to marry their sons, for fear that their titles of nobility would be tarnished by mixed unions. More white women came to Martinique, but evidently the *belles mulâtresses* were very beautiful,[4] for miscegenation continued, the mulattoes increased numerically, and their economic situation improved.

Ultimately, in 1685, a special set of laws known as the Code Noir was issued by the French government in an effort to control the rising class of *mulâtres* and to establish firmly the domination of the French in the islands. Contrary to previous practice, the children of mixed unions now acquired the status of their slave mother instead of their free father. The freedom of these children could no longer be bought, nor could their mother ever be manumitted. Both a slave mistress and her children by a European father were to be sold in public auction for the benefit of charity. A free man who was proved to be the father of a child by a slave woman had to pay 2,000 pounds of sugar as a fine. The slave owner who permitted such a union with one of his slaves was also fined the same amount. Only if the white man married his slave mistress might he avoid the fine and gain freedom for the mother and child. Legal marriages between whites and slaves had long been looked down upon, and only a few white men actually contracted such marriages after the appearance of the Code Noir. Legal unions between white and black, master and slave, decreased sharply, but the French government erred in thinking that miscegenation could be stopped by passing laws. Illicit, and now illegal, relations between blacks, whites, and mulattoes continued as before. By making such unions illegal, the Code Noir simply reinforced a pattern of concubinage which had long been a pattern in French society.

The Code Noir, in attempting to stabilize the relationships between master and slave, indeed made the latter a chattel, but granted him at the same time legal privileges which he never received in the British possessions. The Code guaranteed the slave the following rights:

---

[4] "It is the *Mulâtresse*—manifesting the amalgamation of the two great black and white races to which Martinique and Guadeloupe essentially owe their population—who is the incarnation of the classic West Indian and whose beauty, in the eyes of West Indians and non-West Indians alike, seems to sum up the particular charm of these islands" (Leiris, *Contacts,* p. 153). Lafcadio Hearn shared this view of the *belles mulâtresses* of Martinique (Hearn).

The slave was to be sufficiently fed; a mother was not to be sold apart from her immature children; sentencing to death, imprisonment, or mutilation (to punish runaway slaves) was not to take place without judgment by regular courts; the working day was to be limited to the period between sunrise and sunset; the sick were to be cared for in a hospital on the plantation. In exchange, the master had the right to have captives whipped and put in chains; gatherings of laborers belonging to different plantations, the carrying of arms, and the use of alcoholic beverages were forbidden to slaves; slaves could be condemned to death for any act of violence or attempt at violence against a free person and for any serious theft—except household thefts, which were punished by whipping or branding. (Leiris, *Contacts,* p. 19)

Any "maroon" (escaped slave) who was caught was to have an ear cut off; for a second offense he was to lose a leg; and for a third, he was to be executed.

Even stricter ordinances were issued by the French government when miscegenation continued, and attempts were made to render manumission still more difficult. A law of 1714 stated that a nobleman would lose his title if he contracted a mixed union. In 1778 marriage as well as concubinage was prohibited between whites and Negroes or mulattoes. In addition, the cost of purchasing a slave's freedom was increased to three times his original value. In 1720 even the kind of costume that slaves and freedmen of color should wear was stipulated. In 1761 and 1764 further laws were issued, this time forbidding Negroes and mulattoes the right of assembling in sacred places, even for weddings and dancing festivals, without special permission. A religious restriction was that only Catholics could own plantations; Protestant marriages were not recognized, nor could non-Catholics practice their rites in public. In 1763 and 1777 slaves and freedmen of color were forbidden to visit France for fear that they would learn about liberty and perhaps gain it.

The eighteenth century also saw a series of laws attempting to limit the range of action of the free mulatto group. An ordinance of 1765 decreed that no mulatto might become a notary or even work for a white notary. All public offices were closed to the mixed group. In 1773 mulattoes were denied the right to use French surnames. By this time, all means of livelihood were closed to them except farming, crafts, and commerce. Nevertheless they seemed to prosper, for one contemporary observer estimated that by 1790 mulattoes owned one quarter of the slaves and one third of all property (Philémon, p. 98). Although this hardly seems possible, the attitude indicates, whether exaggerated or not, how threatening the mulatto appeared to the whites.

On the eve of the French Revolution, Martinique society had crystallized into a rigid caste-like structure. Generally speaking, there seem at that time to have been four well-defined classes or "castes": the *grands blancs,* white slave-owning planters; the *petits blancs,* white small farmers, craftsmen, and even professionals; the *mulâtres,* the free group including various shades of color; and finally, at the bottom, the slaves. Each of the groups formed an endogamous unit at least as far as legal marriage was concerned, and social mobility from one group to another was extremely difficult. Unofficial sexual unions, of course, continued to occur. The attraction of *les belles mulâtresses* knew no class lines, and it was customary for whites of both classes to keep a mulatto as a mistress despite laws to the contrary. In terms of social mobility, however, the two white groups were clearly separated from those of color, and upward passage into the white classes was practically impossible.

Furthermore, by this time a "white bias" (Henriques, p. 44) seems to have been accepted by most people of color, slave and free alike. They adopted as their ideal the concept of the greater beauty of Caucasoid physical traits—light skin, straight hair, "fine" facial features, and the like—for these were symbolic of higher status and the amount of French culture acquired. Thus, both the slave and free colored castes were internally ranked. Especially among the free mulattoes, slight nuances in complexion and hair texture were important as criteria of social classification and a complicated set of terms was employed to distinguish the various shades and textures.[5]

[5] The categories set down by Moreau de Saint-Méry for Haiti in 1797–98 and applied in 1823 to Guadeloupe by Boyer de Peyreleau (1823, pp. 122–23, *n.*) are representative of the complex racial distinctions recognized throughout the Caribbean area. Saint-Méry decided that all men were composed of 128

Social grades were recognized even among the Negro slaves. As elsewhere in the Americas, the domestic servants seem to have felt superior to all others because of their greater amount of Western culture. Alongside them were the *nègres à talents,* slaves with special abilities such as a knowledge of carpentry, who were above the *nègres à culture,* the ordinary field workers born in the colony. At the bottom of the slave hierarchy stood the *nègres pièces d'Inde,* who were recent arrivals from Africa—pagans and savages, lacking any veneer of French culture. Père Labat (p. 63) remarks that slaves would marry only within their own category.

The Revolutionary Republic in 1794 granted freedom to all slaves in the French possessions. But the planters of Martinique were not prepared to accept the principles of the French Revolution. If they did not actually invite the British to take over the island, they at least offered no resistance to the invading forces. By this means, slavery endured in Martinique throughout the revolutionary period. Yet the slaves became increasingly restive, especially after the successful revolt and emancipation of Haiti in 1804. With the example of free Haiti to stir the slaves and drive fear into the hearts of the whites, Martinique entered a period of considerable tension, punctuated by open rebellions in 1822 and 1824.

From the point of view of metropolitan France, the maintenance of the slave system in Martinique thus became a progressively unrewarding arrangement. In order to keep the island's seventy-five thousand slaves under control, a permanent garrison of three thousand troops had to be stationed in Martinique. Furthermore, with the growth of the beet-sugar industry in France, cane sugar had lost

---

parts, which in Caucasoids were all "white," and in Negroes all "black." From the various combinations possible with Negroes, whites, and all people in between he devised a list of categories. Just barely above the Negro was the *saccatra,* who had anywhere from 112 to 120 "black parts." The child of a Negro and a *saccatra* was a *griffe,* who presumably carried from 96 to 104 "black parts." Next in the scale was a *marabou.* Then came the last of the series considered more "black" than "white," the *mulâtre.* The first type described as slightly more "white" than "black" was the *quarteron.* Above him in order of rank then followed the *métif,* the *mamelouc,* the *quarteronné* and finally the *sang-mêlé.* These last had only maximum of three "black parts" (Moreau de Saint-Méry pp. 82–87).

much of its appeal as a colonial product. Finally, in 1848, despite the bitter opposition of the planters, slavery was abolished.

With emancipation, most of the slaves deserted the plantations, although a few were induced to remain when granted ownership of small garden plots. Many migrated to the coastal cities of Saint-Pierre and Fort-de-France where they sought a living as day laborers, domestics, and artisans. Large numbers went inland into the hills and high mountains where they lived as independent farmers. In the interior, these freed slaves seemed to wish to forget the crowded plantation conditions; they did not form villages or even small nucleated settlements. Each man and each family settled on unoccupied land at a distance from his neighbors. A saying arose, that a neighbor should be far enough not to hear people talk among themselves, but near enough to hear a message when it was shouted.

To ease the financial stress caused by abolition, the French government granted an indemnity of six million francs to the planters and guaranteed their debts. Nonetheless, many were forced to sell their estates to French corporations or to small holders. The remaining *grands blancs,* deprived of their slaves, needed a new source of cheap labor if they were to survive. In the years immediately following abolition this problem was resolved by reintroducing the indenture system. About ten thousand Africans, twenty-five thousand East Indians, and smaller numbers of Chinese and Annamese were brought into Martinique as indentured field hands after abolition. Gradually however, the planters were able to depend more and more upon the island's own population for their supply of workers. When the price of sugar rose, the *grands blancs* expanded their holdings, placing more acreage under their control. In bad times, if forced to sell, they banded together to prevent purchase by Negro or mulatto bidders. As the plantation holdings expanded, and as the Negro and mulatto population increased, an adequate pool of landless agricultural workers supplied labor for the operation of the white estates. Thus, by 1936, 61 percent of the island's arable land consisted of estates of over one hundred hectares (247 acres). Three fourths of all the arable land was by then divided up among only 365 holdings, whose owners, with rare exception, were descendants of the *grands blancs* (Revert, p. 268).

II

Today, the descendants of the aristocrats are still in economic control in Martinique. They are now called the *békés,* and sometimes, if very wealthy, *gros* or *grands békés;* or even, as of old, *grands blancs.* Whites of less wealth and less certain ancestry may be referred to as *békés goyaves* or *békés pays,* terms similar to Brazil's *brancos da Bahia* or *da terra* (see Pierson, p. 148), used for people of Caucasoid appearance but of known colored ancestry. People of the "middle class" are spoken of as *mulâtres.* And the *nègres* are thought of, in general, as belonging to the large lower class. Thus, in its essential structure, Martinique society has changed little since colonial days. But there are factors at work which make its system of stratification less rigid than formerly, and much more complex. Important among these factors is the present legal position of people of color. Since Martinique is a department of France, all native-born people are citizens of France with all the rights that this status implies before the law. There are no longer any legal restrictions against intermarriage, against holding public office, against freedom of movement. In the school year 1951–52, public elementary schools were attended by some forty-two thousand pupils (Leiris, *Contacts,* p. 73), and there are many courses for illiterate adults which draw a large attendance. Furthermore, although the whites control the economic life of the island, people of color have by now entered into commerce and the professions. They hold public office on nearly all levels of local government.

Segregation because of color is not visible today in Martinique, and to the casual visitor there is little or no prejudice shown by the whites. On official occasions, such as the dedication of a church, a rich white may sit next to a mulatto and show him every sign of respect and friendship. The people of color have an intellectual elite which has produced such figures as Aimé Cesaire, the well-known French poet; and whites attend lectures given by mulatto and Negro scholars. On the surface it would seem that the official policy of France had gone a long way toward its ideal of total assimilation. But, like most of the West Indies, Martinique suffers from economic problems which make this goal more difficult to attain. The island is one of the most densely populated areas on earth, exceeded in the Caribbean only by Barbados and Puerto Rico. About 239,130 people occupy 427 square miles, which gives a density of about 600 per square mile. Such figures do not show completely the gravity of the problem, for the surface of the island is not uniformly habitable. Actually, one quarter of the surface is occupied by nine tenths of the population. The rugged mountains of the north, dominated by Mont Pelée, have been a powerful barrier to human settlement. The mountainous backbone gives way to a low fertile plain only to rise again to mountains in the extreme south. Only a part of the west coast is habitable, the rest being a drought area of thorn forests. Much of the island is the other extreme, tropical rain forests, so that there are only a few main areas naturally suited for habitation. These areas, however (the level lowlands), have been taken over by the sugar plantations. The mass of people, as a result, have been compelled to live in small cabins at the edge of the plantations which employ them, to crowd into the capital with its 66,000 people, or to live on subsistence plots ranging from one-quarter to two acres each in scattered localities along the fringes of the hills.

The bulk of plantation hands are employed only during the harvest season, from January to June. Between harvests there is a dead season when the laborers are hard-pressed to find work. Even the independent farmer in most cases must supplement his income with odd jobs, for the acreage under his control is not as a rule sufficient to assure a living.

Only very recently has there been any agriculture not centered around the plantation and the sugar factories (*usines*). Bananas have recently become an important crop, one which provides cash for the small farmer rather than for the plantation owner, and which gives a money return at more frequent intervals than does sugar. There are now 5,000 banana planters to whom the government is extending credit in the hope of stimulating the growth of a new peasant class (Leiris, *Contacts,* p. 37). The one complaint of this group is that maritime transport is a monopoly and the freight rates too high. Furthermore, white planters are entering into banana production and are thus competing with the peasants.

Relatively minor sectors of the economy are occupied by fishermen and forest gatherers. Much of the retail trade is carried out by Syrians. In the agricultural economy women bind the cane into bundles as it is cut and, between harvests, they work at weeding, planting, and manuring. The lowest-paid people are those who have no land but have not yet moved to the city—the rural proletariat. Some are so poor that they go from harvest to harvest regardless of the wages, unwittingly acting as strikebreakers. Only five thousand laborers live on estates, their position being considered the least desirable.

The over-all result of such conditions is that the rich whites control 85 percent of all exports, which consist almost entirely of sugar and rum. About 1,000 families, mostly white descendants of the colonial aristocracy, enjoyed in 1949 an annual revenue of over 200,000 francs, while some 150,000 to 170,000 people earned less than 10,000 francs yearly (Revert, p. 42). Of the 4,000 native whites living in Martinique, some 3,500 are descended from the colonial upper class.

Overpopulation, inequality of land distribution, and lack of industrialization render Martinique a typical underdeveloped area. At the heart of the poverty suffered by the island's more than a quarter of a million people lies the monocrop sugar plantation. There is no hope that conditions will change as long as sugar continues to dominate the economy. The processing methods of the French islands cannot compete in a free market with those of the large West Indian islands, such as Cuba, which is the world's largest sugar producer.

The economic stagnation of the island has meant that the people of color have in general not been able to improve their material situation despite their legal equality. Today the Negroes and mulattoes form the mass of people of the lower social strata, and because they are poor they have less education. If they can afford the time, they can obtain a free primary education. But secondary and advanced schooling are beyond the reach of most of them. There are only two *lycées* on the island, one for males and one for females. And except for the recently established (1948) Institut d'Etudes Juridiques, Politiques, et Economiques, and a teachers' training school, those who wish professional education must go to France. Nevertheless, educational opportunities, recently augmented by a system of scholarships, have helped some of the *mulâtres* to improve their positions.

Traditionally, the *mulâtre* group in the French West Indies is the one from which members of the professions are recruited, and which furnishes much of the staff in both public and private sectors; for a long time, the Creole whites have not for the most part been interested in furthering their studies beyond the minimum required for the management of their enterprises, and the Negroes have found themselves in practice deprived of all avenues of culture, while for a number of *mulâtres* education appeared as a means by which they could rise socially. (Leiris, *Contacts,* p. 152)

As a result, the people of color now form the majority of those doctors and technical and administrative personnel who are participating in efforts to improve local conditions.

Together with the backward economy, there has also been a persistence of old traditions and attitudes deriving from the colonial slave society. As indicated above, a hierarchy of racial categories, which became social categories, exists in Martinique, which is in many ways analogous to the ideas prevalent before 1848. As before, these categories are "racial" in that the highest value is placed upon what is white and the lowest value upon what is Negro, but today the categories are fewer in number. People are either *béké* (white), *mulâtre blanc* (white mulatto), *mulâtre brun* (brown mulatto), *câpre* (darker than a mulatto but lighter than a Negro), or *nègre* (Negro). The term *chabin* is also used to distinguish those individuals who have "good" Caucasoid physical traits but are known to have colored ancestors.[6]

[6] Reporting upon his personal experience in Martinique, Guy Dubrueil has this to say about "social-racial" terminology: "People are either *béké* (white); *mulâtre* (a distinction being made between *mulâtre clair* or *mulâtre blanc*— i.e., light or white mulatto—and *mulâtre foncé* or *mulâtre noir*—i.e., dark or

Contrary to what a description of these categories might lead one to believe, however their membership is not self-evident.

Whether or not he has a knowledge of anthropological facts, the observer who is not a native of Martinique or Guadeloupe discovers, on coming to these islands, that he is often mistaken in judging, simply on the basis of the appearance of a person with whom he comes into contact, in which racial category the latter is locally ranged. An individual whom he might consider a white is actually classed among the *mulâtres;* another whom he might take for a *mulâtre* is actually a white Creole; another whom he might think a Negro is labeled a *mulâtre,* etc. . . . . He will see, furthermore, that members of the same family often exhibit great differences although they are all ranked in the same category. (Leiris, *Contacts,* p. 160)

As before, the whites form an endogamous unit that resists marriage with people of color.[7] White men often have informal alliances with mulatto mistresses as they did in the past, but the legal marriage of a white with a *mulâtresse* even today often leads to the rejection of a man by his own kin and by white society. He becomes a *béké sauté barrière* (a white who has jumped the fence), or a *béké dissident.* Furthermore, even though there are deep friendships between whites and others, it is not usual for a white to invite his *mulâtre* friend to his home for dinner when he is entertaining other whites. And white women are supposed to avoid any kind of relationship with men of color which involves their being alone together. Racial barriers between the two major groups are still strong in those spheres which

black mulatto); *nègre* (Negro); *Congo* (very black with "bad" features). This last term refers to those who are supposed to trace their descent from the latest Africans to arrive in Martinique. The terms *câpre* and *chabin* are also used. The former refers to an individual with straight hair and mulatto or Negroid physical traits. The latter distinguishes those individuals who tend to have Caucasoid features along with light hair. Another expression is found: *béké goyave.* It is a pejorative expression referring to those who are apparently white and who sometimes boast about their 'race' but who actually have Negro ancestry. Most of the creole *békés* are thought to be *békés goyaves* by the peasants. As a matter of fact, if a white does not have blond hair, he may become racially ambiguous in the countryside." (personal communication)

[7] "A *grand mulâtre* of Martinique, married to a white from the continent and having such relations with the whites that one could almost say he had passed over the line, described the whites of Martinique as a group of families who own lands and factories (in person or through corporation shares) and practice endogamy to preserve that patrimony. . . ." (Leiris, *Contacts,* p. 133)

involve intimate family life—marriage and recognition of offspring; these are the spheres which might endanger the separate survival of the two groups.

Relative rank within the small middle-class group depends not only upon physical appearance but also upon economic, occupational, educational, and genealogical criteria. Thus, a *mulâtre blanc* tends to have a higher rank because of his physical appearance than does a *mulâtre brun,* but if the latter is a medical doctor he has higher status than a *mulâtre blanc* who is a notary. A mulatto doctor tends to associate with lighter mulattoes, and if he is not very Negroid in appearance, he is probably classified as a *mulâtre blanc.* Color then loses some of its socially negative connotations when it is associated with high economic status or a higher-ranking profession. However, color prejudice is clearly expressed among the upward-mobile members of the middle class in the selection of wives. A mulatto who is trying to improve his social standing seeks a mate whose color is lighter than his own. The racial characteristics of the children of such a marriage will have considerable influence upon their position in the socio-economic hierarchy. Although they tend to regard the aristocracy as a group which has degenerated through excessive inbreeding, many of the values of the aristocratic elite have been taken over by the mulattoes, including color prejudice.

Among the poorest group, which as we have said consists mainly of Negroes, racial distinctions are less important. But there are a few, such as the *Congos* or *neg' Guinins,* descendants of the latest African immigrants, who are looked down upon for being less "civilized." Then there are the "coolies," descended from the East Indian indentured laborers who suffer from stereotypes, such as that they are weak, untrustworthy, and that they "eat dogs and feces." But in general, according to Michel Leiris, this class is divided into two broad groups: *travailleurs casés,* or workers living in houses furnished by their employers on the estates; and *travailleurs non casés,* or independent workers (*Contacts,* p. 36). The *travailleurs non casés* are often just as poor as the others, but the fact that they have greater freedom of movement gives them more prestige. They can live on their own plots or they can gain more status by moving to the villages clustered along the recently built roads. Occupation and income overshadow physical appearance among such people. Since they are unable to compete with most whites on any ground, their racial ancestry becomes less crucial in assigning social rank. It is among the people who have higher incomes and better education, and are employed in white-collar occupations, that the question of color becomes important, because they do compete with the whites.

Color rarely stands out as an important issue for most of the lower-class peasants and manual workers. The preoccupation with finding a wife whose physical characteristics are less reminiscent of former slave status does not occur among the lower-class men. Indeed, as in most of the Caribbean area, the members of the lower classes do not even contract formal marriages until rather late in life, if at all. Among these people there is a 50 percent illegitimacy rate; most of the children are born from relatively permanent but informal consensual unions. Similar mating patterns are to be found on the other islands. The practice is called *plaçage* in Haiti and "keeping" in Trinidad. In Martinique, the expression is *en ménage*. Children born from an *en ménage* arrangement suffer no special stigma; children of fathers who have left the household are fully integrated within the maternal family. Living *en ménage* is correlated with low economic status. Church and/or civil marriage tends to replace it as the economic pyramid is climbed. Christian marriage remains the ideal for most people, and couples sanctify their unions by church (and civil) marriages when they can afford the luxury.

Most whites in Martinique will deny that race is a barrier to upward mobility. The *grands blancs* attempt to deny prejudice by talking of the high poetic, musical, and choreographic genius of the Negro. They speak of the loyalty of Negroes and of the affection they feel for their childhood nurse, their *da*. On the other hand, at the same time they diagnose the poverty of the Negro to be the result of indolence. The mulattoes, they say, are too ambitious and have a proclivity toward revolutionary ideas produced by their "mixed blood." And it is still thought that the *mulâtresse* is by nature sensual and sexually lax.

As we have seen, the mulattoes share the whites' beliefs about the

Negro. The ambivalent mulattoes also scorn the decadent aristocracy, whom they accuse of degenerating through excessive endogamy. It is not a surprise, therefore, to find that the most "French" of the people are the educated mulattoes. The mulatto of Martinique is noted for his polished Parisian accent and elaborate figures of speech. For him, "refined" behavior and "educated" speech are weapons against color prejudice. It is notable that the first Martinique authors neglected native subjects. Nineteenth-century newspapers printed little but news from Paris. Only in the last generation have intellectuals modified their identification with French values and fashions, daring to treat native subjects and venturing to describe life as it is.

III

Our two previous case studies of American Indian minorities were concerned with groups whose separate identity is in general a matter of pride, and who possess an intense in-group feeling on the community or tribal levels. These Indian groups with their special social structures, values, and ideologies, and their rather limited experience with "strangers," are strongly ethnocentric. Characteristically, they resist change, especially those modifications which might weaken their separate identity—even when, as in the case of Mexico, the attempt to change them has risen from benevolent intentions. The people of color in Martinique present quite another picture. Although people of color are quite conscious of the fact that they all suffer from the stigma attached to being non-white, they do not form, either on the community or insular levels, a unit intensely devoted to the idea of preserving their separate identity. On the contrary, a major concern of the dark-skinned people of Martinique is to avoid identification with those people on the island who have the most pronounced Negroid features. Light skin color and Caucasoid facial and hair characteristics have over the years come to be accepted as the ideal standard of beauty by everyone. This preference is visible in the elaborate system of ranking which divides the island's population into a series of horizontal strata closely associated with skin color. Generally speaking, the closer an individual's racial features approximate those of the whites, the higher up in the ranking system will he be found. There are many exceptions, however, since skin color and other physical characteristics are not the only critieria recognized as indications of class position. Wealth, occupation, and education are also important, with the result that a man who looks like a very dark mulatto but who is wealthy or is a university graduate may actually move in upper-middle-class circles and even be known as a *mulâtre blanc*.

As in most of the New World, the people of dark skin color in Martinique are somewhat prejudiced against those who are darker than themselves. Yet when it comes to establishing social position, these color prejudices are not too important since very dark types are readily accepted as belonging to the colored elite if their qualifications of a financial or educational nature are sufficiently outstanding. Thus if a poor Negro boy should somehow overcome the obstacles posed by the meager economic opportunities of the island and achieve a measure of financial success, there is every probability that he will crown his success by marrying a girl much lighter than he. Certainly the children of a wealthy Negro couple will seek, and without difficulty find, light mulatto mates. The trouble is that such cases of upward mobility are relatively infrequent (when compared for example, with the Negro in the United States). The nature of the island's economy is such that there are very few opportunities for poor people ever to improve their material and social position. Consequently, Negro is largely synonymous with "poor," and mulatto with "middle class."

When it comes to the attempt of the people of color to rise into the upper class, however, a new factor enters. Here the upward advance of the colored people, light mulatto as well as Negro, comes to an abrupt end. Color and racial ancestry exert a much greater influence than the factors of wealth and education. Marriage with the small upper-class white elite, which controls the greater part of the island's agriculture, industry, and commerce, is next to impossible for all persons of Negro descent.

Thus while mulattoes, Negroes and whites are represented (unequally) in the middle and lower classes, none but whites belong to the really top echelon of Martinique society. It is this fact which distinguishes the position of the people of Negro ancestry from that of the whites, and divides the society on racial grounds into a colored minority and a white majority. True, the minority itself is divided and even prejudiced against some of its own members, but such internal differences are not at all an unusual feature of minority situations.

Today perhaps the greatest disadvantage which all of the lower socio-economic groups of Martinique, both colored and white, suffer, is the lack of economic opportunity. The limited resources of the island and the stagnant economic system offer little opportunity for economic mobility. If and when such opportunities are available, it would seem that, under the circumstances, color prejudice would be reduced and might ultimately disappear. When Negroes and mulattoes are found in the same proportions as whites in all economic and occupational levels, it will no longer be possible to confuse a social and economic position with color. No longer will Negro be synonymous with poor and mulatto with the struggling middle class.

If we accept the possibility that in the future people of color will share proportionate control over the island's lands and factories, a special fate seems to be in store for today's white majority. With the economic basis of white endogamy removed, it seems likely that miscegenation and intermarriage between whites and mulattoes will increase. The result will be the eventual blending of all racial types. The small white majority in Martinique, in other words, probably will eventually be absorbed by the colored people who now constitute a minority.

RECOMMENDED ADDITIONAL READINGS

Hearn, Lafcadio. Two Years in the French West Indies. New York: Harper, 1890.
Labat, R. P. Voyages aux Isles de l'Amérique (Antilles) 1693–1705. Paris, 1931.
Leiris, Michel. Contacts de Civilisations en Martinique et en Guadeloupe. Paris: Unesco, 1955.
Revert, Eugène. La France d'Amérique, Martinique, Guadeloupe, Guyane, Saint-Pierre, et Miquelon. Paris, 1949.
——. La Martinique; Étude Géographique. Paris, 1949.

THE NEGRO IN THE UNITED STATES

Perhaps one of the most highly publicized and thoroughly studied minority groups in the world is the American Negro. In the nation which has the world's highest standard of living and a heritage of equality of opportunity for all men regardless of race, creed, or national origin, approximately fifteen million Negroes in the United States have suffered from some of the most severe forms of economic, residential, educational, and personal discrimination. The paradox of racism in the United States has become known as the "American dilemma," the title of Gunnar Myrdal's masterful study of the Negro in America. In this book Myrdal writes:

The Negro in America has not been given the elemental civil and political rights of formal democracy including a fair opportunity to earn his living upon which a general accord was already won when the American Creed was taking form. And this anachronism constitutes the contemporary "problem" both to Negroes and whites [in the United States]. (Myrdal, p. 24)

The situation of the Negro in the United States is even more of an anachronism when compared to that of ex-slave Negro groups in other areas of the New World. For, as a group, the United States Negroes probably have a higher standard of living and a higher level of education than the people of color in almost any other American nation. A dynamic expanding economy combined with a malleable social system has allowed frequent and easy economic and social mobility in the United States; and the Negro has shared in this advantage. But he has never received what might be even remotely considered an equal share. Barriers have arisen in the United States to set the Negro apart from the rest of the body politic. These barriers are more rigid and more restrictive than those found in any other American country. How they developed is a strange and paradoxical story.

I

The first Negroes who came to the North American colonies came not as slaves but as indentured servants. In 1619, when Negroes were first imported to Virginia, "there was neither law nor custom then establishing the institution of slavery in Virginia nor the other colonies" (Davie, p. 19). Some of these early comers actually earned their freedom after a certain number of years of service, in the same manner as did numerous European indentured laborers. But soon the concept of slavery was fixed. By the end of the seventeenth century a series of special laws governing and recognizing slavery were part of the legal code of many of the colonies and by "1750 slavery was recognized in the law of every North American colony" (Davie, p. 20).

By 1790 there were already 697,624 slaves in the North American colonies, and these increased rapidly until in 1860, on the eve of Abolition, the census figures showed almost four million, mainly concentrated in the southern part of the United States. Exactly how many of this number were imported and how many were a result of the normal increase of population, it is hard to say. But it is estimated that about four hundred thousand were brought in prior to 1808, when the slave trade became illegal; and between 1808 and 1860 perhaps a somewhat larger number were brought into the United States illegally. It seems that the total number imported did not exceed one million.

The slave trade in the United States exhibited several features not found in other American areas. These influenced the form slavery assumed in the United States and, indirectly, the process of assimilation of the Negro to American society. The majority of the slaves who were imported came late into the United States as compared with most other areas of the New World. Cuba seems to be an exception. The slave population of Cuba was built up mainly in the nineteenth century. In Brazil, the importation of slaves began as early as 1550 and by the beginning of the eighteenth century the flow of

Africans was past its peak, especially since Brazil had lost its monopoly on sugar. In the French West Indies, as we have seen, the slave trade reached its maximum in the early eighteenth century. In the United States, however, it was toward the end of the eighteenth and during the first half of the nineteenth centuries that the majority of the slaves were imported. This was a period of great development of capitalistic and commercial enterprise.

A very significant number of slaves came to this country not from Africa, but from the West Indies where they were already "seasoned." Thus, many of the American slaves, unlike those in the West Indies and in South America, had already been acculturated toward a European way of life. Those who did come directly from Africa found themselves in a milieu in which the Negro slaves were already culturally distant from their native land. This circumstance is important for understanding why perhaps less of African culture has survived here than in any other part of the Americas.

Despite these differences, an underlying sameness united the pattern of race relations in the United States under slavery with the patterns of the other New World slave areas. As elsewhere in the Americas, race relations in the United States were determined by a plantation system. Plantations everywhere in the New World arose from similar economic and ecological conditions and gave rise— whether in Brazil, Martinique, or the American South—to a set of social relationships which had fewer differences than similarities. The basic situation underlying the growth of these slave-operated plantations may be defined as an abundance of virgin land coupled with a shortage of labor. In order for agriculture to yield large profits, crops had to be produced on a large scale. Large tracts of land were required and, before the advent of mechanized agriculture, a large labor force. In the Americas the land was to be had cheaply, but hands to work the land were hard to find. Since land was to be had practically for the asking, free men would work in agriculture only as independent farmers, not as wage-earners. What was needed everywhere was some system whereby the labor force could be anchored, forming a caste of human beings who would stay put while the world moved westward past them.

The pattern of social relations between master and slave on the North American plantation did not differ in any substantial way from the pattern which prevailed in the other slaveholding areas of the New World. The uniquely poor record of race relations in the United States after emancipation was not matched by a correspondingly poor record under the plantation system. In general it appears that Southern planters were no more cruel and no less humane than their counterparts throughout the Americas. Individual cases of brutality were offset by individual instances of warmth and benevolence. As elsewhere, the Southern plantation was a highly self-sufficient microcosm within which master and slave lived at close quarters. In the little world of the plantation the human nature of the slave inevitably had to be taken into account by his master. The white master tended to rule this world as a paternal figure, equally capable of despotism and benevolence, and the slave often responded with sentiments of loyalty and dependence. Warmth and intimacy were especially characteristic of the relations between masters and those slaves who worked in the house, rather than in the fields. The traditional Southern "mammy" had her counterparts known as *baba* in Brazil and as *da* in Martinique. She was sometimes the wet nurse of the master's children and was in charge of them from early infancy to adolescence. She dressed and washed them, scolded them when necessary, and taught them manners and obedience. The children in turn regarded her with deference, kissed her when the family left or returned home, and remembered her kindness and devotion well into adulthood. As the plantation system developed, the relationship between the two races was regulated by a complex system of social ritual and etiquette which tended to humanize the legal status of slaves and to produce striking similarities from country to country, despite contrasting national legal codes.

The distinctive features of race relations in the United States today are not the result of any special peculiarities of the Southern plantation system. The unique pattern of race relations in the United States took form only after the plantation economy had collapsed. Yet the origins of this pattern were present in latent form from an early date, and there were many signs which pointed to the bitter times that emancipation would bring. Clearest among these were the harsh legal codes which defined the status of the Negro, both as a slave and as a free man.

At first there was no precedent in English law for slavery and, as stated above, it seemed for a time that Negroes were to be given the same status as indentured whites. Gradually, however, through court judgment and statute, the legal personality of the Negro servant was distinguished from that of white servants. In the beginning, slavery was thought to be proper only if the Negro concerned had not been baptized, but this objection was overcome in most of the colonies by the beginning of the eighteenth century. In 1667 Virginia passed a law which said "that the conferring of baptism doth not alter the condition of the person as to his bondage or freedom; that diverse masters, freed from this doubt, may more carefully endeavor the propagation of Christianity by permitting children, though slaves . . . to be admitted to that sacrament . . ." (Frazier, p. 24).

As the moral doubts about the enslavement of Christian Negroes vanished, the status of the slave crystallized into that of a sub-human creature and, eventually, in some of the Southern states, into that of an inanimate piece of property. In South Carolina slaves were considered personal chattel; in Louisiana, real estate. The laws of Maryland equated slaves with "working beasts, animals of any kind, stock furniture, plates and books" (Tannenbaum, *Slave,* p. 79). The slave in the Southern states could not acquire property, could not make a will, could not buy or sell, could not testify in the courts. Slave marriages had no legal standing. A slave spouse could not maintain an action against the violator of his or her bed, and there were no legal restrictions either upon the separate sale of husband and wife, or upon that of children and parents (Tannenbaum, *Slave,* pp. 73 ff.).

Even more significant contributors to a distinctively North American pattern of race relations were the various legal strictures aimed at impeding or discouraging the process of private manumission. As early as the seventeenth century the legal attitude was that Negroid features were presumptive evidence of slave status. The burden of proof fell upon the Negro. Throughout the American South the legal structure aimed at keeping the Negro enslaved, or at reducing him to slavery if he was free. Harsh laws discouraged or prohibited unions between freedmen and slaves. In many states private manumission could take effect only if the free Negro left the state within a stipulated period. In Mississippi, Alabama, and Kentucky manumission by testament was illegal. In South Carolina and Georgia manumission of any kind was only valid with the consent of the state legislature. In many states manumission was discouraged by the requirement that large bonds be posted to guarantee the freed slave's good behavior. Elsewhere, the slightest debt incurred by a freed Negro or mulatto was cause for enslavement by his creditor (Tannenbaum, *Slave,* pp. 65 ff.).

In addition, there were laws which forced legal and political inequality upon the free Negroes. These provisions are most revealing with respect to the North American failure to provide mechanisms for the integration of ex-slaves and their descendants into the normal social order. The free Negro posed a problem to the whites, both North and South, even before the end of slavery. His status was anomalous and difficult and he was subject to many disabilities which had no counterpart in the Spanish and Portuguese countries of the New World. There were laws restricting his emigration, and his right of assemblage. Free Negroes could not carry firearms, were forbidden to purchase or to sell liquors, and could not testify in court except against each other. They were disenfranchised, and were subject to differential legal penalities: corporal punishment, enslavement, and banishment from the state. Louisiana in 1806 provided by law that "Free people of color ought never to strike white people, nor presume to conceive themselves equal to the white, but on the contrary they ought to yield to them in every occasion, and never speak, or answer to them, but with respect" (Davie, p. 36).

In his brilliant little book, *Slave or Citizen,* Frank Tannenbaum has pointed out that throughout the English-speaking colonies, the moral and legal climate of enslavement stemmed from a different tradition than that which prevailed in the Spanish and Portuguese areas. The easier transition from slavery to freedom which characterized race relations outside the United States and the British West Indies can be attributed in part to the fact that, unlike the English, the people of the Iberian Peninsula had institutionalized slavery in their own countries as early as the thirteenth century. The laws governing slavery in Spain and Portugal actually represented an almost unbroken heritage from Roman times. These laws were transferred to the New World and determined the legal personality of both the Negro slave and freedmen in Latin America.

The basic postulate of the Iberian codes was that all men are spiritually equal in the sight of God, that the condition of slave or master was an accident of material existence, and hence that a slave might be a better man than his master (Tannenbaum, *Slave,* p. 48). In the United States the slave, like an animal or piece of property, had no rights except through his master. Under the Latin codes, the slave was simply an unfortunate human being who had rights of his own which required protection by the law. Thus the law provided that slaves might marry against the will of the master, and that such marriages were as binding and as holy as any others. Wife and husband could not be separated, slaves could appeal to the courts for protection against undue punishment, and under certain circumstances could testify against their masters. More important still, by way of contrast, was that the Latin American legal and moral climate favored freedom. Slavery, not freedom, had to be proved before the courts. Manumission was encouraged by law, custom, and the Church. Slaves could own property, could buy and sell, and by paying the original purchase price could buy freedom for themselves or for others. "A hundred social devices narrowed the gap between bondage and liberty, encouraged the master to release his slave, and the bondsman to achieve freedom on his own account . . ." (Tannenbaum, *Slave*, p. 55). The most important distinction between the Latin and North American systems was that once free, the Negro enjoyed a legal status equal to that of any citizen of the state, even while millions of his brothers were still enslaved. Negroes could find public and private employment and through education and wealth could achieve high social rank. But in the United States, instead of finding the channels of integration and assimilation open for his use, the Negro emerged from slavery as a pariah.

Undoubtedly part of the contrast between the pattern of race relations in the United States and the pattern in Latin America is related to the moral and ethical climate associated with Protestantism on the one hand and Catholicism on the other. Many of the provisions favoring manumission were strongly influenced by the Catholic Church and its doctrine of spiritual equality before God. Protestantism, especially when affected by Calvinist and Puritan principles, tended to burden the slave and not the master with the moral onus of the institution. With its emphasis upon worldly success as a sign of special grace and its concept of the "elect" who are spiritually superior to others. Calvinism provided a useful rationale for the treatment of slaves as sub-human creatures and of Negroes as pariahs. Within Protestantism, although the Church can help the penitent to find God, the ultimate "acceptance" of God, and hence salvation, is an individual affair. But within Catholicism, from baptism up to the point of death, redemption remains equally feasible for all through the medium of confession and the other sacraments.

Under Catholicism, there was never any doubt as to whether the slave should be baptized or not. Baptism and religious instruction, guidance away from sin, and initiation into church practices were obligations enjoined upon the master on behalf of the slave. The Catholic Church recognized but one Christian community, and with baptism the slave belonged to that community as much as his master did. Since the Catholic slave was married in the Church, and the bans were regularly published, his family had a moral and religious character unknown to the slave in the United States (Tannenbaum, *Slave*, p. 64). The reluctance of the Protestant in the United States to accept the Negro as his moral and spiritual equal is clearly seen in the early rise within the various Protestant denominations of a policy of segregation, the still embarrassing "caste in the church" (Davie, p. 177). Not only do individual churches follow caste lines as a matter of policy in the United States (exceptions in the North should be noted), but frequently the very organization of the Negro denomination as a whole constitutes a separate division or jurisdiction within the central body (Davie, p. 177). And there are also, of course, many purely Negro Protestant sects unaffiliated with any white denomination. Although attendance in Catholic churches frequently follows racial (actually class) lines in Latin countries, segregation as a policy is incompatible with the Catholic doctrine of the Universal Church.

In addition to the ideological obstacles to Negro assimilation in the United States, a powerful array of economic forces worked against a smooth transition from the status of slave to that of free man. Here abolition came at a time when the institution of slavery was in its economic prime—when the production based upon it was in its most lucrative phase. In those countries which are most noteworthy for their avoidance of caste status for the Negro, slavery had had a long history of economic decline prior to legal abolition. In Brazil, for example, the most lucrative phase of the sugar plantation had ended by the close of the seventeenth century, almost two hundred years before slavery was legally abolished. Slave-worked sugar plantations as well as other plantations, such as those producing coffee and cocoa, continued to be profitable enterprises right up to abolition, but for the most part the level of production was at a standstill, or actually declining, due to increasing foreign competition. The high rate of manumission in the Catholic areas of the New World is thus probably due in part to the fact that the freeing of a slave did not represent as great a loss to the plantation owner as it did in the American South. In the United States, from the beginning of the nineteenth century to the Civil War, slaves were in increasing demand for the production of cotton. It might be said therefore that there was a shortage of slaves when the institution came to an end, whereas during the same period in Brazil, for example, a surplus of slaves had existed for many years.

Although slavery was legal and slaves existed in all thirteen original American colonies, the institution proved to be economically lucrative only in the South. In the North, where slaves were used mainly as domestic servants, slavery ended early. By 1804 the Northwest Territory and all the original states north of Maryland, with the exception of Delaware, had provided for the abolition of slavery. The traditionally more favorable status of the Negro in the North is thus clearly based on economic factors. Where slavery was not profitable, it was eliminated despite the fact that the ethical and religious heritage stressed by Frank Tannenbaum prevailed in both the North and the South. In the North, as in Brazil, the rate of increase of the free Negro population was greater than that of the slave population; and, again as in Brazil, by the time abolition took place in each of the Northern states free Negroes outnumbered the slaves. But in the South the rate of increase of the slave population was far greater than that of the free Negro population right up to the moment of abolition. When abolition took place there were nearly four million slaves in the United States as against a free Negro population of less than five hundred thousand (Frazier, pp. 39, 62). It is important to remember that these slaves represented an investment of many hundreds of millions of dollars for their owners in the South.

Intensely bitter feelings toward the Negro prevailed among white Southerners at the end of the Civil War. The newly organized state governments in the South proceeded immediately to pass legislation which, despite the nominal freedom established by the Thirteenth Amendment, actually amounted to reenslavement of the Negro. This body of legislation, known as the Black Codes, made it possible forcibly to apprentice Negroes (preferably to their former owners), reestablished the inequality of Negroes before the Courts, provided for differential punishment, effectively prohibited them from owning and renting farm land, and placed severe restrictions upon their freedom of movement. For the embittered South, persecution of the freed Negro was an act of vengeance. Carl Schurz reported:

Wherever I go—the street, the shop, the house, the hotel, the steamboat —I hear the people talk in such a way as to indicate that they are yet unable to conceive of the Negro as possessing any rights at all. . . . To kill a Negro, they do not deem murder; to debauch a Negro woman, they do not consider fornication; to take the property away from a Negro, they do not consider robbery. The people boast that when they get freedmen's affairs in their own hands, to use their own expression, "the niggers will catch hell." (quoted in Frazier, p. 126)

In an attempt to destroy the Black Codes, the United States Congress displaced the immediate postwar state governments and established a regime of military rule. With armed force behind them, Southern Negroes briefly enjoyed a measure of political and judicial equality which has yet to be attained again in the North or South. During this period of "reconstruction," Negro voters sent many representatives to the state legislatures, twenty Negro representatives to the lower house of Congress, and two to the Senate. Unable to suppress the legal, political, and economic rise of the Negro through local legislative action, the South carried on a mounting resistance movement based on terror and intimidation. Congressional action, military occupation, and domination of Southern politics by the Republican party sharply increased rather than diminished the incidence of outright racial conflict. It was during the Reconstruction period that the Ku Klux Klan was organized as a terrorist force dedicated to the reestablishment of "white supremacy." Many thousands of Negroes were killed during the Reconstruction period, which Guy B. Johnson characterizes as a "prolonged race riot" (quoted in Myrdal, p. 449).

During the last quarter of the nineteenth century the Democratic party emerged victorious in every Southern state, and the "Solid South" was born. The affairs of the freedmen were once again in the hands of those whose principal social objective was to "put the Negro in his place" and "redeem" the South for the white man. New state constitutions were drawn up excluding the Negro from the electorate through a series of devices designed to circumvent the Fifteenth Amendment. Among these were poll taxes, "literacy" and "understanding" tests (administered by white officials), and "grand-father clauses" (restriction of the vote to those whose ancestors had been electors). These constitutions also established various "Jim Crow" provisions, which required the separation of the races in all public conveyances, schools, charitable institutions, and jails. Para-doxically, the triumph of white supremacy in the South marked the end of the worst period of violent, overt racial conflict. The white majority had won superior status over the Negro. The latter's re-sistance seems to have been broken by all the years of murder, riot, pillage, lynching, and terror. Although the Negro did not concur with the full implications of his status as viewed by the white man, he appears largely to have abandoned the hope of realizing the measure of equality promised by the actions of the Federal government after the Civil War. The Negroes in the new "Solid South" overtly accepted their position as members of a subordinate caste, violence diminished, and a *modus vivendi* prevailed. Their attitude is illustrated by the famous proposal made by Booker T. Washington for peaceful ac-commodation between the two races: "In all things that are purely social we can be as separate as the fingers, yet one as the hand in all things essential to mutual progress" (quoted in Myrdal, p. 65). Since the Negro no longer threatened white supremacy, the whites could afford to relinquish open force as a method of gaining their ob-jectives. Thus lynchings, which had increased steadily during the period before the new white supremacy and Jim Crow constitutions were passed, declined steadily after the new state constitutions were in effect.

The struggle to prevent the Negro from achieving social and political equality becomes fully intelligible only when considered in relation to postbellum economic developments in the American South. At no time in the South did the majority of whites own slaves. In 1850 only about 30 percent of Southern families had one or more slaves, and it is estimated that the entire planter class numbered no more than three hundred thousand people. A large portion of the non-slaveholding white population consisted of marginal agriculturists occupying inferior lands, or lands which had been ruined by exclusive cultivation of cotton and left behind as the plantations moved westward. This group of people—often loosely referred to as the "poor whites"—derived no benefit from the slavocracy; on the contrary, their marginal existence was a direct product of the monopolization of good lands by the plantation system. Emancipation was as momentous for the "poor whites" as for the slaves.

Beneath all the fervent appeals for the preservation of the white man's power in the South ran, and still continues to run, the underlying thought that for every good job or acre of good land occupied by a Negro there is one less good job or acre available for the whites. Competition between Negroes and whites for the land and for jobs has been a persistent but covert factor in the perpetuation of the subordinate status of the Negro (see Vance, pp. 112–15).

It is probably true that this competition would have been just as fierce had the population been racially homogeneous. In speaking of the poor diet, sub-standard housing, precarious tenure, the economically marginal situation and general insecurity of the Negroes in the South, it must also be noted that the South as a region—the white population as well as the black—suffers from such conditions as a whole. Given the ruinous comcentration upon "King Cotton," the depletion of resources, the regime of large estates, the industrial backwardness, and the cataclysm of the Civil War, it is apparent that some large segment of the population was going to have to pass through many years of privation and social misery before changes in the economy and social philosophy brought relief from these conditions. In purely economic terms, there has always been a large portion of white Southerners whose lot was as poor as, or worse than, the lot of the Negroes. In 1940, for example, there were 781,197 white families who were tenant farmers and 484,983 Negro families of the same status in ten Southern cotton-producing states (Davie, p. 66).

If the slave population in the South had consisted of Caucasoids rather than Negroes, there is every probability that similar economic conditions would have prevailed after emancipation, although the minority situation, if it existed at all, would have been greatly modified. But with the indelible stigma of physical type acting as a convenient identification of slave background, what might have been a simple case of a depressed economic class seeking to fight its way to a more equable share of the nation's wealth was rendered something totally different. Despite the fact that most Negroes and a large group of whites in the South found themselves in the same economic situation, little progress was made toward pooling social and political forces to achieve common improvement. Toward the end of the nineteenth century when the South, like the rest of the country, was swept by an appeal for agrarian reform, there was an attempt to align the depressed white classes with their Negro counterpart. In Georgia, for example, a Populist appeal to the whites to unite with the Negro farmers was made by Tom Watson in the following terms:

Now the People's Party says to these two men, "You are kept apart that you may be separately fleeced of your earnings. You are made to hate each other because upon that hatred is rested the keystone of the arch of financial despotism which enslaves you both. You are deceived and blinded that you may not see how this race antagonism perpetuates a money system which beggars both." (quoted in Frazier, p. 153)

Race hatred, however, triumphed over common sense, and the forces of white supremacy succeeded in convincing the mass of Southerners that what was most needed to improve the welfare of the South was not agrarian reform but "putting the Negroes in their place."

Up until the end of the First World War most of the American Negro population was concentrated in the rural areas of the South. Under the impact of industrial and other types of urban labor shortages created by the two world wars, great demographic shifts occurred. Today there are more Negroes in urban areas of both the North and South than in all rural areas of the United States. And there are almost as many Negroes in the North, practically none of whom are agriculturists, as there are Negroes, urban and rural, in the South.

The urbanization of the American Negro, of which the great north-ward migration is but an instance, has been accompanied by rapid and profound changes in the cultural and economic patterns of this minority group. The outstanding result of urbanization and north-ward migration has been the creation within the Negro minority of a wide range of occupational and social differences. Despite continuing economic and social discrimination, the growth of segregated Negro neighborhoods in the larger urban centers has led to the develop-ment of a substantial Negro middle class of businessmen and pro-fessionals. Negro stores, restaurants, banks, insurance companies, newspapers and magazines, doctors, lawyers, and dentists have pros-pered within the segregated neighborhoods of the larger cities. An opportunity to move upward socially has thus been made avail-able. Urbanization has meant that it is no longer possible to identify the Negro minority with a single low-level occupational or economic status. The Negroes form a "caste" in American society but nowa-days the occupational limitations of this caste are rapidly disappearing.

A further result of urbanization has been a steady increase in the effectiveness of legal and political moves made by Negroes to combat the worst forms of discrimination. The increased purchasing power of urban Negroes, especially those among the middle class, has been used in part to buy education and professional training. A substantial group of Negro intellectuals has grown up within the last few decades, and it is this group which has spearheaded the attack against the legal bulwarks of "second-class citizenship." The rise of the Negro as a city dweller has also been associated with steady improvement in general living conditions, housing, standards of consumption, health, and educational facilities. Despite these many changes, however, urbanization has yet to bring the prospect of social assimilation and the end of the minority status into sight in the near future.

When the Negro first began to settle on a large scale in the metro-politan centers of the North during and after the First World War, over one third of the population of these cities was foreign-born. Most of these immigrants came from cultural backgrounds that differed more from the dominant American culture patterns than the culture patterns of the Southern Negro. Like the Negro, these European im-migrants had at first been forced to live in ghetto-like slums and to perform the more menial and unskilled jobs. Yet their descendants within the space of two generations have reduced their minority disabilities to a mild form—or even have been assimilated totally into the larger society. But the Negro, after four decades of exposure to the "melting pot" of the large urban centers of the North, has just begun to alter the barriers that perpetuate his minority status. By far the major reason for the slower rate of social assimilation of the American Negro is his physical appearance. The actual reason is not, of course, his physical appearance *per se,* but the importance placed upon Negroid features by American society as a stigma and as the most "visible" criterion for membership in the subordinant Negro "caste." No matter how successfully the children of Southern rural Negroes have adopted the "typical American" behavior patterns, they cannot (without intermarriage) alter their physical characteristics. Thus, although all evidence indicates that the urban Negro is thoroughly acculturated to the dominant American culture patterns (except perhaps for a few Negro patterns which represent a response to minority status itself), they remain highly visible even in the heterogeneous environment of the great cities.

Another factor which has slowed the rate of Negro integration and assimilation is related to the timing of the migration from South to North. The Negro came in large numbers to the North just at the time when the epoch of large-scale European immigration was drawing to a close and a new era in the American labor movement had begun. During the First World War the demands of wartime production, coupled with the isolation of the Eastern European sources of immigrants, created a severe manpower shortage in the Northern cities. Negro workers from the South rushed into this vacuum. When the war ended, however, the greatly strengthened labor movement sought to put an end permanently to the influx of cheap foreign labor. Immigrant labor, whatever its source, was regarded as a device to lower the wage scale. The occasional use of Negroes as strikebreakers helped further to convince the Northern white wage-earners that Negro labor was also a threat to their bargaining power. The immigration act of 1924 signaled the removal of the labor market from

the sphere of unrestricted competition. Thus, when the Negro arrived
in the Northern cities, the "fire" under the "melting pot" had all but
gone out.

In 1919, when millions of servicemen returned and looked for their
old jobs, no fewer than 26 race riots broke out in American cities.
The worst of these took place in Chicago. Twenty-three Negroes were
killed, and 178 whites and 342 Negroes were injured (Myrdal, p.
567). A second rash of race riots developed during and after the
Second World War, coinciding with a second wave of Negro migration
from the South to the North. Economic insecurity of the whites and
fear that the Negro is "rising" have been the principal causes of these
outbreaks. As Myrdal points out, this type of violence is primarily
an urban phenomenon, with lynching as its rural counterpart. It is
more characteristic of the North than of the South, since "it is only
when the Negroes think they might have something to gain that they
will take the risk of fighting back. . . ." (Myrdal, p. 567).

II

Although there are many differences in race relations in different
regions of the United States, certain basic features are common to all
sections of the country. The Negro minority is everywhere a caste-like
segment set apart from the rest of the nation. This segregation has
both spatial and institutional forms, and is inevitably associated with
social discrimination. In some cases segregation is authorized by legal
code; in others it is enforced by informal covenants and codes of
etiquette; in still others it is accomplished in defiance of the law.
Segregation and discrimination affect the Negro in every major category of social and cultural life: in making a living, in getting married,
in setting up a household, in getting an education, in practicing a
religion, in participating in political functions, in recreational activities, in protecting health, and even in disposing of the dead.

The most important aspect of segregation, from the viewpoint of
its role in perpetuating the "high visibility" of the minority and the
obstacle which this presents to social assimilation, is in the realm of
marriage and the family. The logic of calling the Negro minority a

"caste" is seen most strongly in the strictly endogamous nature of the group.[1] In the South miscegenation is widely prohibited by law, and even in those Northern states where there are no legal barriers, intermarriage is a statistically insignificant phenomenon. The taboos regulating marriage and sexual pairings between the races are heavily charged with emotion. These taboos are backed by a series of stereotypes concerning Negro and white sexuality and sexual relations which are often quite ambivalent. One familiar stereotype is that the Negroes have a stronger sex drive and greater sexual endowments than whites. It is also widely believed that the Negro male has a particular desire for the white female but that white females have a certain physical revulsion for the Negro male. Thus, according to these ideas white women must be protected from sexual contacts with Negro men at all costs. White men are said to be attracted to Negro women but their relations must take the form of illicit intercourse and not of marriage. In the South, illicit sexual contact between youthful white males and Negro women seems to be rather expected at an early phase of the male's sexual experience (Dollard, *Caste,* pp. 134 ff.).

Miscegenation is discouraged in the United States by the belief that the offspring of mixed unions are Negroes rather than a new racial type. This remarkable distortion of biological fact lies at the very heart of the peculiarity of North American patterns of race relations. The United States is one of the few countries in which the white majority fails to endow its mulatto groups with intermediate statuses. For most of the occasions, instruments, and agents of segregation and discrimination—legal, customary, or illegal—a man, woman or child in the United States is either white or black. As far as the whites are concerned, nothing lies between these extremes. In

[1] There has been considerable disagreement among sociologists and anthropologists as to whether the term "caste" may be used appropriately for the biracial system of the United States. Some students insist that it should be limited to the social categories of India. The present writers agree with Everett Hughes, who writes: "If we grant this, we will simply have to find some other term for the kind of social category into which one is assigned at birth and from which he cannot escape by action of his own; and to distinguish such social categories from classes or ranked groups, from which it is possible, though sometimes difficult, to rise." (Hughes, *Peoples,* p. 111)

the popular mind, miscegenation is a form of pollution of the "blood" for which there is no known purificatory rite.

One of the most harmful areas of segregation and discrimination has been employment.[2] Until recently only those jobs which are not sought after by white workers have been open to Negroes. Within many industries there are occupational specializations which, because of their dirty, laborious, or otherwise disagreeable nature, are set aside for Negro workers. "The heavy pungent dust of tobacco; the dust and odor of fertilizing plants; the dampness, stench and gore in slaughtering plants; and the blistering heat of open-hearth sections of steel factories are still 'protected' for Negro workers" (Johnson, p. 93). Negroes are generally confined to menial and unskilled jobs. There are few Negro supervisors and foremen in industry or the building trades. Negro white-collar workers are extremely rare except in businesses and governmental bureaus in the North. Negro secretaries and typists are hardly ever found in white employ in any part of the country. In general, for all regions of the country, the industrial or service groups in which the incidence of Negro workers is smallest are those which represent new technical developments, such as synthetics, television, aircraft, electronics; those which involve large amounts of white-collar work, such as telegraph and telephone systems, advertising agencies, banking and brokerage houses; those in which there are good opportunities for rapid promotion; jobs in which there is face-to-face contact with the public, such as those of salesmen, store-clerks, meter inspectors, streetcar, bus, and subway conductors and motormen; and certain food industries, such as those producing butter, cheese, condensed milk, candy, and baked goods (Johnson, p. 87).

A vicious aspect of segregation and discrimination in employment is the frequent occurrence, particularly in the South, of wage scales which differ according to race. Despite the depressive effect this practice has had on wages in the South and the difficulties it presents

[2] The patterns of segregation are changing fast. The following description of Negro-white segregation may be out-of-date in regard to details before this book reaches the public, but it will still provide a picture of the basic pattern of segregation during the last decade or so.

for effective unionization, wage differences are maintained as much
in the interest of the white worker as for the benefit of the employer.
Differential wages permit the identification of "Negro jobs" and preserve the superior social status of the white worker. They are based
on the assumption that whites and Negroes have, and ought to have,
fundamentally different living standards and requirements (Johnson,
p. 90).

Whereas there has been some improvement in the distribution of
Negroes throughout American industry as a result of labor shortages
during the Second World War, one half of Negro male workers and
two thirds of the females are still employed in occupations below the
semi-skilled level, as contrasted with one sixth of the white male and
female workers (Hope, pp. 50, 308). Recent studies of Southern
industry indicate that the racial division of labor has been remarkably stable over a long period of time, and that Negro workers continue to be excluded from white-collar and supervisory jobs. Moreover, white and Negro workers are rarely employed side-by-side in
identical operations, especially not in the South (Hope, p. 205). As
a result of occupational discrimination, the average income of all
Negro families in the United States in 1949 was still about half the
average income of all white families.

Segregation in public and semi-public institutions and services constitutes an important area of differential treatment for Negroes. Discrimination in this category is particularly blatant in the South, although in other sections of the country similar results are produced
through more subtle means. In the South the attempt to keep the
races apart is extended to almost every conceivable situation. Li-
braries in many cities either refuse to lend books to Negroes, maintain separate reading tables, or operate separate and inferior Negro
branches. Public playgrounds, ball parks, and fairgrounds are usually
developed for whites only. Even the parks in most Southern cities
are "off limits" to Negroes. In Houston, for example, Negroes can
visit the zoo only on special days. Racial distinctions are maintained
in public buildings, such as post offices, courts, and town halls, with
the provision of separate elevators, toilets, and drinking fountains for

Negroes. Negroes are forced to sit in separate sections of all public auditoriums, but the usual practice is to schedule Negro meetings on different days from white meetings. On Negro days toilet facilities are frequently locked. All Southern states have laws separating white and Negro passengers in public conveyances. Waiting rooms in railroad stations are separate and served by different entrances. Negroes are generally refused accommodations altogether in Pullman cars, sit in separate coaches, and eat in separate portions of the dining cars. In streetcars and buses, special sections are reserved for each race. In Atlanta, Georgia, taxicabs operated by white drivers customarily do not accept Negro passengers. Instead, there are Negro taxicabs, usually retired from white service, and driven by Negro drivers.

Medical services are sharply different for the two races throughout the South. Negro patients are admitted to hospitals through separate doors, are confined to the use of freight elevators, are rarely attended by white nurses and sometimes by no nurses at all. Private hospitals will turn even emergency cases away, and apparently under most conditions public hospitals follow the color line in deciding upon priority for treating emergency cases. There are probably hundreds of unrecorded instances of unnecessary death caused by discriminatory practices in handling emergency cases throughout the South.

Hotel accommodations throughout most of the country are strictly segregated. There does not appear to be a single hotel in the entire South that will admit Negroes along with whites. Even in New York City, where segregation is illegal, most of the principal hotels would in some way refuse overnight accommodations to Negroes. Similarly, throughout the country strict separation is maintained in most eating places. In Northern cities there is a tacit understanding that Negroes will not attempt to eat in certain restaurants. Those who seek to break the racial policy are given tables in the rear, made to wait, given inferior service and poor food, or are otherwise advised that their presence is not welcome. In the South, refusal to serve Negroes in all but specially designated establishments is the invariable rule. Some restaurants catering to white patrons admit Negroes through rear doors and serve them at special tables in the kitchen. In the South, but not in the North, movie houses uniformly maintain separate sections for white and colored patrons, and sometimes there are separate entrances and box offices. Even in some Southern banks there are often special windows to which all Negro patrons are directed. Throughout the country, marked separation is maintained in mortuary and burial services, beauty parlors, barber shops, and offices of doctors and dentists.

The South is especially well-known for its discriminatory patterns relating to judicial, penal, and political institutions. Negro judges, jurors, and higher police officials are extremely rare. Where Negro policemen are found, they are restricted to Negro districts. Southern Negroes tend to regard policemen not as civil servants dedicated to the preservation of order and the protection of persons and property, but as the fearful embodiments of arbitrary law. Some towns and cities in the South have been reported to have curfew laws for Negroes (Johnson, p. 33). Impartial trial by jury or by judge in the South is often denied Negro defendants accused of crimes. Juries are usually composed mainly of white men and the testimony of Negro witnesses is often not taken seriously, especially when contradicted by whites. Control of the police and judicial system by the white majority is a major instrument in the maintenance of the caste division. Southern Negroes grow up in an environment where physical reprisal constantly threatens those who deviate from accepted patterns, whether these be legalized or merely contained in unwritten codes of etiquette. The casual traveler to the South sees on the whole an apparently calm and orderly social arrangement. The calm is maintained not only by the traditional *modus vivendi* between the two racial groups but also by naked force.

Despite marked improvements during the last decade, the Southern Negro still continues to suffer from discriminatory pressures which prevent him from exercising the political franchise guaranteed by the Federal Constitution. A number of devices have been used by Southern whites to restrict the Negro vote. The poll tax is probably best-known. A great many whites as well as Negroes have been prevented from voting because of the accumulation of poll-tax arrears. The result has sometimes been not only the disenfranchisement of the Negro minority, but political subordination of the entire Southern lower class. More devastating than the famous poll tax has been the white primary. Until recently, Negroes have been prevented from voting in the primaries of the Democratic party by statutory laws of both the party and the states. Since only Democratic candidates have any chance for election in the South, the primary is, in effect, the only time when a choice between candidates can be made. Additional tactics to deny the Negro his right to vote involve unfair administration of literacy tests, and various forms of threats and intimidations too numerous to list. The net effect of these practices up until the last five years was to render the Negro totally ineffectual as a political force in the South. Thus, out of a potential of several million Negro voters in 11 Southern states, only 250,000 voted in the general election of 1940, and only a tiny fraction of these had managed to vote in the primaries for the selection of local candidates (Myrdal, pp. 487–88).

Another major area of discriminatory practices in the South is the educational system. Strict segregation was the legal rule throughout the South until recently. In 1954 the Supreme Court decided that such practices were unconstitutional, but it has deferred until some time in the future its decision as to how desegregation is to be accomplished in the face of overwhelming insistence on the part of the majority that the separation of Negro and white children be maintained. Some states have threatened to abandon their public school systems entirely rather than submit to desegregation. Moreover, it should be noted that segregation in schools may be accomplished quite effectively in most American communities without legal provisions simply by virtue of the prevalance of residential segregation and the exercise of zoning powers on the local level. Negro schools throughout the South suffer in comparison with white schools in terms of physical plant, students per classroom, and quality and quantity of pedagogical equipment. Negro teachers are paid less than white teachers and there is a considerable disparity between the amount of money spent on Negro pupils and on white pupils. Discrimination on the basis of race in the apportionment of educational funds has been most glaring in the appropriation of state funds for the assistance to land-grant colleges. In 1951, the amount allocated per white student in white land-grant colleges amounted to 765 dollars, while each Negro student was apportioned only 470 dollars (Walker, p. 452). In graduate and professional schools, strong discriminatory policies are followed throughout the nation. Although recent legal action seems to be making considerable progress in reducing discrimination in educational institutions, particularly in the so-called "border states," it also seems to have strengthened the determination of people in the deep South to maintain segregation.

No summary of discrimination patterns in the South would be complete without mentioning the body of informal, traditional codes of behavior which govern everyday, face-to-face contacts between Negroes and whites. These patterns represent direct survivals of the etiquette forms which existed on the plantations during slavery times and are designed to maintain subordinate status for the Negro on all occasions of interracial contact. Negroes in the South are rarely called "Mr." and "Mrs." when being addressed by white persons. Men are usually called by their last names, and in addressing Negro women, it is customary to use their first names. "The pressure for omission of certain titles of respect is so strong that in the presence of white persons Negroes are reluctant to use a title when referring to other Negroes. Instead they say 'Brother Smith' or 'Sister Jones'" (Johnson, p. 139). Many Negro women of middle- or upper-class status try to keep their first names hidden from white persons by using their initials or the names of their husbands. In situations where it is bad for business or where circumstances demand some show of respect, whites will compromise by using "Doctor," "Reverend," or "Professor," instead of "Mr." or "Mrs." Similar ceremonial validations of the superior status of the whites pertain to the removal of hats, priority in entering and leaving through doors, yielding the right-of-way while walking in the streets, and waiting to be served in stores. Great stress is laid upon the taboo which prevents whites and Negroes from eating or drinking together at close quarters. Some of the bizarre results of racial etiquette patterns are revealed in the story of what happened when four white men and a Negro guide once went out for a day of fishing in a boat. When it came time for lunch, the white men moved to one part of the boat and laid a stick across to separate them from the Negro (Johnson, p. 143).

In almost everything he does and everywhere he goes, from birth to death, in sickness or in health, the Negro is confronted with the color line. Caste lines are maintained even in religion. The overwhelming majority of Negro church members belong to churches consisting entirely of Negro members. Although in doctrine these Negro churches parallel the major white denominations, they are in fact separate organizations. The Negro Baptists form the largest church body, followed by the African Methodist Episcopal Church, the African Methodist Episcopal Zion Church, and the Colored Methodist Protestant Church. The white denomination to which the largest number of Negroes belong is the Methodist Church. Of the estimated three hundred thousand Negro members in 1948, however, only 640 were members of local white churches.

An extremely important type of segregation is the separation of Negro and white neighborhoods. In many Southern cities such as Charleston, South Carolina, Negro dwellings are scattered almost at random throughout the city as a result of the large number of Negroes who are employed by whites as domestics and who live in back-alley quarters close to the houses in which they work. Here, traditional ways of maintaining social distance between the races work well enough to satisfy the whites. But in the larger and newer cities of the South, where the effects of industrialization and urbanization have made it difficult to adhere to the letter of traditional racial etiquette, and in practically every Northern city, where both the legal fabric of discrimination and the main body of racial etiquette are absent, residential segregation is the main key to caste restrictions. In these Northern cities, such as Chicago and New York, most of the Negroes are found in a few tightly packed, sharply delimited areas. These ghetto-like neighborhoods are usually filled with sub-standard dwellings and are afflicted with all the evils of big-city slums. Unlike the inhabitants of white slum areas, however, many people in these Negro "cities within cities" are financially capable of living in decent lower-middle-class or even upper-middle-class neighborhoods. They are prevented from moving, however, by widespread restrictive policies maintained by white property owners.

The most common formal device for excluding Negroes from white neighborhoods has been the use of restrictive covenants. These are agreements whereby white property owners and real-estate agents pledge themselves as a group not to rent or sell to Negroes. Until 1948 such covenants were legal contracts enforceable by court order. In that year the Supreme Court ruled that the covenants violated the Fourteenth Amendment and denied the lower courts authority to enforce them. This ruling, however, did not question the constitutional right of property owners to enter into restrictive agreements which are adhered to by voluntary subscription. Hence, for the most part, restrictive covenants have been unaffected by the court's decision and still constitute the major formal barrier to Negro infiltration of white areas.

In the absence of legal enforcement procedures, these agreements are largely maintained by the fears of the propertied interests that Negro occupancy will reduce the value of their property. These fears are frequently well-grounded under the present circumstances because the entrance of Negro tenants sometimes means the exodus of white tenants. This result is achieved not by any formal agreement on the part of the white tenants, but is simply a reflection of the underlying "caste mentality" which pertains as much to Northerners as to Southerners. Both Negroes and whites are caught in a vicious circle. If a few Negro families are admitted to a white building, the white occupants are immediately gripped with fear that the whole neighborhood is about to change. They begin to move out and the Negroes begin to move in. Once underway, the complete change-over can occur with remarkable rapidity. There is tremendous demographic pressure built up inside the Negro neighborhoods as a result of residential segregation, and each opportunity for improvement in housing conditions is immediately seized. The first breach in the white's defenses usually occurs in sections adjacent to the boundaries of the Negro ghetto. Generally the first break-through is achieved as a result of a white landlord selling out to a Negro buyer. The price in such initial transactions is usually well above the current value of the property, since Negro landlords have difficulty buying real estate and are willing to pay more than whites. The new landlord rents to Negroes, and the circle begins. Sometimes white speculators deliberately precipitate the panic. In any event, the forces operate with regularity and result in regular patterns of expansion. The farther a location is from the original nucleus of the Negro settlement, the better will be the neighborhood and housing conditions, since these are the latest to have been taken over from the whites.

It is clear that the Supreme Court ruling on restrictive covenants is by itself incapable of ending residential segregation, yet it has been beneficial to the Negro. Since such agreements cannot be enforced by law, it has become easier for Negroes to move into white neighborhoods; some of the pressure is taken off the Negro neighborhoods; and better conditions are provided for the Negro middle class. But segregation in housing continues to be maintained, and the penetration of Negro tenants in white neighborhoods has precipitated interracial violence in the North, playing a role analogous to the violation of the taboo on interracial sexual relations in the South.

The rigidity of residential segregation in the North frees the white Northerner from many embarrassing situations. As a well-known social psychologist has pointed out:

In the North, the Negro is granted theoretical equality, but there is little personal contact between the races and little interest in the Negroes on the part of the whites; in the South there is considerable personal contact and frequently direct assistance of Negroes by whites. Southern writers emphasize the kindliness of Southerners to individual Negroes, whereas Northerners tend to emphasize the theoretical equality in the North as contrasted with the denial of equality in the South. (Horowitz, p. 194)

Northerners like to think of themselves as practicing less segregation and discrimination than they actually engage in. On the other hand, white Southerners have more contact with Negroes in their everyday affairs than do Northerners, and these contacts are largely governed by the traditional codes of etiquette handed down from plantation days. Although the rules of etiquette are designed to maintain proper social distance, their effect, when adhered to by the Negro, is frequently that of establishing an ease of social intercourse largely unknown between the races in the North. Confinement of the Negro to his "city within a city" in the North cuts down the need for formal segregation and discrimination patterns, and increases the chances for legal reforms.

Many commercial and semi-public places are able to say that they do not exclude Negroes simply because they are never put to the test. Others admit Negroes, secure in the knowledge that the occasions will not be very frequent. As a result of the invisible wall which surrounds the urban Negro enclave, Negroes buy largely in stores that cater to Negroes, eat mostly in Negro restaurants, attend predominantly Negro schools, go most frequently to Negro movies and night clubs, usually drink in Negro bars, commonly belong to Negro churches, play in predominantly Negro parks or sections of parks, and use Negro doctors and dentists. In all of these cases there are many parallel white facilities which the Negro uses habitually without incidents, such as the major downtown shopping centers, the large chain cafeterias, lunch counters, and all major publicly owned places and services. Interracial use of such facilities is lubricated by the great impersonality, isolation, and anonymity characteristic of the modern metropolis. The whites themselves constitute such a heterogeneous group that it is difficult for them to form a solid front against the Negroes; the caste line is thus blurred or entirely effaced in many important sectors of activity. Yet in all matters and places defined as "intimate," Negroes and whites seldom mix. Private life rigidly conforms to the caste cleavage. The friends of Negroes are Negroes; the friends of whites are whites. Yet Negroes and whites mix freely in the ball parks, the buses, subways, and railroad stations.

In a sense, the social distance between the two races in the North is as great as, if not greater than, that in the South. What has happened in the North as a result of urbanization is that the Negro has thrown off his old dependent relations to the whites. Without the plantation tradition behind them, the Northern whites have never taken to regarding Negroes simultaneously as inferiors and wards. Their attitude toward Negroes partakes more of indifference; they are not obsessed, as the Southerner is, with validating their superior status. Thus as long as the Negro does not overtly threaten white jobs or white property value, the Northerner is perfectly willing to accept the egalitarian verdicts of the courts and the liberalizing laws of the legislatures. The scope and intensity of discrimination and segregation in public services, places, and situations have steadily diminished in the North as a result of progressive legislation, yet socially the Negroes still form an out-group. The Northerner discriminates and segregates in a conscious fashion on relatively few occasions; for the most part, he is simply disinterested (see Marden, pp. 256–57).

III

The past few decades have witnessed some profound and extremely promising changes in the minority situation of the American Negro. The rise of large segregated Negro neighborhoods in the Northern cities has produced an increase in the number and effectiveness of protest organizations and has led to the emergence of forceful Negro leaders in many areas of social life, especially in law and politics. The increasing number of professional men and managers in the social hierarchy within the Negro minority has destroyed many of the old attitudes of dependence upon white people. Armed with a new conception of himself, the Negro has begun to challenge the position of the majority wherever legal and political pressure can be brought to bear. The increase in the numbers of university-educated and professionally trained Negroes has also tended to weaken the conception held by whites that the Negroes are an inferior race.

Important changes in the relationship of the Negro to American life came with the increased control of the national economy in the aftermath of the great depression. Under Roosevelt's New Deal administration, there was a vast expansion of the dominion of Federal government. Federal aid programs and numerous new agencies exerted a steady pressure toward uniformity in matters relating to racial policies. This does not mean that there was no discrimination in carrying out the New Deal programs, but that such discrimination violated Federal policy. As government has been given an even wider role in regulating national life, a situation has gradually developed in the South which in some respects is similar to the period immediately following the Civil War, when liberal policies were enforced by military occupation.

The Second World War also had an important influence in bringing about modifications in the Negro's status. The ideological pretensions of an enemy which called itself the master race served to focus attention on the racial problem at home. The Negroes' role in the Armed Forces during this war led finally in 1948 to an executive order, issued by President Truman, which declared it "to be the policy of the President that there shall be equality of treatment and opportunity for all persons in the armed services without regard to race, color, religion, or national origin." He appointed a committee, known as the President's Committee on Equality of Treatment and Opportunity in the Armed Services, which carried out a study and in its report recommended a four-point program for desegregation of Negroes in the Army. In 1950 the program was accepted by the Army, and these recommendations have rapidly been put into effect (see Simpson and Yinger, pp. 451 ff.). During World War II the American Negro also improved his situation economically. Especially during the later years of the war, Negroes entered into many positions from which they had previously been excluded.

Improvements have occurred in recent years in the educational, employment, and housing situations, in political participation, and their use of public and semi-public facilities, mainly as the result of progressive legislation or new interpretations of the United States Constitution by the higher courts. In great measure, the success of this uphill fight is a tribute to the perseverence and energy of the new generation of Negro leaders. Outstanding has been the role of the National Association for the Advancement of Colored People

(NAACP) whose membership has passed the half-million mark (Walker, p. 468). The Association's lawyers have waged a relentless struggle on behalf of civil liberties, and to them have fallen some of the most dramatic court victories in the history of American law. Also effective in the recent changes has been the work of numerous social scientists, both Negro and white, who have hammered away at the lies and half-truths of racist doctrines. These scientists have not only exposed the fallacies of racism, but have constantly sought to communicate objective knowledge about the Negroes' plight to larger and larger audiences. As a result, an enlightenment of considerable proportions has been taking place in the United States. It has been furthered by the expansion of educational facilities and the raising of the general educational level of both the Negro and the white. Although many of the advances made through the courts and the legislatures are merely formal declarations of opposition to prevailing habits of segregation and therefore unlikely to be immediately effective in controlling the deep-seated prejudices and mores of the mass, they are nonetheless the sign of a definite shift in the climate of opinion among large segments of the population.

The fight against discrimination in education has been waged on three fronts: against disparity in teachers' salaries; against disparity in segregated schools from the standpoint of equipment and curriculums; and against segregation itself. Discrimination in teachers' salaries first came under attack in the latter part of the 1930's. A suit supported by the NAACP was brought against Maryland county officials in 1939, and was decided in their favor by the United States District Court. The court declared that Negro teachers must be paid the same salary as white teachers when they perform the same duties. The campaign to equalize salaries spread to other states, and additional favorable court decisions were obtained (Davie, p. 153). Although in some states the average salary of white teachers is still almost double that of Negro teachers, there has been much improvement as a result of this litigation. In 1950, in ten Southern states and the District of Columbia white teachers received an average of $2,710 and Negro teachers $2,143.

The legal basis of segregation in public-school systems was set in 1896 by the historic decision of the Supreme Court in the case of *Plessy v. Ferguson*. It was the court's decision at that time that a state law requiring the segregation of Negroes in railways does not deny them the equal protection of the laws. The decision gave rise to the famous "separate but equal" doctrine. It led to the interpretation that segregation in public education was legal as long as the facilities to which the Negroes were confined were "substantially equal" to white facilities. The failure of the Southern states to maintain equal facilities while rigidly enforcing the separation part of the doctrine has led, over the years, to scores of cases before the higher tribunals. Progress along these lines through litigation was necessarily slow since a separate court order had to be won for equalization in each instance where unequal facilities could be shown to exist. Dramatic results began to be achieved, however, when the number of Negroes seeking admission to professional and graduate schools reached proportions which existing segregated institutions could not handle. The Southern states at first tried the expedient of providing scholarships for attending out-of-state schools, but this practice was challenged by a Supreme Court decision in 1938. In that case (*Lloyd Gaines v. University of Missouri*), which involved an applicant for admission to the Missouri Law School, the court ruled in effect that "equal facilities" had to be provided within the state and not outside it. As a result, the state of Missouri was forced to establish a law school, and within the next two years, a Negro school of journalism and a graduate school were added (Walker, p. 570). Similar pressure was applied for the creation of advanced professional and graduate schools for Negroes in Maryland, Texas, Oklahoma, and North Carolina. Although the decisions in these cases did not end segregation, they did promote the rapid expansion of postgraduate education for Negroes throughout the South. Moreover, this campaign to equalize separate facilities did weaken the whole fabric of segregation. On the postgraduate level, duplicate institutions for Negroes are extremely burdensome for state finances; and, rather than support new facilities, many states began to admit Negroes to formerly exclusive white schools. Thus it was estimated in 1952 that well over one thousand Negro students were enrolled in Southern institutions of higher learning which, a few years previously, had maintained strict segregation.

As the decisions compelling states to provide equal facilities began to pile up, a new interpretation of "equality" slowly emerged. When Oklahoma was challenged in 1948 for its failure to provide a law school for Negroes, not only did the Supreme Court rule that such facilities had to be granted, but that they had to be granted to coincide with the beginning of the term in the white law school. It was decided that the state had to provide the Negro plaintiff with an opportunity for a law education "as soon as it does for applicants of any other group." Since the beginning of the term was not far off, the state had to decide either to admit the applicant to its law school or to create a new one within a few weeks. The latter alternative was actually taken, and a makeshift "law school" was set up for Negroes (Walker, pp. 470–71).[3] But the attitude of the court was a sufficiently clear indication of which way the wind was blowing; as a consequence, Arkansas and Delaware announced a few weeks later that Negroes would be accepted in white schools for enrollment in courses not given in the Negro colleges. In 1950 a further step was taken toward outlawing segregation itself: in a unanimous decision involving the University of Texas Law School, the court held that a separate Negro law school did not provide equal facilities for Negroes because it was inferior in faculty, in courses offered, and in "those qualities . . . which make for greatness in a law school." This trend culminated in the epoch-making decision of May, 1954, when the same principle was applied to segregation in all levels of education. It was ruled that segregation itself inevitably entails educational inequality, since it prevents the segregated student from full participation in the

[3] Actually, "The Board of Regents hastily roped off a space in the state capitol as a 'law school' for Miss Sipuel [the plaintiff] and all others similarly situated and assigned three instructors to the school." Miss Sipuel did not enroll, for the school clearly did not satisfy the requirements of the American Bar Association and the Association of American Law Schools. (see Simpson and Yinger, p. 597)

intellectual and social milieu which is an integral part of the educational process.

It will be many years before educational segregation ends in fact as well as in principle. A few communities in the South, and especially those in the border states, have already begun to desegregate their primary and secondary schools. The great majority, however, particularly those in the deep South, have gone on record as being opposed to desegregation in the immediate future, if not forever. Some states have even readied their legislatures for the passage of laws which would make their school systems privately owned and would provide for financial support directly to the pupil rather than to the system. In recognition of this resistance, the Supreme Court allowed for delay in the enforcement of its momentous decision until it had a chance to hear proposals as to when and how desegregation might most peacefully be accomplished.

Whatever the plan adopted, desegregation in education will confront many obstacles before it becomes a reality. As has been indicated, residential segregation permits zoning of school districts so that virtual segregation is achieved in the North although it has no statutory basis. In most Southern communities the actual number of Negro pupils who could not be zoned out of white schools is probably very small. Yet it is revealing of the contrast between Northern and Southern race relations that the South is fighting not for partial segregation, but for total segregation. In the South the superior status of the white tends to be a matter of pride and a constant "point of honor"; in the North, it is usually an unconscious corollary of informal and private barriers.

The status of Negroes in political affairs has been helped by progressive court decisions and legislative changes. In recent years real gains have been made in the struggle for political enfranchisement of the Negro in the South. In the general election of 1940, less than two hundred and fifty thousand Negroes in eleven Southern states voted. In 1948 the number had risen to seven hundred and fifty thousand, and for the election of 1952 it is estimated that over a million and a quarter Negroes registered to vote in the South (Walker, p. 467).

This steady growth of the Negro electorate reflects in part the weakening or destruction of some of the more important statutory devices for voiding the Negro franchise. As a result of political agitation, poll tax laws have, between 1920 and 1949, been repealed by six states. Only five states still retain the poll-tax requirement for voting. In addition, a long series of suits before the Supreme Court, which began in 1927, have destroyed the legal basis of the white primary. In 1941 and in 1944 the Supreme Court handed down decisions which, in effect, established that primaries are an essential part of the election process and that the exclusion of Negroes from Democratic primaries was a violation of the Fifteenth Amendment to the Constitution. In South Carolina, the legislature countered this move by repealing all laws relating to primary elections in order to make it appear that the Democratic party was a private club and not an integral part of the state's election machinery. Further litigation resulted in a 1947 decision by a Federal court, which was not reviewed (and thus was indirectly confirmed) by the Supreme Court, to the effect that the primary was the only practical means for expressing a choice among candidates and was therefore subject to Federal control.

The relaxation of voting restrictions has also been due to certain more general factors. One of the most important of these has been the redistribution of the Negro population. Negroes constitute a declining proportion of the total Southern population, and this decrease has removed some of the urgency of keeping them from voting as far as the whites are concerned. There is considerably less fear that the Negro vote will be decisive and, therefore, a greater degree of complacency about the individual Negro voter. Another relevant demographic fact is that the proportion of Southern Negroes residing in cities has increased from about 15 percent in 1900 to almost 50 percent in 1950. Urbanization in the South has tended to weaken the effectiveness of white supremacy policies, to render them less vital for everyday affairs, just as it has in the North. Moreover, the development of Southern industry, which has been associated with the urbanizing trend, has brought to the South a new class of commercial and industrial managers, many of them from outside the region. This group tends to be Republican and constitutes a growing threat to the one-party system of the South.

Along with the basic social and economic changes taking place in the South as a result of urbanization, there has come a political awakening among Negroes themselves. The disposition of Negroes to struggle for their civil rights has increased markedly since the 1940's. The dissipation of much of the political apathy formerly characteristic of the rural Southern Negro is due in part to the general rise in the educational level of the group, and, in part, to the rise of a new leadership interested in the organization of the Negro voters. The intensification of interest in the credo of democracy, stimulated by participation in World War II, has also played a role.

The growing participation of the Negro in American politics may be further indicated by reference to the increase in Negro office-holders since 1900. At the turn of the century there were only two Negroes serving as members of state legislatures in the entire country. Since 1930, Negroes have been elected to state legislatures in at least seventeen Northern and Western states (Davie, p. 279). During the past decade Negroes were elected to membership on about twenty city councils, five of these in Southern cities. Their appointment to positions in local and national agencies is additional evidence of their growing political importance. The New Deal was responsible for the greatest increase in appointive positions held by Negroes. Some of them functioned as advisors to Federal administrators on matters involving the interests of Negroes. This group of administrative assistants, which became known as the "Black Cabinet," paved the way for appointments of Negroes to responsible positions in government outside of fields involving competence in race relations. In the North, Negroes have received appointments as judges, attorneys, tax commissioners, and administrators of various state agencies. Although the South has yet to match this record, there is evidence that the recognition of the Negro voter has tended to make local government officials more disposed to improve community facilities which are provided for Negroes on a segregated basis.

Since the Second World War the situation of American Negroes has improved with respect to employment in private industry and business. Particularly encouraging has been the emergence of state legislation designed to prevent discrimination in hiring by private businesses. The agencies charged with the prevention of discrimination in the various states had for their prototype the Federal Government's Fair Employment Practices Commission, which, in turn, was an outgrowth of the attempt to achieve full manpower utilization during the war in industries holding Federal contracts. Although this commission was largely ineffectual in the South, in the North it was responsible in some measure for the fact that between 1940 and 1944 the number of Negroes who held skilled jobs in American industry doubled, whereas at the same time there was a marked decrease in the proportion of Negroes who were employed in domestic services and agriculture. With the expiration of the Federal commission in 1946, control over employment practices was left to the state governments. There are now eleven states (all outside the South) which have enacted laws designed to eliminate discrimination in employment.

Perhaps still more promising has been the steady improvement in the attitude of organized labor toward admission of Negroes to formerly white unions. Here again recent legislation and litigation have played important roles. In 1944 the Supreme Court held that a union could not act as an exclusive bargaining agent for all persons in a craft unless it admitted members without distinctions based on race (Walker, p. 461). A year later the same court upheld the constitutionality of the New York State law which prohibits discrimination in any labor union. Similar laws and decisions have been passed in Kansas and California. Furthermore, the unions themselves have begun to take the initiative in outlawing segregation and discrimination in their own ranks. From the time of its founding in 1935, the Congress of Industrial Organizations (CIO) has enforced a policy of nondiscrimination which was incorporated as a chief aim in its constitution. Although there has been much resistance owing to the traditional prejudices of its members, excellent results have been achieved, especially in the crucial CIO affiliate, the United Automobile Workers. Strong stands against discrimination have also been taken by certain affiliates of the more conservative American Federation of Labor (AFL), especially those representing garment workers, plasterers and bricklayers. Most of the AFL affiliates have followed a policy of accepting the prevailing pattern of discrimination characteristic of the industry and locality which they serve, without attempting to eliminate it if it exists, or to introduce it if it does not. Nevertheless, it has been the national policy of both the CIO and the AFL to argue strenuously for a federal anti-discrimination law which would apply both to labor and to industry. Such an ideological stand may well be taken as a harbinger of further real improvement, especially in view of the recent merger of AFL and CIO.

Less substantial gains have been made in housing, but here again, no picture of contemporary race relations in the United States would be complete without reference to some of the more hopeful signs. As in the case of education, politics, and employment, government agencies are responsible for initiating the trend toward improvement. One of the most significant successes to date, the abolition of legal status for restrictive covenants, has already been mentioned. Public housing authorities throughout the North and West have recorded some successes in the building and operating of interracial housing developments. Some of the attempts along these lines have led to outbreaks of violence, as in Detroit and Chicago, but by far the majority of them have proved successful as experiments in overcoming some of the most deeply rooted prejudices on the part of white people. Successful interracial housing projects—i.e., where Negroes and whites live in the same buildings—have been established in New York, Los Angeles, Boston, New Haven, Cleveland, Seattle, Oakland, Springfield (Ill.), Lima (Ohio), and Lansing (Michigan). Additional encouragement is to be drawn from the success which a number of large privately owned interracial projects have had in New York City, and from the fact that similar projects are planned for Chicago. While interracial housing amounts to but a small fraction of publicly financed projects and of the total of private dwellings, they indicate a definite trend toward a policy of nonsegregation in both public and private housing.

IV

During the last decade the Negroes in the United States have registered gains in almost all spheres of American life. Dramatic "firsts" have occurred from motels to organized baseball. Yet probably the most profound change has escaped the headlines and goes unnoticed by the majority of whites. This change has to do with the growth and intensification of emotional unity among Negroes of different social strata and geographical regions. A new *esprit de corps* has been generated in the wake of progress achieved on the economic and educational fronts. Few American Negroes today would accept Booker T. Washington's self-effacing recommendation to be satisfied with segregation in "all things that are purely social." Today the Negro in the United States grows daily more unwilling to accept segregation and discrimination in any form which reduces his opportunity for material betterment and spiritual satisfaction. Negro spokesmen of the Negro group have sounded a clarion that is being heard from one end of the country to the other. They have made it clear to the whites that the Negro is no longer prepared passively to accept inferior housing, health, education, and subordinate political status. As time goes by and more progress toward equal justice and opportunity is achieved, we may expect an increasing sentiment of solidarity among the members of the Negro group. Today, more and more emphasis is being placed by Negroes themselves upon the heritage of Negro life and the great cultural and economic contributions which Negroes have made to the American scene.

Paradoxically, one of the concomitants of the new, active, even militant role which the Negro in the United States has recently begun to play is the probably indefinite prolongation of the Negro as a distinct racial group within the American population. For the integration which the Negro seeks, and in some considerable degree is reaching, is premised upon the continued separation of the races in marital and family life. In his program of equal civil and economic rights, there does not appear to be any place allotted to intermarriage as a solution to the Negro's problems. In marked contrast to Martinique and other areas of Latin America, miscegenation now appears to be unacceptable not only to the whites but to many Negroes as well. All indications are that Negro-white marriages are few in number and that they may even have slowly but steadily decreased since the beginning of the century (see Davie, p. 410; and Wirth and Goldhamer, pp. 276 ff.). "Passing," whereby borderline physical types defect from the Negro group and enter the ranks of the whites, also seems to be insignificant and perhaps declining (see Davie, pp. 401 ff.). It seems clear that the assimilation of the Negro by American society is a long way off.

Although integration appears to be much closer than ever before, the deep-seated prejudices and powerful institutions arrayed against progress toward that goal must not be underestimated. It has been a long road which the Negro in the United States has walked since the bitter days of slavery and the violence of reconstruction. All indications are that a long road still lies ahead.

RECOMMENDED ADDITIONAL READINGS

Ashmore, H. S. The Negro and the Schools. Chapel Hill, N.C.: University of North Carolina Press, 1954.

Cash, W. J. The Mind of the South. New York: Knopf, 1941.

Davie, Maurice R. Negroes in American Society. New York: McGraw-Hill, 1949.

Dollard, John. Caste and Class in a Southern Town. New Haven: Yale University Press, 1937.

Drake, St. Clair, and Horace Cayton. Black Metropolis. New York: Harcourt Brace, 1945.

Frazier, Edward Franklin. The Negro in the United States. New York: Macmillan, 1949.

Herskovits, Melville. The Myth of the Negro Past. New York: Harper, 1941.

Johnson, Charles S. Patterns of Negro Segregation. New York: Harper, 1943.

Klineberg, Otto, ed. Characteristics of the American Negro. New York: Harper, 1944.

Myrdal, Gunnar. An American Dilemma, The Negro Problem and Modern Democracy. New York: Harper, 1944.

Powdermaker, Hortense. After Freedom. New York: Viking Press, 1939.

Tannenbaum, Frank. Slave or Citizen, The Negro in the Americas. New York: Knopf, 1947.

III

The European Immigrants

THE final two cases presented in the chapters that follow concern minorities of European origin whose physical appearance is approximately similar to that of the dominant groups in their respective societies. They are thus set apart from the dominant groups by characteristics other than race—such as language, religion, national origin, or simply differences in cultural background. They are minority groups of different types from those composed by American Indians or Negroes. Their problems are different in many respects and must be solved by different means. The two minorities of European origin selected as cases for this book, namely the people of French origin living in Canada and the Jewish people living in the United States, are but two among innumerable similar minorities in the New World.

All white Americans in both the southern and northern hemisphere are, of course, descendants of immigrants from Europe. But in each colony, the people of the "mother country" soon came to form the dominant majority; thus the early Portuguese arrivals became the Brazilians; the early English became the North Americans; the early Spaniards became the majority in the Argentine. But in the nineteenth and early twentieth centuries an added flow of European immigrants came to the Americas. They came in great numbers to areas where industry and agriculture were expanding and there was a need for labor. They came to the northern United States, Argentina, southern Brazil, and Canada. In all these areas, the sparse aboriginal populations had either been completely exterminated or pushed back into isolated areas, leaving the land open for European settlement. These were areas of the Americas in which the plantation system with slave labor had not taken root; they were all in the temperate zone and were thus more adaptable to European agricultural techniques and to European crops. And each of these areas—the northern United States, Canada, Argentina, and southern Brazil—was in turn the scene of a rapidly expanding frontier and finally of considerable industrial development. These two separate areas of the New World at opposite ends of our continents received the majority of the recent European immigration and thus are noted for their minority groups of European origin.

This late wave of European immigration came earliest and in greatest numbers to the United States, for it was there that the frontier expanded most rapidly and that industralization was the most intense. From about 1820 to 1880, there was a constant influx of European immigrants into the United States. They joined the older colonists of predominantly English ancestry who already formed the dominant majority. These immigrants, sometimes spoken of as the "Old Immigrants" (Walter, pp. 252–53), were primarily northern Europeans, therefore they tended to be Protestant in religion and similar in other respects to the dominant national group. They included German, Irish, Scotch, Swedish, Dutch, as well as additional English immigrants. They came during the epoch of an expanding western frontier, and most of them rapidly spread out over the country, many of them to the West. A few of these "Old Immigrant" groups long persisted as enclaves throughout the country, and settlements of German, Swedish, and Dutch descendants are still found in the Midwest. Most of these "Old Immigrants," however, soon accommodated themselves to the dominant English-American culture patterns which were then taking form, and were assimilated quickly and peacefully into the American population. The surnames of the "old families" of almost any midwestern American town bear witness to the successful assimilation of these "Old Immigrants" from northern Europe who came in the nineteenth century.

In the latter decades of that century, however, a change occurred in the type of immigration into the United States. As the frontier was gradually populated and as industry began to develop in the cities of the northeastern part of the country, there was a great demand for cheap labor. A wave of "New Immigrants" came after 1880, not from the northern part but mainly from the southern, central, and eastern parts of Europe. They did not come to the rural zones and the frontier, but crowded into the big cities. They were Italians and Greeks from the Mediterranean area; Serbs, Croats, Czechs, and Poles from central Europe; and Jews from southeast Europe and Russia. Culturally, these "New Immigrants" differed far more from the dominant national groups of the United States than did the "Old Immigrants." They were Roman Catholics, Orthodox Catholics, or Jews; they spoke languages strange to the ears of the "Old Immigrants," who were by then overwhelmingly English-speaking; and their home countries were generally less industrialized than those of northern Europe so that they were less skilled mechanically. In America they took over the low-paying jobs in industry or were relegated to certain occupations or small business enterprises. In America they continued to live in relative poverty, and their level of education was low. They were forced to live in "little Italies," "Hunky Towns," or similar districts of big cities where they could continue to speak their own languages. But despite these unfavorable conditions in America, they continued to come from Europe in increasing numbers; during the early twentieth century they came almost one million strong each year. By 1930, over fourteen million people who were born elsewhere were residing in the United States, and most of them were these "New Immigrants" from Europe living in north-eastern American cities.

Because of linguistic and cultural differences and as a result of the competition for jobs, considerable prejudice grew up against the "New Immigrants" on the part of the earlier comers. Southern and central Europeans were believed to be "racially inferior" to northern Anglo-Saxons; they were accused of being more inclined to crime, of being unable to adjust to the American culture, and of wishing to overthrow the American institutions in favor of European powers and systems. The growing prejudice against these recent arrivals to America was intensified by periods of economic depression, and it finally culminated in the immigration laws which established quota controls on immigration in the 1920's and which stemmed the tide of great mass movements of Europeans into the United States. By now the great majority of these "New Immigrants" have in varying degrees become assimilated. Their descendants who are now second- and third-generation Americans have married descendants of the older groups of immigrants. They speak English of the American variety, and have entered a wide range of occupations and professions. Thus, it might be said that the "melting pot" has to a great extent been a success, although certainly not with the rapidity and lack of tension ideally depicted. Now there is a series of even newer immigrants, such as the Puerto Ricans and the Mexican Americans, to be assimilated in the United States. Along with the Negro, these very recent arrivals—and not the Europeans who came in the late nineteenth and early twentieth century—are the groups who suffer most as minority groups in the present-day United States.

The "New Immigrants" of the past century also came to Argentina and Brazil, although they arrived somewhat later and in smaller numbers than they did in the United States. As indicated above, this was a result of the later agricultural and industrial development of these countries. Just as English colonists had set the dominant culture patterns of the United States, the Spanish colonists set the dominant patterns for Argentina and the Portuguese set the patterns for Brazil. But in the late nineteenth and particularly in the twentieth

century, these earlier European arrivals were joined by large numbers of additional Spaniards, Portuguese, Italians, Poles, and Germans. This new European immigration began in 1856 in Argentina,
but the first appreciable surge of immigration came after the humid
pampas had become an important producer of wheat. Between 1857
and 1930, 6,300,000 people migrated to Argentina. Many of these
eventually returned home to Europe, yet at least some three and a
half million remained. Of these, some 1,300,000 were Italian and
1,025,000 were Spanish. Similarly, Brazil received over four million
immigrants from 1884 to 1939. Italians represented 34 percent of
this total, Portuguese 29 percent, Spaniards 14 percent, and Germans 4.1 percent. The major part of all these immigrants came to
southern Brazil—to the states of Rio Grande do Sul, Santa Catarina,
Paraná, and São Paulo.

The "New Immigrants" of Argentina and Brazil encountered a
somewhat different situation from that found by their compatriots in
the United States. In the first place, neither Argentina nor Brazil was
as highly industrialized as the United States. Furthermore, most of
the agricultural lands were already held by large estates—the famous
estancias of Argentina and *fazendas* of Brazil. Thus, among the "New
Immigrants," only the very successful were able to acquire land for
themselves. Despite the weak development of industry, however,
many of the immigrants drifted to Buenos Aires, Pôrto Alegre, and
São Paulo, producing a rapid increase in population of these cities.
In fact, it has been said that immigration of European peasants to
Latin America has been, in one sense, part of a general exodus of
rural peasants to the cities.

Although the Europeans who migrated to Argentina and Brazil
were few in number when compared to those who went to North
America during the same period, they had a profound effect upon
this South American region, since numerically they came to represent
such a high percentage of the total population. In 1880 the total
population of Argentina was but two and a half million people, com-
prising descendants of Spanish colonists, of Indians, and of a few
Negro slaves. The influx of millions of Europeans after 1880 com-

pletely changed the character of the Argentine population. In southern Brazil a similar phenomenon occurred. Particularly in the state
of São Paulo, the "New Immigrants" almost overwhelmed the earlier
sparse population; today southern Brazil still presents sharp cultural and racial contrasts with the rest of the country.

These "New Immigrants" became minority groups in Brazil and
Argentina just as did their counterparts in the United States. But in
South America, with the exception of the German and Polish groups,
there has been more rapid assimilation and integration of these minorities and the relations between the majority and minorities has been
less strained. As indicated above, many of the "New Immigrants"
themselves came from the home countries of the majority. Although
Argentina and Brazil had diverged markedly from Spain and Portugal since the colonial period, the new arrivals did not find it any more
difficult to adjust to the dominant culture patterns of the respective
countries than did late English migrants to North America. Moreover, the Italians were not strangers to either Brazilian or Argentine
customs. They were Catholics in predominantly Catholic countries;
they learned Spanish and Portuguese easily; coming from another
Mediterranean country, they shared many culture patterns, beliefs,
and attitudes with the "Old Immigrants" of their new homeland.
Like the Spanish and Portuguese late-comers, the Italians assimilated
fast. Only the very late arrivals in the large cities and the pockets of
Italians in the rural zones of southern Brazil are today set aside as
minority groups. On the other hand, the Germans and the Poles,
differing from the dominant majority in language, culture patterns,
and sometimes religion, have offered greater resistance to the forces
of assimilation.

The case studies of minority groups of European origin included
in this volume, namely the French Canadians and the Jews in the
United States, are but two from among the many that might have
been selected. They were chosen for several reasons. First, they are
among the most thoroughly studied minority groups in the Americas. There is a vast literature concerning the history and the contemporary situation of the Jews in the United States. Several eminent

students of minority groups have studied the French Canadians, and scholars of French-Canadian origin have written profusely upon their situation. In contrast, much less has been published to date on the Italians in Argentina and Brazil or even on the Germans in southern Brazil. Second, these two groups were selected because they represent rather widely divergent historical situations. The French Canadians are "Old Immigrants" who became a minority group by the realignment of colonial boundaries in the New World as early as 1763, when England extended its rule over French North American territory. Most of the Jews in the United States, on the contrary, are "New Immigrants" who came during the late nineteenth century from central and eastern Europe.[1] The two groups contrast in other ways. Although today there are French Canadians living throughout Canada, over 80 percent of them reside in Quebec Province, which is their territorial stronghold. This physical isolation has been important in allowing the French Canadians to maintain their unity and their cultural and linguistic distinctiveness over a three-hundred-year period. The Jews in the United States, on the other hand, live intercalated among the majority population, although they are more numerous in the northeastern states.

The French Canadians are traditionally rural and agrarian and the Jews are traditionally commercial and urban. The French Canadians have almost complete political autonomy in Quebec and a strong political voice throughout Canada. Their rights to use their language, to maintain their own schools, and to follow their own religion are guaranteed legally. Yet the French Canadians experience discrimination in economic spheres and there is a disproportionate number of French Canadians, as compared to English Canadians, in the lower economic brackets of the nation. On the other hand, the Jews have prospered in the United States; taken as a group, their income and standard of living is probably higher than the United States average. In the United States the Jews, however, have no

[1] There have been Jewish settlers in the United States since the seventeenth century, and many of the descendants of American Jews, especially those from Germany, arrived well before the influx of the "New Immigrants" in the nineteenth and twentieth centuries (see below, last chapter).

special legal protection guaranteeing their right to be different; neither their Sabbath nor their traditional religious holidays are respected by law. Although Jews have held many of the highest offices of the land, such as that of governor of a state, justice of the Supreme Court, and member of the president's cabinet, it is doubtful that a Jew would be elected president.

The situation of both groups is relatively favorable in comparison with that of other minorities (e.g., the Puerto Ricans in the continental United States, the Negro in the United States, the Indian in Mexico, and many others), yet both groups feel the pressure of prejudice. There is a fundamental difference between the "prejudice" shown by English Canadians toward the French Canadians and that experienced by the Jews in the United States. The prejudice of the English Canadian toward the French Canadian is, so to speak, indigenous to Canada; it derives from the French Canadians' lower standard of living, a difference in language, and difference in culture. It does not derive from a hatred of the French by the British in the Old World. On the other hand, the prejudice shown toward the Jews in the United States is the continuation of the ancient anti-Semitism of Europe. When the Jews arrived in the United States, the Protestant majority had already formed antipathetic sentiments toward them, without ever having known a Jew. Moreover, the "New Immigrants" in the United States also had the European derogatory stereotypes of the Jew readily available to them. In addition, the Jews in the United States, unlike the French Canadians, tend to have a feeling of unity with Jews in other countries. Particularly since the resurgence of anti-Semitism in Germany and the wholesale slaughter of European Jews, this sense of identity and solidarity with Jews elsewhere has increased. These and many other differences between the two European minority groups provide added variations of minority-majority situations for our study.

THE FRENCH CANADIANS [1]

Canada is officially a bilingual country within the British Commonwealth of Nations. Over four million people, some 30 percent of the total population, are of French descent. They are culturally and linguistically distinct from the English-speaking majority, and as Catholics they are further set off from the descendants of British colonists, who are predominantly Protestants. By far the majority of these "French Canadians," as they are called, live in the Province of Quebec. In 1951 there were 3,327,000 people of French descent in Quebec, compared to 491,818 people of British descent and 236,735 others of various national origins. Only 692,000 French Canadians are scattered throughout the other Canadian provinces.

These French Canadians are not an uprooted people who came to the New World as strangers in the midst of an established society. They were in fact the first Europeans to settle in the area which is today eastern Canada, and they formed a separate colony for two centuries until the area was ceded to the English in 1763. Nor are they politically subordinate to the English-speaking majority. Although they lived in an English colony for many years and now are a part of the British Commonwealth, they have been able to secure and to maintain equal political participation with English Canadians and the right to carry on their own way of life. Two French Canadians have been prime ministers of Canada. Both English and French are spoken today in the Canadian legislature. In their home province of Quebec, their numerical majority provides the French Canadians with overwhelming control of the government. In this province they have their own government-subsidized Catholic schools in which in-

[1] The authors gratefully acknowledge the assistance rendered by Mr. Guy Dubreuil of the University of Montreal in the preparation of a research draft for this chapter. Mr. Dubreuil, however, is not responsible for errors of fact or interpretation.

struction is given in French, and English is only a second language. There are two well-established French-Canadian universities—the Université Laval and the Université de Montréal. Today French Canadians are found in all socio-economic levels of Canadian society. On the surface, it would seem that Canada has successfully achieved a pluralistic society in which the two major linguistic and cultural groups, the English Canadians and the French Canadians, coexist and cooperate on an equal basis.

Yet French Canadians still consider themselves to be an under-privileged minority group. They feel that the English Canadians are prejudiced toward them because of their different culture, language, and religion. Many state that they are discriminated against eco-nomically, and some French Canadians even claim that they are "second-rate citizens" suffering from an endemic poverty deliberately provoked by the dominant English-Canadian group. It is dubious whether such extreme allegations can be substantiated. Still, it is certainly true that there are significantly more French Canadians than English Canadians in the lower economic brackets of the country. More important is the fact that French Canadians consider them-selves a minority group suffering from prejudice and discrimination. This subjective attitude is just as important as the objective reality of the situation in determining the relations between English and French Canadians. It is equally clear that the linguistic and cultural antithesis between these two groups constitutes a constant source of discomfort. "Once Canada became an English possession," writes a Canadian historian, "the profound antithesis [between English and French Canadians] emerged, the vast conflict of philosophies, which ever since has kept the country divided and which, in presenting it with a problem of such proportions, constitutes the principle theme of Canadian history" (Lower, *Colony*, p. 66).

I

French Canada's history began in 1534, when Jacques Cartier officially took possession of the country in the name of the king of

France. This part of North America, extending from the Gulf of the Saint Lawrence to the Great Lakes, was indeed a huge territory. But it was sparsely populated by tribes of Indian hunters and gatherers, and had little to offer of the natural resources sought after in that period, such as minerals and exotic spices. Despite their initial enthusiasm, the French soon realized that New France, as it was called, would yield no gold nor afford the passage to the Indies. During most of the colonial era France was so involved in her own political consolidation, in her religious quarrels, continental adventures, and also in her rich sugar-producing West Indian colonies, that little energy was left to devote to North America, which represented more of a liability than a source of profit. As late as 1636 there were only 200 Frenchmen in Canada. From 1608 to 1660, only 1,200 immigrants came. Toward the end of the seventeenth century, when New England's population was about two hundred thousand, there were but ten thousand French colonists to the north. The fur trade was practically the only industry in New France prior to the first quarter of the eighteenth century. A small number of homestead farmers furnished the colony with its main means of survival—diversified, subsistent agriculture. These farmers, or *colons,* gave French Canada much of its distinctive character, one which is still idealized today by French-Canadian writers and politicians.

These *colons* came from various French provinces, mainly Normandy, Perche, Brittany, and Îsle-de-France. They shared two important traits: they all spoke French and they were all Roman Catholic. Colonists for New France were recruited under the initiative of trading companies, and were placed on the land in a semi-feudal relation to landlords (*seigneurs*) to whom *seigneuries,* or fiefs, had been granted. In New France however, the landlords never succeeded in forming a powerful aristocracy comparable to that of the *grands blancs* of the French West Indies. Most of the *seigneurs* were drawn from the petty nobility or were given their titles after they had emigrated to New France. They were not wealthy when they came to the New World and conditions in New France seldom improved their economic situation. They had little real control over the colonists on their domains (*habitants*), and many of the so-called privileges granted to the members of the *seigneur* class actually became burdens to them. The right of *corvée,* for example, which in France might mean as much as three days' work a week without reward from the lord, was limited in Canada to six days a year and the unfortunate *seigneur* was obliged to feed the workman. Furthermore, the agricultural products of these Canadian *seigneuries* could not find any profitable market in the home country, nor did the rents paid by the *habitants* to the *seigneurs* ever amount to much. The lot of the *seigneur* in New France "was frequently one of decidedly genteel poverty, unless he were rescued by war or were a merchant who had bought the *seigneury* to enhance his dignity" (Lower, p. 41). Everything seemed to favor the peasant. In reality he was in control of his land. Contrary to the situation of the *petits blancs* and free mulattoes of Martinique, the peasants' lot gradually improved and in many cases they were better off economically than the *seigneurs*. By the beginning of the eighteenth century, peasants were in possession of almost one third of the *seigneuries* of New France.

The *habitants* of New France could depend solely upon their own efforts and that of their sons to clear the forest and cultivate their lands. The indigenous peoples of the region, such as the suspicious and hostile Iroquois, were too few to furnish any labor supply. Very early, therefore, the *famille souche*—that is, an extended family consisting of a man, all his sons, their wives and children—came to be the nucleus of French-Canadian society. Such families were from the very early days of the colony exceedingly large; in the seventeenth century, the French Crown actively stimulated early marriage for the *habitants* of New France. Women known as the "King's girls" were sent over from France to become the wives of settlers. Bounties were given to boys who married before they were 20 years of age and to girls who married before 16. Fathers who had not married off their sons and daughters by these ages were fined; bachelors were barred from hunting, fishing, and trading. Special bounties were granted to families with 10, 12, or 15 children. These policies seemed to have been successful, for the birthrate was evidently very high (see Miner, p. 5).

These large families became almost autonomous economic units devoted to agriculture and directed by the father. Agriculture was primarily a mode of life engaged in for subsistence and seldom for profit. "With the exception of the occasional crop failures, there were no large calamities [on these family farms]. As a rule, there was plenty of maple syrup, bread and pork available for everyone. Cooked with beans, *fèves au lard,* this latter became a kind of national diet" (Lower, *Colony,* p. 46). The highest ambition of the father, the leader of such families, was to "transmit the goods of the family to some one of its children, although favoring—according to the measurement of its resources—the establishment of the other children outside the family foyer [home]" (Gérin, cited in Hughes, *French Canada,* p. 4). Given the small size of the landholding of the *habitant,* and the large size of his family, the effort to establish sons on farms resulted in a markedly equalitarian society among the French-Canadian rural peasants. The English conquest of eastern Canada left the French-Canadian social system essentially untouched; even at the end of the nineteenth century a French-Canadian sociologist could still write: "The French-Canadian countryside presents itself as a simple juxtaposition of families who are nearly all equal; nearly all engaged in farming; nearly all sufficient unto themselves . . ." (Gérin, cited in Hughes, *French Canada,* p. 4). This is the mode of life that persists even today in many isolated rural areas of Quebec.

The grants made to the *seigneurs* were long and narrow, often beginning on a river front and running inland for many miles. The sites ceded to the *habitants* followed the same pattern. Today the individual farms are long and narrow, often no more than 100 to 200 feet wide but as much as a mile and a half long. All these farms border upon a road where each family has its house. Since the fields are very narrow, the farmhouses are only a few hundred feet apart and give the impression of a village strung along the road. This kind of village is called a *rang* (see Miner, pp. 45–46). Within the *rang,* most of the inhabitants are apt to be related by blood or marriage and even nonkinsmen are tied to the group by neighborly obligations and cooperative work parties.

Leadership for this embryonic rural community of New France was provided by the Catholic priest. The *curé* and the church, not the *seigneur* and his mansion, became the center of community life. As an individual the priest was usually foreign to the community in which he settled, but his presence was eagerly desired by the peasants. To them, Catholicism was a set of beliefs and rituals which attained their maximum efficacy only when practiced by a priest. When the priest came, a respected position was spontaneously accorded him. Religious rituals, such as Sunday Mass, baptism, marriage, and first communion, were also social meetings where community problems were discussed. Very few social gatherings could do without the *curé*. Fields, farms, houses, and animals were blessed by him on special occasions. Prayers were organized to gain spiritual support when special work was undertaken. The *curé* served as arbiter, advisor, and as judge. There were no problems in the community of which he was unaware, for he had personal relations with every family member. The *curé* and the family heads were partners in many spheres of activity, especially in the matter of children's education. Actually, he was an honorary member of every family and as such was in a position to control the whole community. He could channel public opinion in the direction he wanted. The power of the priest as a local leader in French Canada has been described by many visitors, often with considerable sarcasm. "One cannot have any pleasure," wrote the Baron de La Hontan, "either at cards or in visiting the ladies, without the *curé* being told of it, and without his denouncing it from the pulpit. His indiscreet zeal goes as far as to name persons; and if he goes so far as to refuse Communion to noble ladies for wearing colored ribbons, for the rest, you can judge for yourself" (La Hontan, pp. 89–90).

The influence of the clergy pervaded French-Canadian social life. Births, marriages, and deaths were recorded by the priests for their parishes, and these records became semi-public institutions. The tithes paid to the *curé* were for a long time the only taxes paid by the *habitants.* Primary education was—and still is—directly or indirectly controlled by the parish priest. It was the priest who gave the community its system of values and its attitudes toward the outside world. In the eighteenth century, the parish *curés* preached against the dangers of the Anglo-Saxon Protestant neighbors who threatened the colony, and even urged using the community militia against them. They taught that the modest economic conditions of the *habitant* constituted more precious wealth than the worldly riches of the Protestants. It is the *curé* who has contributed to the conservatism of the French-Canadian *habitant* and to the ideal of "unchangeableness" in regard to French Canada. Perhaps more than any other factor, the leadership of the clergy has strengthened the in-group feeling of the French Canadian.

This leadership by the Catholic clergy in New France went beyond the local parish. In fact, it could almost be said that New France had a three-headed government: the governor, who represented the king of France; the *intendant,* in charge of justice, internal order, and finance, who represented colonial interests; and the bishop, who represented the Church. The bishop's influence at times completely overshadowed that of the civil authorities. Toward the end of the seventeenth century Bishop Laval, for example, was able to gain the recall of three governors and even of the *intendant* Jean Talon. With powers based upon the control of the *curé* over his parishoners, the Church was an integral part of French-Canadian society, while the civil colonial government of New France seemed more and more to be a superimposed structure representing "foreign interests." As the well-known historian Francis Parkman said, "The royal government was transient; the Church was permanent. The English conquest shattered the whole apparatus of civil administration at a blow, but left her untouched" (Parkman, p. 203).

With the threat of English conquest, the weakness of the link between New France and the mother country became more apparent.

Emigration from France virtually ceased in 1672, yet by 1765 the population had increased more than tenfold to approximately 70,000 and almost every *habitant* could trace his Canadian ancestry for several generations. Long residence in a new land had created an embryo nation whose sense of an identity separate from the mother country was already full-blown. The *canadiens* were French in origin and heritage, yet vigorously Canadian in interests and outlook. (Innis, p. 13)

It is not surprising, then, that the people of New France did not resist the English encroachers out of loyalty to the mother country: it was the Church that fired them into resistance. The Bishop de Pontbriand warned them against "the unfortunate witness of the detestable errors of Luther and Calvin invading this diocese, whose faith was always so pure. You will therefore fight," he ordered, "this year not only to preserve your goods, but also to protect this vast country against heresy and the monsters of iniquity that it generates at every moment" (cited in Brunet, pp. 506–16). This became a patriotic holy war for the *canadiens* against a people whom propaganda had painted as brutes. But the French Canadians were a mere handful against the large Anglo-American colony to the south. In 1760 the French forces capitulated, and in 1763, by the Treaty of Paris, Louis XV ceded the whole of Canada to Great Britain.

Between 1760 and 1763 relations between the *canadiens* and their English conquerors were strangely peaceful, in view of the strong hatred engendered before and during the war. The first English military governor of the provisory military regime gave orders to his soldiers to respect the local people and the *seigneurs,* and the clergy offered their cooperation. Help was given to depressed communities and even to convents of French nuns. The *habitants* were left to themselves and the whole French-Canadian population reacted with remarkable submissiveness to English rule. By 1763, however, when a royal proclamation was issued to establish a civil government for New France, now to be called the Province of Quebec, it was obvious that the relations between the two groups was not to be as happy. The order not only sharply reduced the traditional boundaries of the colony but it was clearly aimed at the acculturation and assimilation of French Canadians into English colonial life. "An old French colony was to be remade into an English colony" (cited in Wade, *Canadians,* p. 54). English laws and English courts were established. Plans were made for a large-scale immigration of English subjects into the new province. Lands were granted to Protestant clergy and schoolmasters, in the hope that Protestantism would supplant Catholicism.

The policies established by the royal proclamation could hardly be enforced, and with their numerical superiority the French Canadians were able to preserve their language, religion, and customs until the Quebec Act in 1774 gave them a legal basis for survival. In fact, French-Canadian passive resistance during the years following English conquest does much to explain the tenacity with which the French-Canadian minority has resisted acculturation and assimilation into the present. French-Canadian merchants, ruined by the war, could not compete with the English merchants who migrated to Quebec and invested heavily in the fur trade and in commerce. There was a retreat into the countryside by many dispossessed *seigneurs* and French merchants; forced out by economic competition, these urban French Canadians joined the *habitants* and adopted their rural patterns of life. As a result, rural life became a conscious ideal among French Canadians; it was considered the only possible way to resist assimilation. Isolated and out of contact with the English, old French-Canadian values were erected as sacred rules. Frugality became a prize virtue and fecundity an evident duty. There was a strong reaction against the proselytizing of the Protestants. The old parish organization under the *curé* was strengthened and the lower clergy came to be comprised of native-born French-Canadian peasants. Almost every family had at least one member in the clergy. As a result of this rural entrenchment, the Church became even more integrated into group life. A myth developed that French Canadians had always been a rural people.

The movement for independence in those British colonies which lay to the south seems to have improved the lot of the French Canadians. As the American cause grew stronger, the English merchants of Quebec tended to side with the proponents of revolution. In an effort to secure the loyalty of French Canadians against the revolutionary tide rising in the south, the English government issued the Quebec Act in 1774. This is often considered the Magna Carta of

French Canada (see Lower, *Colony,* p. 74). The Quebec Act allowed French Canadians to hold public office without taking the hated anti-Catholic oath. It established that in civil matters the "Laws of Canada" should be resorted to, that the priests should again have their tithes and the *seigneurs,* their dues. There were no provisions that guaranteed the use of the French language and it was evident that the Act favored the clergy and the *seigneurs;* it therefore did not secure the loyalty of the *habitants* "who showed themselves singularly indifferent to the quarrel among *les sacrés anglais* and did not appreciate the restoration of their symbols of servitude" (Lower, *Colony,* p. 74). But the Act did restore to the French Canadians their traditional religion, and some of their laws and institutions; and by pleasing the elite it did leave the situation more favorable for the survival of French Canada as a British colony.

The years of the American Revolution were difficult ones for French Canada. On the one hand the *seigneurs* and the clergy remained loyal to the Crown. The clergy was afraid of the Protestant-American attitude toward the Catholic Church and the *seigneurs* had more affinities with the English functionaries than with the French-Canadian *habitants.* On the other hand, French Canadians were subject to passionate appeals from the American rebels to join their cause in the struggle for liberty, representative government, and freedom from economic persecution; and in fact, a few French Canadians did join the American forces. But on the whole the rural *habitants* were indifferent; they both resisted enrollment in the militia when ordered by the British government and at the same time definitely turned against the American forces when these attempted to requisition supplies or to pay for them with paper money. But in the end, England was able to retain Canada and the French Canadians remained under British rule.

Following the War for American Independence, there was a wave of immigration of Loyalist English colonists into Canada. More than thirty thousand entered Nova Scotia and the area which was later to become New Brunswick. The Montreal region received some one thousand Loyalists, and the region which became the Province of Ontario was settled by nearly six thousand Loyalists from the south (Burt, p. 82). The English merchants welcomed these new-comers, seeing in them a sign of future English numerical dominance over the colony. For the first time the colony assumed a dual char-acter as English-speaking inhabitants settled beside the French. The British mercantile class soon clamored again for an elected assembly. Although the majority of the electorate was French, the British counted on the growing English-speaking settlement in the upper St. Lawrence region and on sufficient French support to control the assembly. At the same time, the seigneurial class opposed the elected assembly, fearful of losing their newly gained powers. The Loyalists on the upper St. Lawrence River demanded a separate government apart from that dominated by the French-Catholic papists. It was the decision of the British home government that the country was too large, and the dif-ference between the French society on the lower St. Lawrence River and the growing English society too great, to be administered as one unit. Thus, the Canada Act of 1791 divided the colony into Upper and Lower Canada (Nova Scotia and New Brunswick were separate colonies). Each was endowed with an appointed council, an elected legislative assembly, and a governor representing the Crown. Lower Canada, with some one hundred fifty thousand people remained theoretically dominated by the French, and remained Roman Catholic in religion. Upper Canada had only about ten thousand people, most of whom were English-speaking Loyalists.

The French Canadians failed to gain political control of Lower Canada despite their great numerical superiority and their strength in the elected assembly. At first a relatively large number of the mem-bers of the legislative council were French, but as time went on they were mainly English or French *seigneurs* sympathetic to English interests. In 1827, 18 out of 27 members of the legislative council were British. In the same year, only 3 out of 10 judges were French, and of 30 judicial appointments between 1800 and 1827 only 10 were made to French Canadians. "In 1834, although they constituted over three quarters of the population, the French held less than a quarter of the public places. This was a serious grievance to a people who

did not have the commercial outlet of the English and looked on
government posts as major goals" (Lower, *Colony,* pp. 217–18).

The French Canadians now felt themselves to be in the midst
of a hostile people who were attempting both to exploit and to absorb
them. They felt that they had no "mother country." Even if France
had offered them help it is doubtful that they would have accepted,
for the clergy had made it clear to them that post-Revolutionary
France was a lost child of the Church. Their reaction was again to
resist change and to develop an ardent dislike for the English. The
more their customs were ridiculed, the more determined they became
to preserve them. They saw themselves being progressively engulfed
by English merchants and bankers who were becoming rich while they,
the "real *canadiens,*" were relegated to being rural peasants and lum-
berjacks. Every political debate took the form of a "racial struggle,"
and French Canadians tended to identify the English as "barbarians,"
"exploiters," "enemies of the race," and "arrogant Protestants." Likewise, the English colonists resented the French. Numbering only
seventy-five thousand in 1834 against some six hundred thousand
French in both Canadas, they had real cause for worry. Most of
these English colonists could not understand why Frenchmen and
Roman Catholics should have a voice in a British colony. They were
irritated by the "antiquated" French legal system, the power of the
Church, and the immobility and conservatism of the French peasantry. The two groups faced each other with fear and distrust and
with equal conviction that Quebec should be theirs exclusively.

Tension reached a peak in 1837 when a rebellion led by the fiery
leader Louis Joseph Papineau broke out in Lower Canada. This
rebellion was terminated quickly, but resulted in the abolition of the
separate elected assembly for Lower Canada. In 1840 the Union
Act again united Upper and Lower Canada under a single legislature
in an effort to check the troublesome French. The failure of this brief
uprising of 1837 had the effect of deepening the already existing
patterns of resistance among the French Canadians. It also reinforced
English misconceptions concerning their countrymen of French origin.
Even the report of Lord Durham, who was sent to Canada after the

uprising to study the troubles, expressed disdain for the French colonists. It seemed clear to him that "sooner or later the English race [*sic*] was sure to predominate even numerically in Lower Canada, as they predominate already in knowledge, energy, enterprise and wealth" (Wade, *Canadians*, p. 203). He referred to the French Canadians as a people with "no history and no literature" (Wade, p. 212).

At mid-century, the French Canadians were still a "troublesome" group with considerable political influence, but as a result of English, Scotch, and Irish immigration into Canada, they had lost their numerical majority. In 1861 they numbered 883,569 people, within a total Canadian population of over two and a half million. Even in Lower Canada, French Canadians constituted only 75 percent of the population. As a numerical minority they became increasingly concerned with *la survivance*—survival of their language and culture.

In 1867 the four provinces—Ontario (Upper Canada), Quebec (Lower Canada), New Brunswick, and Nova Scotia—were united under one central government. These provinces were later joined by six others. The British North American Act, which established this union, allocated many important powers to the separate provinces. Each province was represented in the upper house of the legislature by appointed representatives, and in the lower house by elected representatives. Each province had a lieutenant governor who, with his cabinet, exercised executive power, and an elected legislative assembly. Among the powers specifically retained by the provincial governments was the ability to control provincial education. For the French Canadians in Quebec this was a vital part of the British North American Act. Through political control of one large province they maintained a strong voice in Canadian government and through their own schools they were able to transmit their language and traditions. Since the establishment of dominion government, Quebec has jealously guarded these provincial rights and the question of infringement upon such rights has often been a crucial issue in Canadian politics.

When Canada's great western prairie lands were opened for settlement, a new wave of immigrants swelled the population. Settlers from the United States "flowed north across the border into the last remaining segment of the fertile western plains . . ." (Innis, p. 16). The majority of the new immigrants, however, came from overseas. The British Isles and the countries of northwestern Europe furnished the bulk of them, but many came from the Balkans and from western and southern Russia. The rate of immigration increased as the nineteenth century came to a close. In 1900 alone, some forty-one thousand immigrants entered Canada, and the yearly number reached four hundred thousand in 1913. "This was the climax of a decade during which nearly 2,500,000 people—a figure equal to nearly half of the population of Canada at the beginning of the century—came to the Dominion" (Innis, p. 16). The rate of immigration declined somewhat during the First World War and continued to do so afterwards. By 1931, world-wide depression and stringent regulations brought it practically to a halt. Some of these "New Immigrant" groups, such as the German-speaking Mennonites from the Volga and the Russian-speaking Dukhobors, formed new minority groups within Canadian society. Most of Canada's "New Immigrants," however, came from the British Isles or from northern European countries. These have been rapidly assimilated by English-Canadian society, thus increasing the numerical superiority of the English-speaking element in the Canadian nation.

French Canada responded to the growth of the English-speaking population with *revanche des berceaux,* the "revenge of the cradles." The birthrate of French Canadians has long been one of the highest in the western world, and even today they still lead all other components of Canadian society in fertility. Their high birthrate, combined with the traditional practice of settling the family farm upon one heir, has obliged many French Canadians to migrate from Quebec Province. Many have entered the United States and have come to form an important minority group in the New England states. But, more important for Canada itself, they have expanded their numbers in other Canadian provinces. They have gradually replaced the English settlers in the so-called eastern townships of Quebec itself. "Large sections of the Ontario side of the Ottawa Valley have likewise become French. In New Brunswick, the French have increased from 15.72 percent of the total in 1871 to 35.81 in 1941" (Lower, *Religion*, p. 476). Furthermore, many French Canadians have migrated to the western provinces, such as Alberta, Manitoba, and Saskatchewan.

Yet it cannot be said that the *revanche des berceaux* will ever enable the French Canadians to regain numerical equality with English Canadians. For outside of Quebec, French Canadians are much more vulnerable to the forces of acculturation and assimilation. They often must attend English schools. They must use English in daily life and they are constantly exposed to English-Canadian influences. The plight of these French Canadians far from their "homeland" has long been a point of irritation to French Canadians in Quebec. Thus, the expansion of French Canadians into other parts of Canada has created two distinct types of contact between French and English Canadians. On the one hand, French Canadians within Quebec and in surrounding localities have the support of numbers and of a unified linguistic, cultural, political, and religious front; whereas those living in alien areas are faced with an overwhelming English-Canadian society.

Since confederation in 1867, there has been a mutual effort on the part of both English and French Canadians to develop a sense of true nationhood despite their differences. On the whole, the Canadian experiment has been a success, as the present dynamic condition of the nation shows. "The fact is," states one well-known Canadian historian, "that a sense of common Canadianism does not depend for its strength on a concept of national uniformity" (Innis, p. 26). The two groups have certainly learned to coexist, but tension and ill feeling have not been eliminated. The cleft between them becomes overt in periods of crisis, such as during wars, economic depressions, and political campaigns. For example, during the First World War troops were sent from Toronto to break up tumultuous meetings in Quebec City held to oppose the national draft laws. French Canadians opposed obligatory service in the army because English was the official army language and French-Canadian recruits found themselves at the bottom of the military hierarchy. The English Canadians accused the French of refusing to "defend civilization against the Huns."

Similarly, there were bitter misunderstandings between French and English Canadians during the Second World War. Nevertheless, the Canadian nation has sustained these and many other stresses between the two groups. In 1957, the prime minister was a French Canadian and an avowed champion of national unity. At present, similarities and symbols of national unity are the preferred theme of most Canadians. As one writer put it: "In finding that they are children of the same soil, with the same political roof over their heads, French and English, Roman Catholics and Protestant, are very slowly discovering their common interests. Nationalism is proving a bridge" (Lower, *Religion,* p. 478). Canada has become an example to the world of a bilingual nation of two cultures, yet latent hostilities remain and French Canadians still think of themselves as a depressed minority.

II

Who is a Canadian? A French Canadian will speak of himself as a *canadien* and refer to the others as *les anglais.* On the other hand, the English Canadian calls himself a "Canadian" and may speak of his neighbor as a "Frenchman" or a "French Canadian." This awareness of difference underlies the fundamental attitudes of the two groups. But one group's opinion of the other varies greatly according to the kind of relations individuals have had with one another, from one county to another, and from one socio-economic class to another. Neither group is today homogeneous. *Les anglais* now include a large Irish-Catholic group, many Scots, and acculturated descendants of Germans, Ukrainians, and other peoples. The *canadiens* are split by rural and urban differences, by marked differences in socio-economic class, and by region (i.e., those of Quebec versus those of the western provinces). Yet each group does seem to hold a set of traditional stereotypes, or "pictures in the head," of the other group—even though these "pictures" are more often exaggerated caricatures than a true likeness.

Perhaps the most derogatory view of the French Canadian is held by English Canadians in the western provinces and in Ontario, where many have never seen a French Canadian. In brief, to these extremists, a French Canadian is a backward peasant, a papist fanatic, a narrow-minded Catholic, and a medieval fossil clinging rigidly to an outmoded way of life. The province of Quebec is to them almost a "reservation" to be visited by tourists; Quebec's insistence upon the bicultural and bilingual basis for nationalism in Canada is but a bit of fantasy to be tolerated but not taken seriously; Canada is an English-speaking country and a part of the Empire. Many English Canadians, even in the province of Quebec, are convinced that Canada will eventually be English-speaking and English-Canadian in culture, and that the French-Canadian group will eventually disappear through acculturation and assimilation (see Sanders). Other minorities learn to speak English and learn Canadian ways of life, they argue; why should the French Canadians have their own schools, radio stations, and associations?

On the other hand, French-Canadian extremists still look upon *les anglais* as men with two countries—Great Britain and Canada. Long ago, when there was agitation for Canadian participation in the Boer War, this fundamental idea was clearly expressed: "We French Canadians belong to one country, Canada; Canada is for us the whole world; but the English Canadians have two countries, one here and one across the sea" (Wade, *Trends,* pp. 145–46). The English Canadians are thought to be imperialist, much more interested in the welfare of the Empire than of Canada. Furthermore, the English Canadian is thought to be imperialist at home; he wishes only to exploit and to assimilate the French Canadians. Since the English Canadians are the majority in the federal Parliament, French Canadians suspect any federal laws or orders of being unfair and directed against French-Canadian interests. They think of the English Canadians as rich and powerful and in complete control of economic trusts which rule Quebec and the French Canadians. Personally, *les anglais* are considered to be materialists—practical men given to business—arrogant, proud of their "race," and lacking in consideration of others. The English are pictured as barbarians—more interested in dogs than in children, in sports than in religion, in money than in arts.

Above all, many French Canadians feel that they are exploited and discriminated against as a group. In fact, there does seem to be considerable evidence that they are an economically depressed group when compared with other Canadians. In their home province of Quebec, which is now being rapidly industrialized, technical, managerial, and financial control seems to be in English-Canadian hands; whereas the French Canadians are concentrated in small industry, commerce, the professions, and unskilled and semi-skilled jobs. Quebec has long been advertised as an area where there is a surplus of cheap labor. It is true that the average income was but $972 per year in Quebec as against $1,290 in Ontario in 1952 (Chapin, p. 50), and that in 1953 workers in Ontario's industries (excluding paper and pulp industries) averaged $6.60 per week more than did Quebec's workers (Beausoleil, p. 48). During the last two decades Quebec has experienced a period of rapid industrial growth, but the capital for this development has come mainly from the outside. It has come from English-Canadian provinces and from the United States. Thus, from the French-Canadian point of view, Quebec "suffers from absentee ownership and entrepreneurship," and "administrative functions have been delegated to a predominantly English-speaking local management with limited responsibilities" (Faucher and Lamontagne, pp. 36–37). This situation is highly resented in Quebec, and a vote-getting rallying point for politicians has been their campaign against *les trustards* (the trusts).

The fact that French Canadians have played but a minor role in industry has been attributed to their cultural background. It is pointed out that French Canadians long ago idealized the simple agricultural life of the rural *habitant* and looked upon themselves as "children of the soil." French Canadians are said to stress conservatism, as expressed in the classic novel *Maria Chapdeleine* by Louis Hémon: "In the land of Quebec nothing must die, nothing must change." It is said that both their religion and their traditional values emphasize the non-material aspects of life more than the material. French Canadians tend to enter the liberal professions rather than business, engineering, and other technical occupations. When the industrialization of Quebec began, the mass of French-Canadian workers were thus unskilled and poorly prepared for jobs in industry. The middle class and educated French Canadians did not have the qualities necessary for good executives; they had not learned the impersonal objectivity necessary for administering large organizations but tended to be highly personal in their judgments and to be "family-oriented," favoring kinsmen over other employees. Furthermore, French Canadians with a little capital preferred to invest in real estate rather than in new business enterprise (see Chapin, p. 45). From this point of view, the present economic disadvantages result mainly from the particular, historically formed French-Canadian culture, which has provided barriers to adjustment to contemporary commercial and industrial conditions.

French-Canadian education has traditionally stressed religion, philosophy, arts, letters, and the classics over science, technology, and other subjects called for by modern industry and commerce. Even today, the educational system is overwhelmingly in the hands of the Church. The majority of primary-school teachers are either Catholic brothers or nuns. Likewise, the secondary schools or *collèges classiques* are Catholic institutions in which priests form the majority of the teaching staff. The structure of the Quebec educational system differs from that in the English provinces: for example, instead of the four-year English-Canadian high school, from which one enters the university, Quebec has the eight-year *collège classique* as well as the parallel course called *Primaire supérieur,* which also allows entrance into the university. Only a small segment of French-Canadian students, however, receives secondary education of either form. According to Léon Lortie, only about 3,500 children complete secondary education each year, whereas in Ontario there were more than 13,000 in the last year of high school (Lortie, p. 186). Until very recently, only those with the *"bachelier"* degree from a recognized *collège classique* were admitted to French-Canadian universities.

To a large extent, the educational system of French Canada has been directed toward the formation of an elite rather than toward a broad program that would prepare the mass of people for the industrial revolution which French Canada has experienced in recent years. Secondary education, especially that which the *collège classique* provides, emphasizes rhetoric, philosophy, Latin and Greek, and other humanistic subjects, rather than science. As a result, those who enter the universities are better prepared for theology, law, medicine, and the humanities than for engineering and science. Of 9,304 students who graduated from the *collège classiques* between 1939 and 1950, slightly over 37 percent entered the priesthood, 40 percent chose medicine, 16 percent engineering, 11 percent law, 8 percent commerce, and only 7 percent "applied science" (Falardeau, p. 110). These educational trends are reflected in a lack of French-Canadian technicians for industry. With about 30 percent of the total population of Canada, Quebec contributes only 2.5 percent of the chemists and 5 percent of the engineers of the country (Chapin, p. 93). The educational system thus is especially weak in just those fields required by modern industry and commerce. It is quite clear that both the educational system and the traditional values of French-Canadian society of which it is a result do not provide the basis for full participation in the new economic life of Canada.

Yet many French Canadians look for a "more materialistic and commonplace explanation," namely, economic imperialism and discrimination against them as a minority group, for their disadvantageous economic situation vis-à-vis English Canadians. They point out that "it is well known that successful businessmen in French Canada as elsewhere, at least in the past, were not necessarily university graduates" (Faucher and Lamontagne, pp. 36–37). They point out that equally trained French-Canadian employees are often ignored for promotions by English-Canadian employers. The very fact that the owners and heads of Quebec's major industries are mainly English-speaking meant that they were inclined to appoint English Canadians as their immediate assistants. Although the situation may have changed in recent years, this seems certainly to have been true in the community called by the fictitious name of Cantonville, in the eastern townships of Quebec, which was studied by Everett Hughes about two decades ago (Hughes, *French Canada*). In 1937, although the population of Cantonville was overwhelmingly French-Canadian, only 2 of the 11 large industries in Cantonville were managed by French Canadians. These employed only 70 people, whereas more than half of the industrial labor of Cantonville, numbering over 2,700, worked for a large artificial silk goods factory owned by a British company. The 25 men of the general executive and technical staff of this mill were all English (British and English-Canadian), except one who was the company physician. Eighteen of them were sent out from England by the British plant because of their special skills and knowledge of the business. "But others, without techniques peculiar to this industry, were sent from abroad" (Hughes, *French Canada,* p. 50). These included the general manager and a labor superintendent. Likewise, only about 30 percent of the foremen were French-Canadian, and in general the French-Canadian "foremen" were in lesser positions.

It was quite clear that the "French Canadians as a group did not enjoy that full confidence of industrial directors and executives which would admit them easily into the inner circles of the fraternity—and fraternity it is—of men who run industry. This situation prevails through the province of Quebec" (Hughes, *French Canada,* p. 53). The reasons given for this lack of confidence comprise a series of derogatory stereotypes, such as "the French have to be told what to do and therefore cannot be trusted with jobs requiring initiative and the meeting of crisis"; or, "they are good routine workers but are inclined to take things easy if left to themselves"; or, "they have so many relatives and friends that they cannot avoid favoritism." The time has probably passed when a French engineer might receive the following answer when he asked his English-Canadian boss why he had not been promoted. "But your name . . . ?" It might have been Beauchemin (Chapin, p. 92). But it is probably true that French Canadians are still at a disadvantage in organizations controlled by English Canadians, British, or Americans. In such commercial or industrial organizations, the French Canadian has a linguistic disadvantage; bilingualism is for him a definite requirement while the English Canadian need not necessarily know French. Both for reasons of cultural background and because the English Canadians dominate economic life and strive to continue to do so, the French Canadians feel strongly what has been termed the "French-Canadian differential" in the economic life of Canada (Falardeau, p. 109).

The inferior economic status of French Canadians as compared with English Canadians produces a situation in many Canadian cities which resembles residential segregation. Actually, as Jean C. Falardeau points out: "Very frequently, the spatial distribution of the French and of the English in our urban communities reproduces their respective position in the industrial hierarchical order" (Falardeau, p. 106). French Canadians and English Canadians live as neighbors when they share equal economic and social status, but because of the economic differential between the two groups there are often predominantly French and predominantly English districts in large cities. In Montreal and even Ottawa, the low rental areas where laborers live tend to be French. Even in cities of eastern Quebec, "segregated by parks, by a river or by a company golf course, one discovers the residential area of the English-speaking managers, technicians, and often foremen of the industries" (Falardeau. p. 106). But even when equality of economic situation allows French and English to live alongside each other they still tend to congregate into neighborhoods along ethnic lines, for differences in language and in culture make it more comfortable to have neighbors of one's own group.

The two groups tend to form dual "societies" which often overlap but into which the members of each can and do retreat. In Montreal, for example, the duality appears to embrace religion, art, literature, business, pleasure, sport, and sex (Chapin, p. 156). One of the great barriers between the two "societies" is language. English Canadians as a rule seldom speak French; it is said that only 3 percent of all English Canadians are bilingual (Chapin, p. 16). Many English Canadians excuse themselves for their inability to speak French by subscribing to the cliché that French Canadians speak a *patois:* "These people don't speak real French" (Chapin, p. 16). On the other hand, French Canadians—especially in Ontario, in the western provinces, and even in Montreal—are often forced to learn English. For despite the recognized use of French in the Parliament, English is important to them in business and in daily life. It is a decided economic advantage for a French Canadian to speak English and it is almost a necessity in some business or professional situations; yet language remains a crucial symbol of group survival to the French Canadians. They are proud of their language and eager to preserve it.

The inability to communicate with each other, combined with differences in cultural values, necessarily limits social contacts between the French and English Canadians. As Everett Hughes wrote some time ago: "People of the two groups . . . meet and greet one another on the streets and in places of business. At theaters, concerts, and at athletic events they sit amicably side by side. Categorical and casual relations abound. Intimate and prolonged contacts are few" (Hughes, *French Canada,* p. 160). In Cantonville only a small "sporty set" consisting of a few French- and English-Canadian couples had frequent social relations with one another. The French- and English-Canadian elite were frequently thrown together at the local golf club and at semi-public social events, but seldom did they entertain each other in their homes. Among men there was a greater ease of social mixing than among the women. When women met socially, "there was something of a barrier between them. Most of the English women cannot converse in French and accuse the French of chattering away among themselves." French women did not take bridge seriously but rather seemed to enjoy the occasion for some lively social interplay (Hughes, *French Canada,* p. 166). Furthermore, in Cantonville, there were different concepts of social status between the English and the French Canadians, deriving from their different cultures. The English (both Canadians and British) were not born in the town, but most of the French were involved in an intricate web of kinship which established their local status and determined their intimate relationships and loyalties. The two status systems were to a certain extent in conflict and were mutually misunderstood. "The French of the lower and middle classes . . . could not mix with the English even if they wanted to. There simply were no English of any class they can aspire to" (p. 168). Finally, in Cantonville intermarriage was exceedingly infrequent; five cases of English industrial workers who married French girls of equal standing and four cases of English executives and white-collar men who married local French girls are cited by Hughes (p. 167).

In the larger urban centers and after more than a decade of rapid social change in Canada, social relations between the two groups seem to have become more frequent and perhaps more intimate. This has resulted from a realignment of the traditional class system of French Canada. While the traditional system persists, the recently enriched French-Canadian merchant and businessman has joined the priest and professional in the higher brackets of French-Canadian society. The members of "new" professions—the architects, engineers, and chemists—and the "new" commercial upper class of bank and corporation management, investment banking, factory ownership, and the like, are enjoying the same prestige as the old upper class. In addition, wealth tends to reinforce the traditional status of the professional groups, while the priestly group lacking in wealth seems to be weakened. French-Canadian society is now confronted with

two overlapping scales of social stratification, each oriented toward a set of values which is in conflict with the other. One of the scales perpetuates the traditional ideal. It recognizes the clergy as the supreme social group and gives priority to spiritual and intellectual achievement. The other also takes the clergy for granted but it is closer to the secular, economic scale of prestige prevalent in the remainder of "North American Money Society." (Falardeau, p. 119)

This has led to closer contact between the French and English Canadians. Success in either commerce, industry, or the professions means increased relations with English Canadians. French Canadians participate in occupational and professional associations and clubs which are organized on a national basis. As French Canadians move upward economically, they may be spoken of as *nouveau riche;* and an aspect of the behavior of a *nouveau riche* to French Canadians is to have commercial, professional, and social connections with the English-Canadians, and to adopt their values and to a certain extent their way of life (Falardeau, p. 119).

Furthermore, in recent years French Canadians have flooded into the cities and into industries as workers where they are inevitably forced into some form of contact with their English-Canadian fellow countrymen. In the cities, the working-class French Canadian is no longer a part of an integrated parish community. The clergy still controls education and other institutions, but the *curé* has lost influence. In the large city, the church is but the place that one goes to Mass on Sunday; it is not the center of the community. Although there are separate Catholic syndicates in Quebec, supported by the Church, many French-Canadian workers belong to national trade unions which unite them with English-Canadian workers. French Canadians are, furthermore, beginning to mix with English-Canadian workers in clubs and in recreational activities organized by industries. They learn that the linguistic, cultural, and religious differences between them are relatively slight as compared to the resemblances brought about by the equivalent socio-economic conditions. Thus, industrialization and urbanization have increasingly broken down the barriers between English and French Canadians.

Although social and economic relations between the two groups have increased and improved immeasurably during the last few decades, there is still an important cleavage between them. The French-Canadian middle class, which is said to constitute the hard core of French cultural survival, usually remains aloof from social contacts with English Canadians. There are no ready figures on inter-marriage between French and English Canadians, but all observers seem to agree that the French-Canadian bourgeoisie is highly endogamous. Especially among the middle class—and even among the elite and the working class—there is a proliferation of organizations which are separate but parallel to those of English Canadians. There are innumerable associations dedicated to French-Canadian interests, even to French-Canadian "nationalism," such as the long-standing *Société Saint Jean Baptiste* and *Comité de la Survivance Française.*

They have their own holidays, both secular and religious in nature. In fact, not long ago considerable tension was built up in Montreal when the municipal council voted that all shops should be closed on Roman Catholic holidays. It was reasoned that since Catholics must close their shops it would be unfair for Protestants to keep theirs open. Many of the large stores continually ignored the law, paying fines each time, until finally they were able to appeal to higher courts to have the law revoked.

In Canada, not all Catholics are French Canadians; in 1941 there were 1,614,000 non-French-Canadian Catholics (Lower, *Religion,* p. 475). Furthermore, the English-Canadian Protestants do not form a homogeneous unit, but are divided among the United Church of Canada, the Church of England in Canada, the Presbyterians, Baptists, Lutherans, and other sects. Yet French-Canadian Catholicism penetrates deeply into French-Canadian life; so much that it might be said, as it has been said for Latin American culture, that French-Canadian culture is Catholic culture. As one Canadian scholar put it:

French Canadian Catholicism . . . retains many of its medieval aspects. The wayside shrines, the numerous churches and the constant sound of bells, the clergy in habits of brown or white or black, the places of pilgrimage with miraculous powers ascribed to them, all heighten the impression of medievalism. It is further reinforced by the prominence given to scholastic philosophy in higher education, by the complete control of education, and by the cheerful allegiance given to the Church. Quebec is perhaps unique in the modern world, a virtual theocracy. (Lower, *Religion,* p. 461)

Perhaps it is religion, more than language, which creates a division between English and French Canadians.

Although Protestants do not form a united group, there is a cohesive, all-embracing opposition to French-Canadian Catholicism among them. Particularly those of the Irish Protestant Orange Order have carried out a continued belligerent campaign against the French-Canadian "papists," but there are frequent blasts from almost all Protestant sects against "priest-ridden" Quebec. The result is an increased counterreaction from French-Canadian Catholic pulpits against the dangers of Protestantism. A Canadian scholar summarizes the situation:

The day has gone by when Catholics and Protestants were constantly "at daggers drawn" but they still feel self-conscious in one another's presence, and on either side are organizations the major purpose of which is to keep the ancient fires alight. In Canada, religion can never be, as it is in England, a private affair. "Going over to Rome" cannot be viewed as merely a personal experience: it is also treason to the group. (Lower, *Religion*, p. 463)

Politics also divide French from English Canadians. Political differences are a reflection of cultural and religious differences, but politics is one aspect of life in which the French Canadian curiously has had an advantage. The solid French-Canadian vote has often been crucial in deciding national elections. In fact, it has been said that "Canada has been governed almost continuously since 1867 by a national party, the nucleus of whose strength has come from a majority of French votes in Quebec, with majority support also from the Atlantic and Western Provinces and with the Ontario majority usually in opposition" (Underhill, p. 347).

The most important political issue for French Canadians is provincial autonomy. For many French Canadians, Ottawa and all the national political parties bear connotations of federal control and domination by *les anglais*. Provincial rights are therefore jealously guarded, and any intrusion into Quebec's provincial affairs becomes a "hot" political issue. In 1956, for example, Maurice Duplessis, Premier of Quebec, rejected federal assistance to higher education on the ground that it constituted an invasion of provincial rights under the Canadian Constitution (New York *Times,* October 28, 1956). Prime Minister St. Laurent had proposed that federal grants to universities be turned over to the National Conference of Canadian Universities for distribution. But M. Duplessis called this a "trespass by the side door." He stated that if Ottawa had money to give to the universities, this only meant that Ottawa was taxing for purposes outside its jurisdiction.

"Let the federal government vacate enough of the taxation field so that provinces can move in and raise the revenues to fulfill their obligations," he is reported to have said.

From their political stronghold in Quebec, French Canadians attempt to safeguard the rights of fellow French Canadians in other provinces. They fight especially for the use of public funds to support separate Catholic French schools in the other provinces. In Ontario, for instance, property taxes are partially devoted to financing separate Catholic schools, but the French Canadians are quick to point out that although these schools enroll 20 percent of the elementary school children in Ontario, they receive but 11 percent of the local school-tax revenue (Fraser, pp. 9 ff.). The school system is a perennially important political issue among the French Canadians, for whom education represents the first line of defense against "anglicization." It is through education and through politics that French Canadians hope to survive as a separate group within Canadian society. Thus, political differences with their English-speaking countrymen add one more barrier to mutual understanding.

There are many cultural factors other than language and religion that still create a lack of understanding between French and English Canadians. The traditional French-Canadian values of the middle class are still very much alive, and these contrast strongly with English-Canadian values. In contrast to the English Canadians, for example, French Canadians still expect highly personalized social relations and strongly focus their social life upon their near and distant kinsmen. A study carried out during 1954 and 1955 in Montreal shows the French-Canadian kinship circle in this urban area to be exceedingly large. A French-Canadian factory worker, for instance, acknowledged 233 kinsmen, 203 of whom were alive at the time of the study. Of these, 93 lived in Montreal; 72 lived in the province of Quebec; and 38 more lived in Ontario and the United States. He met, on the average, 45 kinsmen each month, and at certain seasons he reported seeing all of his 93 relatives living in Montreal as well as others whom he went to see at greater distance or who came to Montreal. Despite this rather intense family life he apologized for lack of further social contact with his kinsmen because he was so busy as a junior executive in his local trade union branch. He stated that his wife "knew more of his own relatives than he did."

It is also clear from the same study that even urban French Canadians depend upon relatives for personal services and assistance. People called upon their relatives for jobs, for the loan of a needed object, for baby-sitting, for help during illness, for advice from a lawyer, for medical service, for help in getting a job, and for religious services at baptisms, marriages, and funerals. This is certainly different from the North American and English-Canadian family pattern.

All informants agreed that there was a French Canadian family ideal. While not aware of all its implications, they would verbalize about it and criticize variations from this ideal on the basis that to cease to behave like a French Canadian was to become "English." These ideals about the family and kinship were not isolated but were part of a cultural complex which included the French language as spoken in Quebec, a specific system of education, membership in the Catholic Church, and various political theories about the status of French Canadians in Canada. To be a member of a French Canadian kinship group implied attitudes and beliefs about some or all of these. (Garigue, pp. 1090–1101)

It is clear that there is still a cultural gulf between most English and French Canadians.

III

The French Canadians are, in at least one way, a unique minority group in the New World. Like the Jews in the United States, they are of the same biological race as the dominant group of the nation and are thus not highly "visible." Again like the Jews in the United States, they have a relatively good economic and social position within the national society, and among themselves they are divived by marked social and economic differentials. They are set off from the dominant group, as are many other minority groups, by religion and by language, both of which in their case are important symbols of group persistence. Their uniqueness comes from none of these dif-

ferences; it is due to the fact that they are the only New World minority with a "homeland" within the confines of the national state to
which they belong. Many minorities in the New World are concentrated in certain areas of the nation in which they live and in some
cases they may form a numerical majority in these areas. Thus,
Puerto Ricans in the United States are concentrated in New York
and in other cities on the eastern seaboard; Italians in Brazil are found
in São Paulo and in other southern Brazilian states; until recently
the majority of Jews in the United States lived on the east coast. But
none of these minorities ever enjoyed the degree of political power
conferred upon the French Canadians by their control of Quebec.

This fact accounts for some curious aspects of the French- and
English-Canadian relations. Within the stronghold of French Canada,
the roles of superordination and subordination are frequently reversed. In many Quebec communities it is the *anglais* rather than the
French Canadian who suffers a loss of prestige, political power, and
even business opportunity. A good illustration is to be found in the
so-called eastern townships of Quebec (between the St. Lawrence
River and the United States border), where French Canadians have
in the last century moved in to overwhelm an earlier settlement of
English Canadians. The earlier English-Canadian population in these
eastern counties became in the local context a minority.

"We feel that we are fighting a losing battle here," said the elder son
of an English storekeeper. "I don't feel that there's any use taking over
father's store when I grow up, because I couldn't carry it on if there
were only French in the village. If a person speaks French it helps. You
could carry on a store a little longer. But even then, you couldn't compete against a French store keeper in the village." (Ross, pp. 281–95)

It is reported that the English feel "French prejudice and possible
discrimination in all areas of the economy."

It is clear that within Quebec the French Canadians can scarcely
be said to constitute a minority group. Of course, all minorities be-
stow at least limited advantages on their "own kind." Thus it is advantageous to be a Jew in the clothing business in New York, to be a
Negro if one is running for political office in Harlem, and perhaps to

be Irish if one is seeking advancement in the New York police force. In the case of the French Canadians, however, advantages—or at least an absence of either advantages or disadvantages—pertain throughout the social fabric of an entire province, and not just within some specialized activity in a restricted local context. It is true that Quebec, especially rural Quebec, has a lower standard of living than the rest of the country. But the endemic poverty of the French-Canadian "homeland" is not the result of prejudice or discrimination exercised by the English Canadians. The poverty of the French-Canadian minority stems, as has been shown, from intrinsic factors of the history of the settlement of Quebec and from the specific values and traditions of the group.

In view of the existence of a French-Canadian "homeland," within which English-speaking residents feel themselves to be the victims of prejudice and discrimination, what justification remains for identifying the French rather than the English as the minority in Canada as a whole? It might be argued, of course, that proportionately speaking more French Canadians than English Canadians reside in "foreign" areas. Therefore, the French, as the people suffering the greatest incidence of prejudice and discrimination, ought to be considered the minority. It would be easy to contest such an argument. The political power of the French-Canadian group extends well beyond the borders of Quebec and frequently makes itself felt upon national or provincial policy with a force that is disproportionate to the size of the French-speaking population. The maintenance of French as a second official language for all of Canada and the use of public funds to support Catholic education are felt by many English Canadians to be unwarranted and undemocratic impositions. Perhaps the ultimate justification for calling the French a minority and the English a majority must refer back to the genesis of Canada's pluralistic society. Historically, it is clear that the French were the conquered group, the dominated rather than the dominant. The history of Canada since the conquest of New France consists in great measure of the attempt of the French group to preserve its identity and to win for itself through political pressure an equal social and cultural status within the Canadian union. The effort to reach a firm conclusion as to whether or not the degree of equality which the French now enjoy has released them from their former subordinate status probably involves subjective considerations alien to the spirit of scientific inquiry. Certainly the French Canadians themselves feel that they have yet to enjoy a satisfactory situation. But many English Canadians feel with equal conviction that the French have more than their share of power, rights, and special privileges. The dispassionate observer must straddle the two positions and refrain from dogmatic conclusions.

The really important conclusion to be reached, therefore, is not whether it is the French or the English who are the minority, but rather whether such a question seriously needs to be entertained. The unique feature of minority-majority relations in Canada is the dynamic, relatively equitable balance which the two principal groups have achieved despite their linguistic, religious, and cultural differences. The relationship between the French and English in Canada represents a fairly successful pluralist solution of a minority problem. In our final chapter we shall attempt to explain why such a solution must necessarily involve a certain amount of intergroup hostility, prejudice, and discrimination, to which both groups contribute.

What will be the future of the French-Canadian minority in Canada? It is obviously not a group that will be assimilated into English-Canadian society rapidly or easily. It is composed of a large population with an exceedingly high birthrate. It has political power in the nation and political control over Quebec. It has its own schools from the primary level to great universities. It takes pride in its French traditions and culture. There is a vigorous French-Canadian intellectual movement in the arts, literature, philosophy, and now in the sciences. There is an active French-Canadian theater. In both Montreal and Quebec there are French-Canadian artists of talent and international reputation, and "polemics [on art] fill any paper that will give them space" (Chapin, p. 151). French Canada has its national sport and its sporting heroes in ice hockey. The French Canadians as a group have all the elements of a vigorous social unit which cannot easily be overwhelmed even by the more rapidly expanding English-Canadian group.

Nevertheless, Canadian society is slowly becoming culturally more homogeneous. With the growing industrialization of Canada, Quebec included, more and more people of French-Canadian descent are being brought into direct contact with their English-speaking countrymen. The very nature of the new industrialism of Canada causes a blurring of the lines of division between the French and English segments of the population. Today, the press, the radio, the cinema, and the automobile have greatly reduced the cultural isolation of Quebec. The influence not only of the English Canadians but also of the United States is now penetrating into the French "homeland." In provinces far from Quebec these influences are felt with much greater intensity and may eventually lead to the assimilation of substantial numbers of people of French-Canadian descent. In Manitoba, where there were 66,020 French Canadians, according to the 1951 census, over 20 percent of them could no longer speak French. In Saskatchewan, 31.5 percent of the 21,859 French Canadians could only speak English. In Alberta, 38.9 percent spoke English; in Ontario 47 percent among over three hundred thousand "French Canadians" spoke only English; and in British Columbia, of those who were called French Canadians, 54.5 percent spoke only English. But even within the province of Quebec there is a sufficient amount of acculturation to raise anxieties among French-Canadian conservatives. Under the title "Le Scandale de Pontiac" a French-Canadian newspaper recently devoted a series of articles to the plight of the French Canadians in Pontiac, a county which lies near the Ontario border and where the French-Canadian population is about 40 percent of the total. There, it was reported, some ten thousand French were in the process of "anglicization." Already, 1,461 French Canadians in Pontiac county had adopted English as their maternal tongue, according to the last Canadian census. The journalist attributed this adoption of English characteristics to the lack of French-Canadian priests. There were 9,924 French-Canadian Catholics among the total of 13,825 Catholics in the county. Yet of 29 priests who served this population, only 7 were French-speaking, and "at least three [of these] have an English mentality." The Irish clergy, according to the writer, was clearly anti-French and the schools, although Catholic, were in the hands of Irish nuns. One of the French-Canadian leaders in Pontiac had gone so far as to question French survival: "It is we who because of our ignorance, lack of courage, and inertia have allowed this situation to degenerate" (La Porte).

Despite the feeling of alarm common among many French-Canadian leaders, there is little likelihood that the French-Canadian minority is any closer to assimilation today than it was two hundred years ago. The rapid acculturation and fairly extensive assimilation of those French Canadians who have left the "homeland" does not alter the prospectus for the group within Quebec. Within this strategic province a considerable amount of culture change is perfectly compatible with the preservation of a strong sense of group identity. The critical role of Quebec in national politics and the powerful organizational effect of the Catholic Church weigh heavily against the forces of assimilation.

RECOMMENDED ADDITIONAL READINGS

Chapin, Miriam. Quebec Now. New York: Oxford University Press, 1955.
Falardeau, Jean C., ed. Essais sur le Québec Conteporain. Quebec, 1953.
Hughes, Everett C. French Canada in Transition. Chicago: University of Chicago Press, 1943.
Miner, Horace. St. Denis, A French Canadian Parish. Chicago: University of Chicago Press, 1939.
Wade, Mason. The French Canadians, 1760–1945. Toronto, 1955.

THE JEWS IN THE UNITED STATES

The Jews are in many ways the classic example of a
minority group. Probably no other single human group has constituted minorities in so many different states and in so many parts
of the world—in Europe, Asia, Africa, and the New World. In the
thousands of years since, and even before, the destruction of the
central temple in Jerusalem, the Jews have lived dispersed among
the nations of the world, usually victims of prejudice and sometimes
of brutal persecution. Jewish minorities continue to form part of
many different nations throughout the world. But today, as a result
of the annihilation of some six million Jews in Europe, those in the
United States form perhaps the largest Jewish minority group of all.

The 5,200,000 people (*American Jewish Year Book,* 1956, p.
295) in the United States who for one reason or another are classed
as Jews actually are a highly variegated group. They come from many
countries and they migrated to the United States at different times.
Except for the fact that Hebrew has been retained as a religious and
scholarly language among many of them, they cannot be said to share
a common vernacular—unless today it is English. Physically they are
all Caucasoid. Despite the many commonly held concepts about
Jewish physical features, "No such grouping of traits has been discovered by any reputable scientist. In every country Jews tend to
approximate the local gentile type because of the intermixture which
has invariably occurred" (Simpson and Yinger, p. 53). Although the
physical appearance of some Jews may still be influenced by the eastern Mediterranean Caucasoid stock from which they are thought
originally to have derived, the persistence of distinctive Jewish physical characteristics after all these centuries seems doubtful.

It is thought that the Jews also gain their unity from the Jewish religion and the associated culture traits, such as food laws, rites of passage, holidays, and the ethical values of Judaism. But throughout their long history the Jews have undergone a considerable amount of cultural differentiation. Despite the continuity of a core of scriptural beliefs and attitudes, Jewish values and patterns of behavior have always been subject to the influence of the different and sometimes sharply contrasting social milieus in which they have settled. In the new state of Israel, one of the deepest problems encountered has been the clash of economic standards and life aspirations of the Jews who have been "gathered in" from Europe, as opposed to the standards and aspirations of those who have been "gathered in" from Yemen and other essentially Oriental areas. Judaism, as a religion, has not been immune to the stress of heterogeneous cultural traditions and philosophical currents of thought. As a result of schisms originating in Europe, Judaism in the United States today consists of at least three major movements: Orthodox, Conservative, and Reform. These movements embrace doctrinal positions which differ as fundamentally as Catholicism differs from Protestantism. Furthermore, there are Jews in the United States who no longer practice any of the rites or customs associated with Judaism, who are thoroughly acculturated to American patterns of behavior, and yet who continue to feel that they have a common cause and share a common burden with Jews as a group.

Jewish affiliation, whether it involves merely being born of Jewish parents or adherence to one of the various forms of the Jewish religion, is a stigma and in one way or another it acts as a brake on upward social and economic mobility. Yet the Jews in the United States have fared exceedingly well in comparison to their co-religionists in other times and places. They have at one time or another held the high political offices of the land: they have been members of the president's cabinet, justices of the Supreme Court, governors of states, and United States senators. Large numbers of Jews have achieved high standing in the arts, sciences, professions, and in the business world. The majority of the Jews in the United

States belong to the great American middle class.[1] Their standard of living and educational level is probably average or even above average, for the nation as a whole. They have come "one way or another . . . to conform to the standards of middle class life in America" (Handlin, *Freedom*, p. 253). As a group, the Jews resemble such religious bodies as the Presbyterians, Episcopalians, and Congregationalists in their educational level and occupational structure (Bernard, pp. 388–89; Pope, p. 356). Yet the persistence of anti-Semitic attitudes and discrimination have kept the Jews in the United States a minority group.

I

Three branches of European Jewry, differing from one another in language, ritual, and many other aspects of culture, have contributed to the Jewish population of the United States. The earliest but numerically the least important is the Iberian branch, known as the Sephardim (from the Hebrew word for Spain). Evicted from Spain in 1492, the Sephardim moved to Holland, France, Greece, England and other far-flung places. A small group made its way to the Dutch outpost of Recife in Brazil. When Recife fell into Portuguese hands, some of the Sephardim fled to New Amsterdam, arriving in 1654. Additional Sephardim came to North America during the colonial era. These were the first Jews in what later became the United States. They were quickly outnumbered, however, by Jewish immigrants from Germany and from eastern Europe.

The Jews from Germany came from ghettos. The European ghetto

---

[1] In Yankee City, studied by W. Lloyd Warner and his associates from 1939 to 1945, only 3.02 percent of the local Jewish minority was assigned to the upper middle class; 41.81 percent to the lower middle; 47.31 percent to the upper lower class; and 7.56 percent to the lower lower class (Warner and Srole, p. 71). At the present, and on a national basis, observers such as Carey McWilliams (pp. 142–61) place the majority of Jews in the "middle class"— using this term not for an equivalent of the European bourgeoisie, but for that widening class of Americans which includes highly paid industrial workers as well as professionals and executives. Recent investigations have tended to show that the Jews of Yankee City were not respresentative of the national average (see Pope, pp. 353 ff.).

was at first a voluntary corporate city-within-a-city designed to protect Jews, and was established at their own behest. Gradually, however, it assumed the character of an instrument of oppression. This transformation occurred throughout western Europe when the mercantile and artisan functions by which the Jews had earned their niche in manorial society were assumed by Christian merchant and craft guilds. As a result, Jews were confined by law to a narrowing sphere of occupations such as usury, pawnbroking, and the sale of secondhand goods. They became, in effect, a guild of moneylenders. Yet it might be said that these occupations paved the way for their ultimate emancipation. As the new capitalistic age got under way, liquid assets rather than land became the basis of the economy and many Jews, despite prejudice, discrimination, and segregation, rose to positions of great power and wealth. As merchants and financiers they had the skills crucial to the new economy. Their aid in establishing the fiscal structure of the emergent centralized national states of western Europe gave them an important role in European history. After the French Revolution and the triumph of bourgeois liberalism, the Jews of western Europe emerged increasingly as secular, cosmopolitan, and acculturated nationals of their respective countries.

On the other hand, the eastern European Jews, coming chiefly from Poland, Latvia, and the Ukraine, shared none of these experiences. The eastern European Jews eventually came to differ markedly from those Jews who lived in the ghettos of western Europe, for society in the East remained dominated by a manorial system of production until well into the nineteenth century. Instead of living in ghettos in large cities, many of the eastern European Jews plied their crafts and trades in small towns from whence they served a rural population of serfs and peasants. Their life included little contact with centers of learning and "high society," in contrast to that of many western European Jews. They continued to speak Yiddish, a language derived primarily from medieval German, and to cling tenaciously to the ancient Hebraic codes and the customs and rites associated with their religion.

The Enlightenment, capitalism, and liberalism moved across the face of Europe in a more or less coordinated fashion from West to

East. Just as serfdom persisted longest in those areas under the control of the Czar, so too in those same areas did Jewish communal life and culture exhibit a greater fidelity to the medieval model. Jewish immigrants to the United States who came from Germany and other western European countries were thus on the whole more likely to exhibit the cultural features which owed their existence to the Enlightenment and the bourgeois liberal revolutions.

But not all German Jews had been affected equally. Throughout the nineteenth century the Jews migrated in large numbers from East to West. Many Western Jews were actually but recent arrivals from points further east. "For the earliest settled groups of Western Jewries, the influx of these newcomers spelled retardation, in some respects a direct reversal of the main trends of their own development, which were often equivalent to salvation from imminent extinction as Jews" (Baron, Vol. II, p. 261). The same trend, and its reversal, was to be repeated dramatically in the United States.

At the time of the American Revolution there were probably less than three thousand Jews in the United States (Learsi, p. 29). Thereafter their numbers slowly increased, and by 1880 there were about 230,000. Between 1800 and 1848 there was a tiny trickle of "German" petty merchants who had often come from ghettos and were of Orthodox religious backgrounds (Schermerhorn, p. 390). Until the abortive revolutions of 1848, the more enlightened and sophisticated German Jews appear to have remained in Germany. Thereafter they moved to the New World in large numbers and became the dominant force in American Jewish life. Often these highly acculturated Jews were accepted simply as Germans by the mass of Americans, and "true to their background, strove for complete integration within the American scene" (Schermerhorn, p. 351). They adapted quickly and, chiefly as merchants, soon acquired a secure place in the expanding economy.

A tendency to abandon Jewish affiliations appears to have been quite marked during the nineteenth century (Handlin, *Freedom,* pp. 75 ff.). Even the doctrinal and ceremonial aspects of Judaism yielded rapidly to cultural conformity. At mid-century, stimulated by similar movements in Europe, a type of Reform Judaism emerged in the

United States which was as different from its historical Orthodox forerunner as Protestantism is from Catholicism. Hebrew was largely abandoned as the liturgical idiom, women were admitted to the pews, organs and choirs were introduced, dietary taboos were renounced, prohibitions against labor on Saturday were relaxed, exogamous marriage was permitted, and the Biblical notion of a return to a national homeland was rejected. In Charleston, South Carolina, a group of Reform Jews declared: "This country is our Palestine, this city our Jerusalem, this House of God our Temple" (Learsi, p. 116).

Before this trend toward acculturation and perhaps assimilation had run its course, the small acculturated Jewish minority was overwhelmed by a sudden wave of immigrants from eastern Europe. Between 1881 and 1914 about two million Jews entered the United States (Simpson and Yinger, p. 288), well over 90 percent of whom were transported directly from eastern Europe (Lestchinsky, p. 60). In the space of an ocean voyage these Jews were called upon to make the transition to modern conditions which their western European co-religionists had experienced a century or more earlier. Their habits and customs set them off sharply both from the native Americans and from their acculturated Jewish brethren, who for the most part remained aloof from them and considered them inferior. Most of the eastern European men kept their heads covered with a skull cap and wore beards; some grew *paoth,* ringlets of hair about their ears. Most of them spoke only Yiddish and about 26 percent were illiterate at least in the language of the European country from which they came. Most of them, however, could read Hebrew prayers. They maintained purificatory baths for pregnant and menstruating women, shaved the heads of brides, and adhered strictly to Orthodox dietary taboos and other customs and institutions of medieval and ancient Judaism. Unlike their German predecessors, however, 67 percent of them were skilled artisans who were not averse to working with their hands as tailors, milliners, or shoemakers (Schermerhorn, p. 393).

What had produced this sudden exodus from eastern Europe? Explanations usually center upon the rash of murderous "pogroms" which were carried out in Russia and Poland toward the close of the last century. These undoubtedly had their specific effects, but the underlying causes were the world-shaking transformations which were affecting all of eastern Europe. With the spread of industrial capitalism famines, disease, and unrest swept through the peasant masses from whom the Jews earned their living. Their position deteriorated with that of the peasants. "By 1900, in Galicia, there was a Jewish trader trying to scratch a living out of every ten peasants, and the average value of the stocks of these merchants came to some twenty dollars" (Handlin, *Freedom,* p. 81). Forbidden by law in Russia to emigrate to the metropolitan centers of the new economy, the Jews found themselves being squeezed out of their earlier role as middlemen and artisans. They had no alternative but to leave the country altogether. If there was any hesitation on their part, it was soon overcome by the terrorism whipped up and directed against them by the Czarist police. As petty but highly visible exploiters of the peasantry, they were easy victims of the pogroms which deliberately aimed at diverting the wrath of the people away from the real sources of their misery.

The arrival of these eastern European Jewish masses in the United States reversed the direction of the change which had been taking place in the nineteenth century. Orthodox Judaism began to flourish among the Jews of the United States as it never had before. By the turn of the century the Orthodox was the largest of the Jewish congregations. Moreover, a strong reaction set in against the "excesses" of the Reform temples and produced the third general division of the Jewish religion, the Conservative movement. Although the Conservatives adopted some of the syncretic features advocated by the reformers, such as mixed pews and sermons in English, they insisted on a stricter observance of the Sabbath and of dietary laws, and on the preservation of Hebrew as the liturgical language. They were doctrinally opposed to the denationalization of the Jewish people, and prayed for the restoration of a Jewish national homeland.

In 1924, with passage of the Johnson Immigration Act, the influx of eastern European Jews came to an end. Subsequent immigration has consisted largely of German Jews fleeing the horrors of the Nazi regime. The result has been a gradual resumption of the trend toward acculturation. Despite the American Jewish agencies which are interested in maintaining Jewish cultural forms, the Jews seem once again to be headed in the direction of becoming culturally indistinguishable from Americans of comparable socio-economic levels and regional backgrounds in everything except their religion.

II

Like the western European Jews, the Jews of eastern Europe have tended rapidly to become acculturated to the majority culture of the United States. Except in New York and other cities which were host to recent Jewish immigration, strictly Orthodox Jews in the eastern European sense are now a rarity. Few Orthodox Jews are today bearded. Only exotic groups such as the Chassidic cult wear ringlets of hair around the ears. The use of Yiddish has decreased and is limited to urban neighborhoods inhabited by Jews born in Europe.

In 1916 the circulation of the Yiddish dailies in the United States stood at well over half a million. In 1952 it had fallen by more than 60 percent (Learsi, p. 189), even though in that same period there was a marked increase in population and literacy. The diminishing use of Yiddish has greatly decreased the "visibility" of American Jews, as has the adoption of standard dress and the loss of European gestural accompaniments to speech. The loss of these cultural traits, together with the fact that the Jews do not constitute a physically homogeneous population, has now made it impossible positively to identify most American Jews simply by inspection or on brief acquaintance when they are in a "neutral" social environment.

Marked changes have also taken place in the manner by which Jews observe their Sabbath. In eastern Europe, labor of any sort— commercial or domestic—was prohibited from Friday at sundown to Saturday at sundown. The Sabbath restrictions barred smoking, writing, playing at sports, riding in vehicles, and handling or using money. Even the labor of cooking was prohibited. The greater part of the day was to be spent in the synagogue at prayer and in the home amid respectable quiet. The eastern European immigrants initially tried to "keep" as much of the Sabbath as possible. Many are said to have chosen to be pushcart peddlers in order to avoid working on Saturday. But inevitably the economic realities of competition forced the abandonment of most of the Sabbath observances. Even the self-employed Jewish retailers rapidly succumbed. State and municipal "blue laws" prohibited commerce on Sunday, and to be idle on Saturday meant the loss of the week's most lucrative shopping day.

The range of activities undertaken by Jews on Saturday is constantly expanding and undermining the day's religious significance. Recreation rather than prayer and rest has come to dominate Saturday among both Jews and Christians. In 1952, while engaged in a concerted effort to reassert the religious basis of the Sabbath, a committee of the Conservative United Synagogue of America nevertheless recommended that dancing and sports be permitted on Saturday (*American Jewish Yearbook,* 1953, p. 102). In Minneapolis it was found that "children use the day for parties, movie-going, shopping, dancing, music, and other special lessons, eating out and in general having a good time. Mothers in ever increasing numbers do their shopping, attend theatres and parties and the like. Fathers go out to the golf clubs, attend football games, indulge in a friendly game of cards, or take the family on an outing" (Gordon, p. 97).

There are now actually two Sabbaths in the American work schedule, both of which, however, are primarily secular in character. As a result of the increase of non-religious activities among both Christians and Jews on their respective Sabbaths, the secularly-oriented "week end" is the emergent reality, despite protests of Jewish and Christian religious leaders. Many of the adjustments made by Judaism to the American scene are simply instances of the increased secularity associated with urbanization and industrialization. As religion among all groups has come to occupy a less important position in everyday life, denominational differences have tended to become invisible as far as daily behavior is concerned.

When they first came to the United States the eastern European Jews had insisted upon the establishment of the traditional Jewish schools (the heders or Talmud Torahs) in America. Today a large and perhaps even increasing percentage of contemporary Jewish children of primary-school age are exposed to some formal training in Jewish religion and tradition, but such instruction is steadily being confined to fewer hours per week and to children of pre-adolescent

age. In a growing proportion of cases, religious training of the young
ceases with the ritual of *bar mitzvah,* or confirmation, and is in fact
regarded primarily as a preparation for these rites. Thereafter, attendance at the synagogue, traditionally a daily requirement, is in the
great majority of cases confined to the festival of the Jewish New
Year and the Day of Atonement (Yom Kippur). "Yom Kippur
Jews" (i.e., those who go to the temple once or twice a year) probably constitute the bulk of those who are formally reckoned as members of Reformed and Conservative congregations, and are abun-
dant even among the Orthodox. The Hebrew calendar continues to
guide ritual observances, but very few Jews are capable of reckoning
time by it or of naming the Hebrew months and days.

For a constantly growing number of American Jews, the period
from Christmas to New Year's Day is the most important festival
period of the year, in terms at least of secular pleasures and gift exchange. The latter are sometimes called "Hanukkah presents," in
reference to the Jewish festival which occurs in December. Many
American Jewish children believe in Santa Claus, although some
parents prefer "Uncle Max, the Hanukkah Man." A few Jewish
parents indulge their offspring with Christmas trees (sometimes
called "Hanukkah trees") and in the suburbs of New York and other
urban cities where houses are decorated with colored lights at Christmas time, some Jews have followed suit by placing "Hanukkah lights"
in their windows.

The observance of the important Jewish festival of Passover (in
commemoration of deliverance from Egyptian bondage) has been
greatly modified in the American context. Traditionally a complete
change of culinary equipment was made for the eight-day period. All
vestiges of leavened bread were removed from the household, and no
food made or handled by equipment used throughout the rest of the
year was admitted to the house. Few contemporary Jews continue to
maintain separate pots and dishes for use during Passover week. Although bread is still widely omitted from Passover-week menus, a
growing number of American Jews simply place industrially prepared
matzos (unleavened wafers) on the table along with the usual food

and utensils. Jews, like all other urban Americans, depend upon industrially processed and packaged foods for their daily provisions. A remarkable development connected with Passover has been the appearance of packaged foods which have been ritually cleansed by specially hired rabbis. In New York City, the major egg, milk, and butter processors have adopted this practice, and during Passover, food products labeled "Kosher for Passover" enter indiscriminately into the homes of Jews and non-Jews alike. In further deference to the large Jewish population of New York City, a high percentage of all beef brought into the city throughout the year is ritually killed, whether marked for sale to Jews or to Christians.

One of the most interesting trends in United States culture since the end of the Second World War is the heightened respectability of formal religious affiliation. Church attendance and participation in community activities sponsored by secular institutions which maintain direct or indirect links with one of the major religious denominations are enjoying a vogue entirely unforeseen by early students of American culture (see Herberg, pp. 59–77). This trend has injected a paradoxical element into the process by which the Jews are being more and more thoroughly acculturated. There can be no doubt that Jewish religious institutions and their secular arms are experiencing some kind of revival or strengthening on a scale fully as great as that of the Christian denominations. Today synagogue membership, construction programs, and all sorts of Jewish community projects are at an all-time high. But whatever else the expansion of church or church-sponsored activities may mean for the Jews in the United States, it clearly does not mean that the rate of acculturation has been slowed. On the contrary, the form and content of the religious "upsurge" among Jews so closely parallels the form and content of the Christian "upsurge" that it is in itself a prime example of the increasing homogeneity of United States culture.

What was the shape and form of the religion of the Jewish Community in mid-twentieth century America? It was characterized by a far-reaching accommodation to the American pattern of religious life which affected all "denominations" in the American synagogue. The institutional system was virtually the same as the major Protestant churches—the same corporate structure, the same proliferation of men's clubs, sisterhoods, junior congregations, youth groups, "young marrieds," Sunday school classes, discussion circles, adult education projects, breakfasts, "brunches," dinners, and suppers. With minor variation, "the arrangement of the synagogue, the traditional appurtenances of worship, and the religious ceremonies showed the effects of change wrought by the American environment." The central place of the sermon, congregational singing, mixed choirs, organs, responsive readings, abbreviated services, the concluding benediction, and many other commonly accepted features obviously reflected the influence of familiar Protestant practice. (Herberg, pp. 205–6)

Today, hundreds of thousands of American Jews live in homes, work at jobs, and receive educations which yield no clue to ethnic ancestry. By manners and morals, opinions and aspirations, costume and speech they cannot be positively identified. But Jews may actually be found at all stages of acculturation, spread out in a continuous band from those retaining the most Orthodox practices and Old World pre-industrial traits to those whose only Jewish trait is a name revealing Jewish descent. In New York City entire neighborhoods, such as parts of Williamsburg and Brownsville in the borough of Brooklyn are strongholds of eastern European customs. Yet, significantly, these neighborhoods are slum or semi-slum areas. Most authorities agree that there is a close correlation between Orthodox, Conservative, and Reformed congregations and the degree of ascent toward upper-middle-class standing. In general, the more acculturated the Jew, the higher his socio-economic status. As traditional and Orthodox Jews improve their financial position, they (or their children) tend to move away from the slum-like Orthodox neighborhoods. In their new surroundings the pressure toward conformity is much greater, and in the next generation acculturation toward the dominant Christian patterns proceeds with ever greater velocity.

Curiously, despite the rapid pace of acculturation, the Jews appear to have an extremely low rate of marriage with non-Jews—one of the lowest rates, in fact, of any immigrant group (Simpson and Yinger, p. 307). It is not known whether this rate, estimated at between 5 and 10 percent (Shanks, p. 370), is increasing, since the data is extremely fragmented and difficult to obtain. But marked changes of attitude seem to be taking place, at least among Jewish college students. A study conducted among Jewish youth at Columbia University revealed that 35 percent favored intermarriage, 43 percent were neutral, and 22 percent definitely opposed it. Moreover, 41 percent of these students had "dated" Christian boys or girls within the past six months. Only 9 percent, however, had "gone steady" with gentiles (Shanks, pp. 372–74). It seems reasonable to conclude that the change in attitude will sooner or later show up in the actual marriage rate, especially if it is true, as one study indicated, that only 25 percent of non-Jewish college seniors "would not prefer to have [a Jew] marry a close relative of mine" (Simpson and Yinger, p. 586).

Of supreme importance for an understanding of the minority status of the Jews is the fact that they are undergoing their acculturative experience in the largest urban centers of the United States. Nearly four fifths of the country's five million Jews live in cities of more than one hundred thousand people (Simpson and Yinger, p. 384). Almost half are to be found in New York City alone. Although acculturated Jews are not highly visible against this urban background, big-city dwellers were in the past highly differentiated from and generally disliked by people who lived in small towns and on farms. (This is less true nowadays.) Hence it was easy for the majority to attribute to the Jews certain features of urban life widely regarded as undesirable. It has even been suggested that anti-Semitism in the United States is actually hatred of the city by a population which is rapidly being forced to surrender its early agrarian heritage (Rose, *America,* pp. 288–89). It is, of course, this new urban industrial system, not the Jews, which is responsible for "the divorce from nature," the fierce competition for status and security, the premium on aggressiveness and the prevailing materialism and impersonality of the great American cities. But a disproportionate number of Jews are involved in the urban struggle. In their attempt to rise to the American urban middle class, they have been in a particularly vulnerable position. They are even more insecure than others in a fluid system of social stratification noted for its insecurity.

The occupational distribution of Jews in the contemporary United States is rather markedly different from the national average. Like all immigrant groups, the Jews arrived in America with some specialized skills and cultural values which were a product of their previous history. The Germans knew how to make beer, the Italians knew how to make wine, and the Portuguese were often fishermen. As already stated, the great mass of eastern European Jews were skilled laborers and craftsmen in Europe and, excluded from the land, many of them specialized in trade and in the role of the small-scale entrepreneur. These facts are reflected in their present occupations.

According to information derived from the American Institute of Public Opinion in 1945–46, covering a sample of approximately twelve thousand Americans, Jews have the highest percentage of business and professional occupations (36 percent), the highest percentage of white collar occupations (37 percent), and the lowest percentage of urban manual workers (27 percent) and farmers (0.6 percent) [Pope, p. 358]. Other surveys show that about three times as many Jews are engaged in trade and commerce and twice as many in professional services as for the nation on a whole. Whereas about 17 percent of the total population is engaged in agriculture, less than 2 percent of the Jewish group is so employed (Simpson and Yinger, p. 384).

Something like 70 percent of the eastern European Jews were skilled laborers—tailors, hatmakers, milliners, and shoemakers (Schermerhorn, p. 393). Upon arrival in the United States, many of these Jews went to work in factories. Yet the proletarianization of the American Jews appears to have been a transitory phase from which the native-born rapidly escaped. Earlier in this century, Jews were the chief source of operatives for the ready-made clothing industry; but by 1923 they constituted less than half, and by mid-century less than 28 percent of those workers. In the meantime, Jews, rising to management and ownership, have achieved almost exclusive control of the entire wearing-apparel industry (Learsi, p. 163).

Jewish concentration in so-called "white-collar" and professional categories reflects an ancient emphasis upon intellectual pursuits. The Jews had a role in transmitting the learning of the Greek, Roman, and Arabic civilizations into medieval Europe. Jewish scholars as a class were exempt from taxation in the European Jewish communities and ghettos. A merchant would be praised for making a scholar a silent partner and giving him his daughter in marriage. In the New World, education (which frees one from manual labor) still appears to be the highest aspiration that most Jewish parents entertain for their children. As a kind of "intellectual investment" which, unlike other forms of capital, cannot be expropriated, this emphasis upon learning may well represent an adaptation to a precarious economic status as well as an ancient traditional value.

In addition to cultural emphasis upon learning, the expansion of certain spheres of the American economy at the right moment also accounts for the success with which Jews have entered white-collar occupations and the professions.

In the United States, for instance, the total number of employed was quadrupled between 1870 and 1940. But during this period employment in the primary industries (agriculture, fisheries and forest products) increased by little more than one-half; the manufacturing group quadrupled, that is, increased in the same proportion as the total population; but those engaged in trade increased more than tenfold, the clerical group more than seventeenfold and the public service group more than twenty-one fold. (Reich, "Modern Jewry," p. 1258)

The rapid rise from factory, wage-earning occupations to those in commerce and the professions has contributed to the stereotype that Jews control the American economy. If this were so, one would look for the locus of such control among the directorships of investment and insurance companies and the great manufacturing corporations. Yet few Jews are to be found in such positions. Jewish participation in heavy industry, the backbone of the economy, is virtually non-existent, and their influence in banking and insurance has been shown to be negligible (*Fortune* editors, pp. 39 ff.).

Generally speaking, the businesses in which Jews are concentrated are those in which a large risk factor is involved; businesses peripheral to the economy; businesses originally regarded as unimportant; new industries and businesses; and businesses which have traditionally carried a certain element of social stigma, such, for example, as the amusement industry and the liquor industry. Not being able to penetrate the key control industries, Jews have been compelled to occupy the interstitial, the marginal positions in the American economy. (McWilliams, pp. 147–48)

Far from controlling American industry and finance, the Jews have been forced into marginal and new industries—such as moving pictures, radio, television—and light manufacturing—such as the clothing and tobacco industries (*Fortune* editors, pp. 17 ff.).

III

Before the separation between church and state was guaranteed by the Constitution of the United States, established churches in many of the English colonies made the enjoyment of full civil and legal status dependent upon religious conformity. The Constitution and the Bill of Rights prevented the Federal government from limiting political rights on religious grounds and The Northwest Ordinance of 1787 guaranteed both political and religious freedom in all states thereafter admitted. But discriminatory statutes which remained among the laws of several of the original thirteen states limited the right to vote or to hold political office to Christians. New Hampshire, Massachusetts, Connecticut, New Jersey, Maryland, North Carolina, and Rhode Island sustained discriminatory statutes into the nineteenth century. Disabling clauses continued in effect in Rhode Island until 1842, in North Carolina until 1868, and in New Hampshire until 1876 (Learsi, pp. 47–50). It must be said, however, that these were not the states with large and active Jewish populations, and such clauses therefore affected but few people. As Carey McWilliams argues, these were often obsolete laws which remained on the books but which were not supported by any demand of the majority or by intergroup conflict. "No amount of historical quibbling," he writes, "can impugn the great historical fact that the United States is the one nation in the Western World that, from its inception, has been without the heritage of the yellow badge" (McWilliams, p. 52).

In fact, until the Civil War and its aftermath, Jews were more fre-
quently admired than they were opposed or discriminated against.
Throughout the American Revolutionary period laudatory sentiment
even seems to have prevailed. The Hebrew exodus from Egypt was
frequently cited as a classic inspiration for liberation from tyranny.
Jefferson and John Adams proposed that the official seal of the
United States be a picture of the children of Israel crossing the Red
Sea, above the inscription: "Rebellion to tyrants is obedience to
God." Samuel Langdon and Ezra Stone, the presidents of Harvard
and Yale respectively, considered the American government to be
derived ·from Hebrew precedents and prophesies in the Bible. The
study of Hebrew was stressed almost as much as that of Greek and
Latin. Many Puritans regarded the Jews as a sacred people, living
proof of the divine origin of the Judaeo-Christian code. Early in the
nineteenth century the Jews attracted much attention when they
moved into new areas. When Jews first appeared in Cincinnati, people
came from miles away "for the special purpose of viewing and con-
versing with some of 'the children of Israel, the holy people of God' "
(Handlin, *Freedom,* p. 175).

Anti-Semitism in the United States has never had government support. On the contrary, the government has frequently intervened on
behalf of the welfare of Jews in other countries. In 1840 the State
Department intervened on behalf of the Jews in Damascus, in 1850
on behalf of the Jews in Switzerland, and in 1879 on behalf of the
Jews in Rumania. All throughout the Nazi reign of terror official
American protests were issued in abundance, while an officially favorable attitude toward the creation of an independent Jewish state
helped the birth of Israel. Clearly the minority status of the American
Jew is neither expressed by, nor the result of, political domination.
Anti-Semitism in the United States has largely consisted of acts committed by private citizens and of short-lived—but sometimes powerful—privately organized movements.

The incidence of both kinds of anti-Semitism gradually began to
increase about a hundred years ago, was rapidly intensified at the
turn of the century, and, save for the interruption of the First World

War, rose steadily to a peak until just before the outbreak of the Second World War. Since then, overt acts of an anti-Semitic character appear to have declined markedly, although anti-Semitic attitudes may still be common.

The trajectory of anti-Semitism may be roughly correlated with the curve of increasing Jewish immigration, but it seems to be more immediately related to the tightening of competition for middle-class status. Between 1840 and 1880 over ten million immigrants entered the United States, among them an insignificant handful of German Jews. Throughout half of this period, the presence of Jews in the United States aroused almost no popular antagonism. As the years passed, a few Jews, starting as peddlers and petty merchants, worked up to powerful financial positions. From the time of the Civil War, the competitive threat from Jewish businessmen attracted more and more attention, and acts of overt anti-Semitism multiplied.

During the Civil War, denunciation of Jews appeared in both the Union and Confederate congresses. The basis of the charges was that Jewish middlemen were exploiting wartime shortages and were mainly responsible for inflation in both the North and South. In the South, the thankless task of managing the economy had been given to a Jewish Secretary of the Treasury, Judah Benjamin. Thus, after the War, the Jew became a convenient scapegoat for the onus of economic disorder and military defeat. In the North, General Grant ordered the Jews expelled from the Tennessee Valley on charges of smuggling and cotton speculation. Underlying this order, which was quickly rescinded, was an intensely competitive commercial situation in which both Jews and non-Jews were involved. Cotton was urgently needed for Northern factories; some trading with the enemy was legal, and was indulged in by military men as well as by civilians. It appears that Grant's order was issued under pressure from non-Jewish merchants who wished to reduce the ranks of their competitors (Learsi, p. 108).

Other instances of anti-Semitism during the nineteenth century might be mentioned. By the 1870's for example, Jews were regularly being excluded from fashionable clubs, schools, and hotels. But the greatest amount and most virulent forms of anti-Semitism in the United States occurred only after the massive exodus from Europe had swelled the ranks of American Jews competing for middle-class standards. As the Jewish population mounted and as the earlier immigrants improved their adaptation to the new cultural milieu, they came increasingly into conflict with the native middle class and with other upward-mobile immigrant groups. With the emergence of a more acculturated and better educated second generation, anti-Semitism rose sharply. A study of discriminatory want ads in Chicago newspapers showed this change. It was found that between 1872 and 1911 advertisements requesting "Christians only" did not occur. But after 1911 they appeared with increasing frequency, amounting to 4 percent of the advertisements in 1921, and reaching a peak of 13 percent in 1926 (Severson, quoted in McWilliams, pp. 28–29).

After 1910, acts of vandalism against Jewish property and molestation of Jewish persons also seem to have increased. Events took an ominous turn in Georgia, where in 1915 a mob aroused by the demagoguery of ex-Populist Tom Watson lynched a young Jewish factory manager who had been imprisoned on trumped-up charges of rape. Powerful backing for the anti-Semitic movement was soon provided by Henry Ford who, after his attempt to end the First World War by sailing to Europe in a "peace ship," came to see the war and America's participation in it as the fault of the "International Jew." From 1920 to 1927 Ford's newspaper, the Dearborn *Independent,* with a circulation of seven hundred thousand copies, conducted a relentless anti-Semitic campaign. Much of Ford's inspiration came from the fantastic *Protocols of the Elders of Zion,* a purportedly Jewish scheme for world domination which was actually conceived and written by the Czarist police. Under threats of lawsuit, Ford recanted. He publicly admitted the *Protocols* to be a forgery, claimed he had been duped, and promised that "henceforth they [the Jews] may look to me for friendship and good will" (Learsi, p. 291).

Concurrently, in 1916 the Ku Klux Klan was revived and embarked on a course of intimidation and violence against Jews as well as against Catholics and Negroes. The Klan, with an estimated four million members during the late twenties, described the Jews as an "unblendable element"; Jewish store windows were broken, and fiery crosses were set up in front of synagogues. During the thirties the Klan conducted a boycott against Jewish merchants with the password SYMWAO, which stood for Spend Your Money with Americans Only (Learsi, pp. 290–91). Other acts of discrimination came from widely dispersed quarters:

In February 1922, the head of placement in a Chicago employment office reported that 67 percent of the requests for employees specified that Jews were not wanted. A survey of teacher agencies in the Middle West in 1925 revealed that from 95 to 98 percent of the calls for teachers requested "Protestant Only." In August 1922, the Sharon, Connecticut, Chamber of Commerce distributed a leaflet requesting property owners not to sell to Jews. A bulletin of the Philadelphia Chamber of Commerce advocated specific restrictions against "The Hebrew Element." The board of directors of a Milwaukee golf club asked eight Jewish charter members to resign. . . . When a four-year-old girl disappeared at Massena, New York, on September 22, 1928, the local rabbi was called to answer charges of ritual murder. . . . The secretary of the Chamber of Commerce in St. Petersburg, Florida, announced that the time had come to make St. Petersburg a hundred percent American Gentile City. (McWilliams, pp. 37–38)

In the thirties, politically oriented anti-Semitism made its first significant appearance in the United States. Depression and social unrest provided large audiences for demagogic agitators who, encouraged by Hitler's success under similar conditions, attempted to ride to power inside the Trojan horse of anti-Semitism. The Coughlin-Lemke third party in 1935 was an example of this trend. At this time there were over one hundred frankly anti-Semitic organizations in the United States. The entrance of the United States into the Second World War weakened or eliminated most of them. Although they were perhaps more numerous in the immediate postwar years than at any other time, since 1941 such organizations have been insignificant in terms of influence and numbers of followers (Simpson and Yinger, p. 291).

In retrospect, the accomplishments of the political-minded anti-

Semitic groups do not loom very large. Their impact on American politics appears to have been transitory; they never rose beyond the point of placing the merest sprinkling of representatives in government, and in their more rabid forms were under the constant surveillance of the Federal government, which seized every opportunity to indict their leaders on criminal charges. But the obvious links between American anti-Semitic movements and those which were decimating and degrading Jews abroad profoundly influenced the assimilative trend in the United States. Although organized anti-Semitism did not attract the backing of the great mass of American citizens, the danger of these movements lay precisely in their undemocratic premises. They did not require mass popular support in order to seize power. A substantial proportion of American Jewry was alarmed by the measure of backing they did achieve. One of the results, as we shall see, was that organized Jewish pressure groups were strengthened, and the emphasis upon cultural pluralism and distinctive Jewish identity was intensified.

What is the extent of discrimination and other forms of minority disability which the Jews suffer in the United States today? Most observers agree that anti-Semitism in its overt forms seems to be decreasing while in its covert forms—attitudes and stereotypes—the situation is at least not deteriorating and may be improving somewhat.

One of the chief ways by which social scientists have attempted to measure the extent of anti-Semitism is through social-distance tests and public-opinion surveys. These investigations show that a considerable body of the American people hold derogatory opinions about Jews. Thus, in a study conducted by Elmo Roper in 1948, it was found that 13.2 percent of the respondents would prefer not to work side-by-side with Jews on an equal basis; 21.3 percent would prefer not to have Jews move into their neighborhoods; and 14.2 percent would prefer not to have Jews as guests in their homes (Weintraub, p. 42). More than a third of the respondents reported that they would rather stay at a resort hotel in which all the guests were non-Jews. Regarding college education, 62.5 percent wanted to see their children go to a college which admits the best students who apply, whether Jewish or not, but 6 percent believed in some kind of quota system, while 14.9 percent preferred a college which admits no Jews at all (Weintraub, p. 56). A study by Robinson and Rhode revealed that between 28 and 53 percent of non-Jewish New Yorkers thought that Jewish businessmen were less honest than other businessmen; between 27 percent and 57 percent thought that there were too many Jews holding government offices and jobs; and between 29 and 43 percent thought that Jews had too much power in the United States (cited in McDonagh and Richards, pp. 754–57). Interviews arranged by the Institute of Social Research of Columbia University with 600 industrial workers in five cities revealed that 20 percent were strongly anti-Semitic, another 20 percent were fully tolerant, and the rest were intermediate (Simpson and Yinger, p. 296). An intensive study of 150 veterans in Chicago showed that 4 percent recommended harsh restrictive action against Jews, that 27 percent harbored strong anti-Semitic prejudices, and that only 41 percent were relatively free of derogatory stereotypes (McDonagh and Richards, p. 298).

Most of these studies show that anti-Semitic attitudes are found with higher frequency among middle- and upper-bracket socio-economic groups (McWilliams, p. 103), but the evidence is by no means conclusive. It is important to realize that verbally expressed stereotypes do not necessarily afford an index of actual, overt discriminatory practices, and that a marked contrast may exist between verbal notions and behavior in real-life situations. Other conditions being equal, however, the existence of unfavorable stereotypes makes it more likely that intensive overt anti-Semitic campaigns can be carried out. It is estimated that "ten percent of the American people might be, under highly disorganized conditions, direct supporters of such a movement, and perhaps half of the remainder could be sufficiently vulnerable to its appeal to give some support or fail to resist it" (Simpson and Yinger, p. 293). But the development of a very dangerous situation for Jews in the United States is dependent upon forces vastly more powerful than the ethnic stereotypes harbored by many people. Only a major crisis brought about by socio-economic events unrelated to ethnic biases could produce such conditions. At the moment, Jews in the United States appear to suffer more from the psychological effects of anti-Semitic attitudes than they do from the embodiment of these attitudes in physical persecution or discrimination. Since the Second World War, such incidents as the bombing of a synagogue and a Hebrew school in Miami, and vandalism practiced by an imitation Hitler Youth gang in Philadelphia, continue to occur, but they are sporadic and in most cases effectively investigated and combated by the police. Most of the violence against Jewish persons appears to be confined to the activities of juvenile gangs, and to flare-ups between individuals in which anti-Semitism is not the principal motive.

Anti-Semitism expressed in political or legal disability also appears to be quantitatively insignificant. Jews do not encounter difficulty in exercising their electoral franchise, nor is there any evidence to indicate that they are at a disadvantage in criminal or civil legal proceedings. If discrimination is a factor in legal decisions involving Jews, it is because of the biases of individual court officials and jurors; overt expression of discrimination in juridical matters incurs the risk of immediate legal reprisal. Discrimination against Jews in public elementary and secondary schools, auditoriums, parks, conveyances, and housing projects similarly does not appear to be significant, and (with the exception of resort accommodations) hotels and restaurants rarely attempt to raise barriers. Overt discrimination against Jews may be found today chiefly in employment, in the admission policies of institutions of higher learning, in resort-hotels, in real-estate practices, and in social clubs and informal social situations.

Jews are reported to experience difficulty in getting employment in many concerns which traditionally have been non-Jewish in ownership and management, such as insurance companies, private utility companies, and banks. The extent of discriminatory hiring practices is hard to determine, but some indications may be seen in want ads and application forms. Among want ads, less than 4 percent express racial discrimination; of these only a small fraction could apply to Jews (Weintraub, p. 81). Potential discrimination revealed in em-

ployment-agency forms is higher: more than 60 percent ask questions
about religion (Weintraub, p. 82). No conclusions can be reached,
however, about the frequency with which employers make use of this
information. In the professions there is no doubt that discrimination
exists, but again adequate objective data is lacking. Discrimination
against Jews seems to be particularly strong in the field of public accounting. For example, it was shown that of 286 accountants employed by 15 important accounting firms in Cincinnati, only 3 were
Jewish (Weintraub, p. 77). On the basis of the same study in Cincinnati, it was found that there is considerable discrimination against
Jews in the engineering profession. The chances for Jews to get top
jobs in law also appear to be poor.

Whatever the true extent of occupational discrimination against
Jews may be, it is evidently not sufficient to force American Jews into
an underprivileged economic status. On the contrary, as already stated,
the proportion of Jews engaged in professional, entrepreneurial, managerial, and clerical positions is considerably higher than that for the
nation as a whole. Clearly the occupational barriers raised against
Jews are not impregnable. There are enough alternatives available
to make it extremely unlikely that any substantial proportion of
American Jewry today suffers economic privation as a result of occupational discrimination. This does not, however, eliminate the effect
of many individual disappointments and humiliations associated with
prejudiced hiring.

Although considerable discrimination toward Jews clearly exists
in American institutions of higher learning, it is difficult to determine
just how great and how extensive it is. Jews, who constitute less than
4 percent of the total population, manage to make up about 9 percent
of the total enrollment in colleges and univerisities. But about half of
these Jewish students attend institutions in New York City, including
its free system of city colleges (see Simpson and Yinger, p. 580).
It is commonly known that many highly regarded colleges and universities maintain a "quota system" by which the number of Jewish
admissions are limited, although the institutions generally deny it.
Thus, many Jews are deprived of the advantages of graduation from

"prestige" schools. Yet despite such quotas, the percentage of Jewish applicants ultimately admitted to colleges and universities is no lower than the percentages of other groups admitted, according to a study carried out by Elmo Roper for the Committee on Discrimination in College Admissions of American Council on Education (see Simpson and Yinger, p. 583). In fact, Jewish applicants in the northeastern part of the United States, where over half of the Jewish population resides, had a higher rate of *ultimate* success in being admitted to college (86 percent) than did Protestant (80 percent) or Catholic (75 percent) applicants. Yet this same study indicated that Jewish applicants make more applications than others—2.4 applications per Jewish applicant, as compared to 1.7 for Protestants and 1.6 for Catholics—and it showed that Jewish applicants succeeded less often in getting into the college of their first choice—63 percent for Jews, as compared to 71 percent for Catholics and 82 percent for Protestants (Simpson and Yinger, p. 548). The admission "quotas" of professional schools are acutely felt by Jewish students for whom the professions—especially medicine—represent the ideal type of occupation. One nation-wide survey estimated in 1945 [2] that American medical colleges were receiving between 35,000 and 40,000 applications annually. These came from about 14,000 individuals, of whom 5,000 to 7,000 were Jews. Approximately 6,000 non-Jews were admitted each year, as compared to 500 Jewish applicants (Kingdon, cited in Simpson and Yinger, p. 602).

Overt discrimination against Jews also appears in resort-hotel practices and in occasional informal residential agreements. It is, of course, difficult to detect restrictions which are informally imposed by hotels or residential restrictions which may simply consist of a mutual agreement among property owners in a neighborhood not to rent or sell to a Jew. In one study in 1948, it was maintained that 90 percent of the first-class resort hotels in Arizona followed a restrictive policy, and that 50 percent of the resorts listed in Cook's

[2] It must be noted that 1945 was the first academic year following the Second World War. A great number of applications from all segments of the American society to all institutions of higher learning was received, and the number of rejections to all types of candidates was consequently high.

Travel Agency for Vermont, New Hampshire, and Maine excluded Jews (Weintraub, p. 26). Although many states prohibit public advertisements which use discriminatory phraseology, commonly understood circumlocutions, such as "churches nearby," "distinctive clientele," and "private references," are widely employed. A spot check in 1948 of resort advertisements in the *Herald Tribune* and New York *Times* showed that 22.9 percent and 11.3 percent of the advertisements, respectively, included such phrases. When letters signed with a common Jewish name were mailed to the resorts using such phrases, the chance of receiving accommodations was 27.2 percent for the *Tribune* and 48 percent for the *Times,* in contrast to 88 percent (*Tribune*) and 90.7 percent (*Times*) for letters signed with a non-Jewish name (Weintraub, pp. 28–31).

In many communities throughout the United States, certain neighborhoods, by mutual agreement of residents and real-estate agents, exclude Jews from renting or buying residential property. (Commercial property is seldom restricted.) Jewish housing, however, from the point of view of facilities and location, is not inferior to national averages for comparable incomes. Jews are not primarily confined to slums. Those Jews who are slum dwellers suffer their plight for reasons not related to restrictive agreements. Restricted neighborhoods involve only a small fraction of the available residential real estate; hence, Jewish choice of housing is more a function of finances than of minority affiliation. The infiltration of Jews into a predominantly gentile neighborhood does not cause a panic among real-estate owners; property values do not plunge downward and there is no exceptionally rapid deterioration of facilities. Substantial numbers of Jews are found in choice residential areas and Jews have not been at a disadvantage in the recent trend toward suburbanization.

Despite their potential freedom of movement, most Jewish families, including those in the middle-income group, live in neighborhoods with a high or almost total predominance of Jews. This concentration results, at least in part, from anti-Semitic pressures. Jews continue to be extremely apprehensive about the possibilities of anti-Semitic encounters, and rather than run the risk of incidents involving them-

selves or their children, they prefer to live in an insulated environment. For many Jews there are still positive cultural factors which
also enter into the choice of neighborhood: proximity to synagogues,
Kosher meat stores, and above all, the presence of people who
share a residue of traditional Jewish customs.

There is also overt discrimination against Jews in social clubs in the
United States. "An examination of the membership lists of the key
prestige clubs in almost any American city," writes Carey McWilliams
(p. 123), "will reveal that Jews have been excluded by long standing
custom or expressed provision." University clubs, town clubs, golf
clubs, cultural societies, college fraternities and sororities, and many
others share this principle. It may be argued that such associations are
based on mutual liking and mutual interests among the individuals
forming such associations and that the exclusion of Jews does not
constitute either prejudice or discrimination toward them; or it may
be argued that such discrimination is petty and inconsequential. But
its effects are more serious than they might seem. As Ralph Linton
has written: "The hope of gaining prestige or the fear of losing it
does more than anything else to hold the average individual to the
proper performance of his roles" (p. 146). Such associations and
clubs are among the most important prestige symbols of modern
American society. They are not only made up of people with social
prestige, but also of those with economic and political power. Thus,
in adition to suffering the psychological effects of such discrimination,
Jews with upper-middle-class aspirations are regularly deprived of
the social status supplied by prestige associations. They again respond
by insulating themselves. Perhaps more than any other minority group
in the United States, the Jews have compensated by creating their own
Jewish prestige associations, such as clubs, cultural societies, fraternities and sororities, philanthropic organizations, and the like.
In these one gains prestige and even power—but mainly within the
Jewish community, not in the larger society.

In the contemporary United States, the disabilities of the Jewish
minority do not necessarily involve any physical, legal, or economic
deprivation or oppression. Most of their disabilities seem to be re-

lated to attempts to restrict the social influence and political power of this socially mobile group. The most serious disadvantage suffered by the Jewish minority is the psychological adjustment of many Jewish individuals and the pressures that make Jews withdraw from non-Jewish society. According to many psychologists, compensatory excesses which are expressed as either superiority or inferiority complexes are frequently found among Jews. One form of compensation is an overemphasis on one's Jewishness, with a consequent underemphasis on one's status in other roles—whether they be occupational, educational, national, or the like. The other form is an attempt to hide one's Jewishness, even to the point of becoming anti-Semitic. According to the psychologist Kurt Lewin, typical signs of maladjustment, such as overtension, loudness, exaggerated aggressiveness, and excessively hard work, are common among American Jews (cited in Simpson and Yinger, p. 304). In a study by A. I. Gordon of Jewish students at the University of Minnesota it was found that 30 percent of the respondents felt that being a Jew was a serious handicap; 40 percent thought that anti-Semitism would interfere with their success and happiness; and 22 percent agreed that "at any moment my feelings may be hurt because I am a Jew" (cited in Simpson and Yinger, p. 301).

IV

Among the case studies presented in this volume, the Jews in the United States are unique in that their minority status is not associated with severe economic deprivations. There is no evidence that the material standard of living enjoyed by Jews is inferior to that of the nation as a whole. This paradox is widely misunderstood by Christians and Jews alike. The success which Jews have registered in many sectors of the highly competitive, urbanized American scene tends to be regarded by the majority as the result of a seditious conspiracy; instead of earning applause from the majority, it arouses fear and leads to an intensification of efforts to make it more difficult for the Jews than for others to achieve high status. The Jews for their part tend to respond by sharpening their competitive effort. The obstacles placed in their path seem to call forth great drive and concentration and earn for them a reputation of aggressiveness. Proudly conscious of their achievements in the face of these obstacles, the Jews frequently tend to interpret their success as evidence of innate "racial" superiority.

Neither Christian nor Jew correctly evaluates the fortuitous chain of events whereby through centuries of forced exclusion from a rural milieu, the Jews acquired a set of values and skills which were finely adapted to the needs of the emerging impersonal, urban-industrial competitive society. "The Jew entered upon the modern world at the time when certain areas of economic activity began expanding at a faster rate than others. It was their good fortune that by tradition and experience Jews were excellently equipped precisely for those activities which were at the threshold of greatest expansion" (Reich, "Modern Jewry," p. 1258). When the socio-economic basis of the western world changed, and the city and city ways became dominant, the previously adopted urbanism of the Jews opened the doors to the paradox of economic success amid social discrimination. The peculiar tragedy of anti-Semitism in the United States lies in the fact that the successful urban adaptation of the Jews has been held against them even though they are in the midst of one of the most thoroughly urbanized and competitive societies in the world.

Semi-official representatives of the Jewish "community" have devoted much time and effort to drawing up rosters of eminent Jewish-American personages in art, science, literature, and government. Such catalogues are designed to encourage the American Jew to take pride in his "heritage" and to confront the majority with the value of the Jewish contribution to American life. The feeling of necessity for such a confrontation undoubtedly stems from the underlying insecurity of the Jewish position, which is a product of centuries of persecution. Nonetheless, these lists, impressive in their length and eminence, also demonstrate a point which their compilers do not often see fit to make, namely, that the Jews in the

United States have made great strides toward overcoming their minority status and are closer to a successful pluralistic adaptation than they have, in such large numbers, ever been before.

The Jews in the United States, however, like the French in Canada and many of the Indian groups in Mexico and Brazil, are today strongly opposed to the loss of their separate identity within American society. For a while during the last century a strong tendency toward both acculturation and assimilation existed. Today, acculturation is still proceeding at a rapid pace, but there is no evidence that the Jews are assimilating in any significant numbers.

It is probable that without the surge of both domestic and foreign brands of anti-Semitism toward the close of the last century, complete acculturation in everything except a few residual religious traits would have been simply a matter of time. If there had been no outbreak of anti-Semitism, a rather unique set of conditions would have confronted the Jews in the United States. For perhaps the first time in history, they would have enjoyed full political, social, and economic equality in a secular and urban environment. These conditions were, of course, merely part of the post-Enlightenment American dream, and never became the facts of reality. Anti-Semitism increased rather than diminished, and only now, at mid-century, has the tide turned once again.

In the meantime, the nature, if not direction, of both the acculturative and assimilative processes has been altered. Jewish associations with a conscious or unconscious vested interest in maintaining the identity of the Jews in the United States as a distinct group with a distinct culture have been heavily strengthened. Powerful crosscurrents were set in motion within the minority as the Jews fought back against prejudice and discrimination. Fear of an increase of anti-Semitism based upon European models, chagrin over actual exclusionist policies, and determination not to yield in the struggle for a measure of political power commensurate with economic standing, are today balanced, to an undetermined degree, by acculturative and assimilative tendencies.

Scores of Jewish community centers, Jewish hospitals, and Jewish charities and welfare institutions have been established in the last few decades. These, together with the synagogues, Hebrew schools, and benefit societies, are staffed by an increasingly large body of professional workers who contribute toward the perpetuation of Jewish in-group sentiment. In the *American Jewish Yearbook* for 1956 there are listed 310 national Jewish organizations. These are distributed under the headings: Civic Defense and Political, Cultural, Overseas Aid, Religious and Educational, Social and Mutual Benefit, Social Welfare, Zionist and Pro-Israel. There are 164 Jewish federations, welfare funds, and community councils, which have the following functions: raising funds for local, national, and overseas service; allocating such funds; coordination of local services, such as family welfare, child care, health, recreation, and community relations with Jews and non-Jews. The *Yearbook* also lists 213 Jewish periodicals in which Jewish problems and viewpoints are aired and disseminated. Seventy percent of the national Jewish organizations, 91 percent of the welfare federations, and 81 percent of the periodicals have been established since 1920.

The increase in the number of institutions which in an organized way are directly or indirectly dedicated to the preservation of Jewish identity has not, however, been accompanied by a tendency toward unity of plan or action. These Jewish agencies are nevertheless in general agreement that the Jews in the United States either are or should be a corporate social group, or to use a frequently applied misnomer, that the Jews are a "community." Increasing support, therefore, has recently been given by the Jews themselves to the concept that they are and ought to remain a separate faction in the American population. In many Jewish circles today further acculturation is regarded as repugnant. Many Orthodox and Conservative leaders maintain that there is a causal connection between the fact that the German Jews were the most thoroughly acculturated Jewish group in the world and that German anti-Semitism was the world's worst. Even some of the Reformed congregations have reversed their long-maintained stand against Jewish nationalism and thrown their weight in with the Zionists. It seems, therefore, that for the moment at least, a large portion of American Jewry is actively opposed to the earlier attempts to become indistinguishable from other Americans in everything except religion. "Jewishness" is being stressed as a virtue, and there is increased hope that social equality may be found through cultural pluralism and a militant, organized effort to enforce civil liberties.

Paradoxically, there is no indication that the organized stress on cultural pluralism is having any effect in slowing down the over-all rate of acculturation. Jewish community centers, Young Men's Hebrew Association centers, Jewish women's federations, Jewish "parochial" schools, Jewish country clubs, and Jewish magazines have multiplied in recent years. Yet the programs and activities of these institutions are remarkably similar to their gentile counterparts and are growing more similar every year. It would seem that as time goes by the doctrine of cultural pluralism, which is at present in great vogue, will inevitably be concerned with less that is genuinely plural in nature.

In America, the Jews are but one of several minorities and despite widespread anti-Semitism they have not been persecuted enough to prevent them from sharing in the general socio-economic rise. Rarely have Jews settled in a society which, despite its obvious inequalities, is less stratified, or more propitious to social, economic, and cultural mobility—that is to assimilation. Nor have they ever lived in a place where the standard of living and the attractions of the dominant group (and intellectual subcultures) have held out greater temptations to surrender the more confining traditional Jewish culture. Moreover, the rapid social and technological change that is distinctive of our age would sorely test the staying power of any set of traditional norms. For all these reasons, extensive cultural assimilation seems more likely than ever before in Jewish history. (Gans, p. 562)

In recent years, Jewish associations, working alone or in cooperation with other organizations, have achieved many notable successes in combating overt forms of anti-Semitism. Jewish lobbies have played an important role in passing the fair employment acts which have been adopted by 12 state legislatures since 1945, as well as in passing measures aimed at reducing discrimination in housing and in other public spheres. By pressing for both prompt and efficient enforcement of existing statutes, and by urging impartial police action, they have done much to help safeguard civil rights for all groups. Whatever may be the actual extent of anti-Semitism in the United States today, there has never been a time or place where the Jews were in a better position to defend themselves. Yet anti-Semitism has only been suppressed rather than eliminated. Its roots still lie firmly embedded in the hostile stereotypes harbored by millions of Americans.

RECOMMENDED ADDITIONAL READINGS

Baron, Salo. A Social and Religious History of the Jews, 2d. ed. rev., Vols. I–VIII, New York: Columbia University Press, 1952–.

Finkelstein, Louis, ed. The Jews, Their History, Culture, and Religion. Philadelphia: Jewish Publication Society of America, 1949.

Gordon, Albert I. Jews in Transition. Minneapolis: University of Minnesota Press, 1949.

Handlin, Oscar. Adventure in Freedom, Three Hundred Years of Jewish Life in America. New York: McGraw-Hill, 1954.

Herberg, Will. Protestant—Catholic—Jew. New York: Doubleday, 1955.

Janowsky, Oscar I., ed. The American Jew. New York: Harper, 1942.

Learsi, Rufus. The Jews in America, a History. Cleveland: World Publishing Co., 1954.

McWilliams, Carey. A Mask for Privilege, Anti-Semitism in America. Boston: Little Brown, 1948.

Conclusion

AN ANTHROPOLOGICAL VIEW

OF MINORITY GROUPS

MOST of the information upon which the preceding case studies are based was compiled by specialists who call themselves sociologists, historians, political scientists, or social psychologists—except when we have been concerned with Indians in Brazil, who are "primitive peoples" and thus lie within the traditional province of anthropology. Whenever anthropologists have turned to the study of minority groups other than enclaves of "primitives," they have been concerned either with acculturation or with race relations. In their studies of acculturation they have taught us much about the process of culture change, especially of a minority culture in contact with a dominant culture. In their studies of race relations, they have clarified the difference between biological inheritance of physical characteristics and social transmission of learned behavior. Beyond these important contributions, a uniquely anthropological approach to the study of minority groups has not been delimited, precisely because anthropology as a discipline merges with other fields of study, such as history, sociology, and social psychology. Yet it does seem to us that there is a unique perspective implicit in the traditional scope of anthropology and that this perspective may be helpful for an understanding of minority groups.

Anthropology is an historical discipline. Traditionally, anthropologists have been concerned with the broad sweep of human history —not only with the brief period for which we have written records, but with the long development of human culture before man learned to write. With this long-term perspective, the anthropologist who attempts to study minority groups finds himself asking questions which other disciplines find it easier to overlook: When in human history did minority groups first appear? To what other social institutions are they historically and functionally related? By what historical process or processes did minority groups take form?

Furthermore, anthropology—especially those subsciences of anthropology known as ethnology and social anthropology—has always been a comparative discipline. From studies of a variety of primitive cultures and civilizations anthropologists have sought to complete a picture of the full range of human behavior and social institutions; they have sought to isolate universals in human societies as well as to explain the presence of the unique. Although the scope of this book is consciously limited to the western hemisphere, and more specifically to only six minority groups, the varieties of distinctive national cultures and of minority-group situations in this area of the world are sufficient to offer a wide range of comparative material. This comparative point of view is especially important for understanding minority groups; to date, most studies of minorities have been carried out within the context of one nation, such as the United States or Canada, or at best within western Europe. From this point of view, the anthropologist attempts to determine whether there are societies and cultures more resistant or more receptive to the presence of culturally discrete minorities, or to the assimilation of stranger groups.

Finally, in their studies of less complex primitive societies and small communities, anthropologists have been concerned with the functional relationships of groups within a society. There is a great difference between analyzing the structure and the functional relationships of groups within these relatively simple societies, and doing the same for minority groups which are subgroups of large states. Yet the basic point of view of functional analysis can be brought to bear on minority groups. In these terms, one must ask the obvious question of how the subordinate position of a minority group relates to the economic system and social institutions of the larger society. Likewise, one must ask the less obvious question of to what extent the sociocultural system of a minority permits adaptive responses to its subordinate status in the larger society and to its struggle for a higher position in the social hierarchy.

Briefly, the point of view taken in this chapter is (1) that specific minority groups need to be seen in the general perspective of the long-term development of human societies; (2) that a knowledge of the pre-minority past of a group, of the conditions surrounding its genesis as a minority group, and of its subsequent historical relations with the dominant majority is often crucial to understanding its contemporary position in the larger society; (3) that given the frame of reference provided by the historical situation, it is necessary to know the functional relations of the minority to the dominant majority (and other groups) in the contemporary scene; and (4) that further light may be thrown at all stages of analysis, on any minority group and its position in a larger society, and on minority groups generally, by comparison with similar situations involving other cultural traditions and other social arrangements. It is from this broad synchronic, diachronic, and comparative point of view, as suggested by the traditional concerns of anthropology, that we should now like to look at minority groups.

MINORITIES AND CULTURAL EVOLUTION

With the knowledge provided by archaeology, ethnography, and written history, it is clear that human societies have progressively expanded in size, in complexity, and in territorial scope as man has extended and perfected his technological control over his environment. For nearly fifty thousand years our species lived in small wandering bands limited in size by their precarious methods of subsistence. During all this time (and much more, if one considers human species other than Homo sapiens) the necessity of hunting for food with inefficient weapons, or of gathering it with ineffective instruments, kept the population sparse. It was not until about ten thousand years ago that man first became a food producer—an agriculturist and a breeder of animals. This "food-producing revolution," to use V. Gordon Childe's term, occurred independently at least once in the old world and at least once in the New World. From the earliest centers, a knowledge of food-producing techniques spread rapidly over most of the globe until a large proportion of all human societies lived by food production, yet in isolated areas and in more inhospitable environments man continued to live by hunting and gathering. With a secure food supply furnished from his gardens and from his domestic animals, there was for the first time a sedentary life in villages. But these village societies were in one important sense as "primitive" as the remaining nomadic hunting and gathering societies. "Throughout both Paleolithic and Neolithic [1] times each little group was largely self-contained and self-supporting, as the surviving primitive societies, whether hunters or growers of vegetable and animal food, are largely self-contained and self-supporting" (Redfield, p. 7). During all of this time there were no minority groups.

About 5,000 years ago a second great "revolution" gave birth to mankind's first cities, to great public works—such as irrigation systems and land reclamation projects—writing, standards of weights

---

[1] In the Old World the hunting and gathering period and the early food-producing period are known respectively as the Paleolithic and the Neolithic periods.

and measures, the beginnings of science, foreign trade, and to specialized labor of all descriptions. This "urban revolution" seems to have first occurred in the Middle East, and at a later date to have spread elsewhere in the Old World. Again the "urban revolution" took place independently in the New World, where such peoples as the Aztec of Mexico, the Maya of Yucatan, and the Inca of highland South America developed their own indigenous civilizations. For the present purposes, the most important feature of this second great change in human history is that it was associated with the growth of a new form of social organization, namely, what we today call the state. In broadest perspective, it was the formation of state societies which made the existence of minority groups possible. Primitive societies are stateless societies. Although a primitive tribe may have considerable formal political organization, such as tribal councils or a chieftain vested with relatively strong authority, social order is achieved by stressing the obligations and rights due to kinsmen by descent or by marriage. It is therefore characteristic that the various systems of classifying kin among primitive peoples have a greater extension than those used by so-called civilized peoples. In primitive societies an individual often has hundreds of "relatives," including individuals only distantly or even fictitiously related (i.e., all my fellow clan members may be my "brothers"). An individual's world in primitive societies is thus populated largely by "relatives," all of whom speak the same language, practice the same customs, and belong to the same physical stock. In the small band and villages typical of the primitive world, the use of ridicule, non-cooperation, and ostracism, reinforced by common bonds of culture, is usually sufficient to insure conformity to the "unwritten law." Coercion, external compulsion, and legal procedure, although not entirely absent, are seldom necessary to maintain internal order (Linton, p. 109). Primitive tribes usually have a definite idea of their own territory, and they resist invasion and trespass with force; but the emphasis of their social organization is on "our people," no matter where they live, and not upon the territorial unit. Primitive social organization thus contains no provisions for incorporating into a single social unit groups of individuals who are not related by descent or by marriage, who follow different customs, who stress distinctive values, and who, in sum, are an alien people.

Only with the development of the state did human societies become equipped with a form of social organization which could bind masses of culturally and physically heterogeneous "strangers" into a single social entity. Whereas primitive peoples derive their cohesion largely from a common culture and from kinship and other kinds of personal ties, state societies are held together largely by the existence of a central political authority which claims a monopoly of coercive power over all persons within a given territory. Theoretically, with a sufficiently strong development of the apparatus of government, a state society can extend law and order over limitless subgroups of strangers who neither speak the same language, worship the same gods, nor strive for the same values.

Yet the growth of the state form of organization did not entirely replace the principles by which unity is achieved among primitive peoples. On the contrary, if a thoroughgoing replacement had indeed taken place, minorities, as we know them today, would not exist. In reality, many of the subgroups have continued to regard themselves as distinctive units within the total society, not because they inhabit the same territory and are subject to the same apparatus of government, but because they share cultural traits different from others and reckon themselves, in a sense, as kinsmen by descent. Moreover, certain of these subgroups, especially the more numerous and more powerful ones, have tended to act as if the population of their state society was like the population of a primitive tribe; have tended to act as if the state society to which they belong ideally ought to consist of their own physical and cultural type; and as if the state were merely the territorial expression of their own people or "nation." Thus, from the persistence of primitive principles of social organization there emerges that strange contradiction of terms known as the "national state." It is the prevalence of this contradiction which guarantees the proliferation of minority situations throughout the modern world.

Of course, there is no absolute reason why a state society cannot also be a nation in the above sense. But the contradiction involved is an historical rather than a logical one. Neither history nor ethnography can provide more than a mere handful of examples of state societies which have consisted solely of racially and culturally homogeneous elements. It need scarcely be said that throughout recorded history the territorial limits of states have been in ceaseless flux, thereby insuring the heterogeneity of their populations. Boundary changes resulting from wars, revolutions, confederations, and conferences have occurred with such frequency as to leave no time for the growth of homogeneous national states. Moreover, the same technological revolution which broke the insularity of the primitive bands and villages and led to the rise of state societies brought with it ever-increasing opportunities for large-scale population shifts. Certainly there is no society in the world today where state and nation may be said to coincide, except as a convenient fiction for novelists and politicians.

And yet, especially during the last few centuries, many conscious and unconscious efforts have been made to achieve the ideal of a national state. In the process, the cultural traditions, the language, and physical type of one of the groups of a state society are proposed as the national language, the national culture, and the national physical type. Usually this dominant or "national" way of life is that of the numerical majority, and the strangers—the minority members— form smaller cultural or racial enclaves. But sometimes a handful of people have, through their superior economic, political, or military power, been able to impose their cultural and physical "ideal" of nationhood on the rest of the society.

All the minority groups discussed in this book are faced by an ideal of national culture and national physical type associated with the characteristics of the dominant segments of the state societies into which they have been incorporated. Although it would be impossible to describe the dominant national ideals of Brazil, Mexico, France, Canada, and the United States within the limits of this book, their main features are easy to discern. In the United States, the national ideal is English-speaking, Protestant, northern European in descent, and light Caucasoid in physical appearance. In Brazil, the national ideal is Portuguese-speaking (with a Brazilian accent), Catholic, Portuguese in descent, and dark Caucasoid in physical appearance. In Mexico, it is Spanish in language, Catholic in religion, Iberian with perhaps a distant Indian ancestor in descent, and mestizo (Causasoid-Indian mixture) in physical appearance. In the French West Indies, the ideal is French in language, Catholic in religion, a descendant of an old plantation family, and Caucasoid in physical appearance. In Canada, despite the fact that the nation is officially a bicultural and bilingual state, the ideal is English-speaking, Protestant, northern European, and light Caucasoid.

THE FORMATION OF MINORITIES

Although the minority status of the groups studied in this book derives generally from incorporation by state societies possessing ideal national cultures and physical types, each group came to be faced with these alien ideals as a result of a unique historical sequence. Nonetheless, despite the diversity of historical detail there are certain broad historical processes responsible for their origin as minorities. With full awareness that the genesis of a minority does not alone explain its present condition, but simply provides a point of departure, let us look at our case studies from this point of view.

Three of the minorities described in our case studies—the Brazilian Indians, the Indians of Mexico, and the French Canadians—obviously trace their origin to the expansionist activities of state societies. Fundamentally, these three minorities are the results of initial acts of conquest by politically and militarily superior societies.

In the case of the Brazilian Indians, the disparity in numbers and in organization between the conquering state and the numerous separate tribal societies resulted in the complete destruction of many of the tribal groups, such as the Tupinamba who lived along the Brazilian coast. Others, such as the Kaingang of São Paulo, managed to survive the initial period of conquest and to persist in greatly reduced numbers as enclaves within modern Brazil. In recent times of course, outright military conquest has not been the main instrument for the subjugation of Brazil's tribal peoples. Perhaps the spread of European diseases has always played a more conspicuous role than actual armed clashes. Furthermore, since 1910 the Brazilian Indian Service has consciously striven to avoid the use of arms and to prevent others from using force against the remaining autonomous tribal groups. This altruistic "pacification" process modifies but does not obscure the fact that pacification means submission to an alien political force. The pacification procedure merely involves the attempt to convince the Indians that further resistance to the encroachment of Brazilian society is futile in view of the vast superiority of the forces against which they are pitted. There is no doubt that if the peaceful methods of conquest employed by the Indian Service had proved unsuccessful, sterner measures would have been demanded by the less altruistic members of Brazilian society.

Before the Spanish Crown extended its control over the territory of what was to become Mexico, the native peoples had lived to a large extent in indigenous state societies within which numerous minority groups were already present. Under the control of the Aztecs of Tenochitlan for example, were the Otomi-speaking and Zapotec-speaking peoples as well as those who spoke Nahuatl, the language of the Aztecs. For many of the Indian peoples of Mexico, the Spanish conquest simply meant the exchange of minority status under one state for minority status under another. But one important difference must be noted. The Spanish conquest was on a larger scale than anything the indigenous organizations had been able to achieve, and its results were more stable. Thus, especially after the birth of the Mexican Republic, it became possible to establish a single national ideal for a great variety of Indian groups. This national ideal does not, as it does in the case of the Indians of Brazil, express only the traditions of the conquerors, but is rather a mixture derived from both European and indigenous traditions.

From the point of view of the formation of minorities, the Spanish conquest of Mexico is perhaps more typical than their conquest of the other great New World center of native civilization in the Andean area. Unlike the loose confederations and alliances characteristic of the Meso-American native states, the Incas of Peru had risen to political and cultural dominion over a region some two thousand miles in extent. Into this true empire, the Inca had welded a vast array of disparate ethnic and linguistic groups. According to the Inca's own tallies, no less than eighty-six "tribes" had yielded their political autonomy to the empire. In Inca society the problems created by these minorities were the subject of much concern on the part of the Inca rulers. Special provisions were made for the control and assimilation of the various peoples who had been incorporated into the state, including special educational programs and large-scale population shifts (Rowe, pp. 185 ff.). Under these circumstances, the Spanish conquest of the Inca actually amounted in some respects to a complication, rather than a simplification, of the native minority problem. In the area formerly controlled by the Incas, there arose after the collapse of the Spanish empire a series of independent states— Ecuador, Bolivia, and Peru—that have replaced the monolithic colossus achieved by the native peoples. Within each of these modern societies there are somewhat distinct national ideals toward which the numerous Indian minorities are now acculturating. As in Mexico, however, the national ideals of these modern states are a composite of European and Indian cultural traits and physical features.

The more typical result of the expansion of European state societies into areas where native states or proto-states already existed has been the extension of political unity over wider areas than had previously been possible. As in the case of Mexico, such "new" states as Ghana, India, Pakistan, and Tunisia owe their present political unity to the conquest process. Like Mexico, and the modern South American highland republics, these formerly colonial dependencies of European powers have recently emerged as independent state societies equipped with national ideals far different from those which existed in the indigenous states. And finally, in each of these areas the emergent state societies are concerned with distinct minority problems—the tribes of Ghana, the religious and linguistic minorities of India, and, one might even say, the French in Tunisia.

While the ancient world had known empires of great extent—

such as the Roman, Chinese, Mongol, and Inca—with the growth of the post-feudal European states, empires of unprecedented proportions came to be formed. By the sixteenth century, the revolutionary development of gunpowder weapons, maneuverable sailing vessels, and navigational devices gave to the European states a marked technological superiority over most of the world's societies. With this new equipment the European states were able to overcome hitherto undreamed-of distances for the purposes of state expansion. Within a few hundred years, Africa, North and South America, India, southeast Asia, parts of China, central and northeastern Asia, Indonesia, Melanesia, Polynesia, and Australia were to become, with varying degrees of permanency, subject to European governments. Colonists were sent into many of these areas to establish permanent settlements and to rule over the indigenous populations. But with the waxing and waning of imperial fortunes and with the growth of movements for independence, the political control of these areas shifted from one state society to another, sometimes with bewildering frequency. Thus, in addition to minorities consisting of conquered indigenous peoples, such as the Indians of Mexico and Brazil, the expansion of European states also created a somewhat smaller number of minorities consisting of European colonists or their descendants whose governments lost dominion over the areas they had formerly controlled. The French in Canada are such a minority.

The origin of the French-Canadian minority differs from that of the two groups previously discussed only in so far as both the English and French, minority as well as majority, were invaders of a territory far removed from the nuclear areas of their respective states. Perhaps the closest parallel to this formative process is to be found in the Union of South Africa where the descendants of colonists from two European powers—England and Holland—have been grappling with the problem of reconciling their divergent concepts of nationhood. The Union of South Africa, like Canada, possesses two official languages, and as in Canada, each of the two major groups controls an important political party. It scarcely needs to be said, however, that the existence of a large indigenous minority in the Union of

South Africa provides an additional set of circumstances which are absent from the Canadian situation.

Three of the minority groups discussed in this book, namely the Jews in the United States, the Negroes in Martinique, and the Negroes in the United States, were not directly formed by the creation or territorial expansion of a state society. These groups migrated, under vastly different conditions, into alien societies. The Negroes were torn from their homelands by force to become slaves on New World plantations, while the Jews to a greater extent "voluntarily" left their European homes to seek a life of greater freedom and economic opportunity. Obviously, however, these migrations are also intimately related to the expansionist activities of state societies. The growth of both the slave trade and the vast migrations from Europe to the New World are, in a sense, merely additional consequences of the post-feudal expansion of Europe. Similarly, the origin of the three minorities previously discussed, the Indians in Brazil and Mexico, and the French in Canada, clearly involves migrations of one sort or another as well as wars of conquest and state expansion. Without these migrations, there would be neither French nor English in Canada, and there would be neither a Portuguese-speaking majority in Brazil nor a Spanish-speaking majority in Mexico.

Although slavery is an ancient institution, found even among primitive peoples, the colossal scale on which the New World colonists and their descendants employed slave labor was quite unique. After the Europeans had decimated or driven out the scanty aboriginal populations who inhabited the southern portions of the English colonies, the Antilles, and the coast of Brazil, they found themselves in possession of great tracts of fertile virgin lands. These areas could be made to grow valuable commodities for which the European climate was unsuited; all that was needed was labor to clear the forests and do the work in the fields. Unable to call upon a dense aboriginal population, as the Spanish were able to do, the lowland planters sought to meet their labor requirements by using the population of another continent. They set up trading stations along the African coast and bartered rum, cloth, and other articles of European and American manufacture for human beings. Encouraged by the avarice of the European traders, the Africans raided deep into the continent for men, women, and children who because they belonged to stranger tribes could be delivered to the traders without qualms. There thus grew up one of the greatest forced transfers of people known in human history. How many people were killed in the African raids by which slaves were captured and how many more died while being transported across the sea under unspeakable conditions will probably never be known with any accuracy.

Among the several forms of migration responsible for the origin of many New World minorities, slavery involved the greatest amount of compulsion and brutality. But there are many other migrant groups in the New World who were to a certain extent "forced" into their trip across the sea. These migrations were prompted by a complex variety of motives; some resulted from various shades and degrees of compulsion other than the extreme represented by the slave trade. Some groups, like the Irish, migrated to escape the threat of imminent death by starvation; others, like the Huguenots and the Quakers, were forced to leave because of religious persecution. Still others, like many of the Germans, hoped for relief from political persecution. Many of the immigrants chose to become indentured laborers in the New World rather than inmates of debtors' prisons in their homelands; untold thousands were recruited by the agents of shipping companies under false pretenses; thousands of others came to avoid serving in European armies. As the economy of the United States and other New World areas shifted toward industrialism, a vast new market for wage laborers grew up, thereby providing an outlet for impoverished, landless, excess populations all over the world. Upon arrival in their new homes, the migrants assumed a variety of statuses fully as diverse as the motives which had prompted their voyages across the sea. Some, as indentured laborers and miserably paid factory workers, lived and worked under conditions not too far removed from the hardships and indignities of slavery. Others found freedom and security, as homesteaders, skilled craftsmen, and merchants. It was Europe, torn by wars, her soils depleted, and with masses of unemployed or marginal workers crowding her cities, which made the greatest contribution to the labor-hungry countries across the sea. Indeed, all of these motives, movements, and results add up to what Robert Park has called the "European diaspora," unquestionably the greatest migratory movement the world has even seen.[2]

Not all of those who took part in the European diaspora assumed a minority status. Some of the migrants were able to establish themselves as majority groups. Thus, the Portuguese became the majority in Brazil, the descendants of the Spanish became the majority in the former Spanish colonies, and the descendants of the English dominated in a large part of North America. But the diaspora spawned minorities on a lavish scale. European migrants who came later found themselves faced by an already dominant group and a developing national ideal. The United States has seen wave upon wave of latecomers such as the Swedes, Danes, Norwegians, Germans, Poles, Irish, Italians, Jews, Greeks, and many others. These peoples came "voluntarily," but, as already indicated, one must remember that emigration from Europe was generally set off by population pressures, land scarcity, glutted labor markets, or political and religious persecution. Thus, the latecomers generally arrived poverty-stricken, illiterate in the language of the new country, and, in the eyes of the people of the new country, with strange and exotic customs.

Some of these latecomers have been completely assimilated into the majority groups. A glance at the surnames in the telephone book of almost any American city will indicate the numerous people of Scandinavian, German, Irish, Italian, and other non-English origin who seem to be scattered within the population; and the incidence of Italian, German, Spanish, Polish, and central European names (President Kubitschek, for example) among "100 percent" Brazilians indicates the extent to which many of these latecomers have been assimilated in that country. Other European immigrants, however, generally but not always the latest to arrive, have persisted as self-

---

[2] "Diaspora is a Greek term for a nation or a part of a nation separated from its own state or territory and dispersed among nations but preserving its national culture." (Park, p. 103)

conscious minority groups. Thus, we still have minorities of Czechs, Poles, Irish, and Greeks in many American cities. In Brazil, the more recent Italian immigrants and the descendants of Germans, Poles, and Italians in southern Brazil remain as minority groups.

Although both the Jews in the United States and the French Canadians were part of this European diaspora, the actual genesis of each of these groups as minorities is the result also of other circumstances. The French Canadians cannot be classed as latecomers among the Europeans migrating to the New World. Rather, they were among the "Old Immigrants" and, as we have seen, their origin as a minority derives from the expansion of one European empire in America at the expense of another. The Jews on the other hand, were a minority group even before their migration from Europe to the United States. For many of the Jews, migration to the New World was a flight from mob violence and brutal forms of state-sponsored persecution. Thus, unlike most of the immigrant groups who first became minorities when they landed in the New World, the Jews had had previous adaptive experience as minorities. Somewhat similar to the Jews in this respect are the Quakers, the Huguenots, and the Gypsies, who have been forced to flee from one state to another and who find themselves minorities in one setting as well as in another. Before they arrived in the United States, the Jews, as minorities in various hostile social environments, had already developed mechanisms and symbols aimed at survival as a distinct group under adverse conditions. But they also encountered in the United States anti-Semitic attitudes and stereotypes of Jews that had developed in Europe and spread to America as part of the heritage of both the "Old" and the "New Immigrants." Just as many people today have preconceived concepts of Turks, of Armenians, of Russians, and of other peoples who have never entered into their lives, the concept of the Jew as the antichrist, the moneylender, and other unsavory stereotypes has long been part of the European tradition. This aspect of the history of the Jews as a minority group in the United States is important to understanding their present situation.

Certain generalizations have already emerged from our analysis of minority groups. First, the appearance of minority groups in the long history of human society is fairly recent and seems to date from the emergence of the state as a form of socio-political organization some five thousand years ago. Second, the origin of specific minority groups is always associated closely with the formation and expansion of state organizations or with migration from one state to another. As Louis Wirth once succinctly wrote: "The genesis of minorities must therefore be sought in the fact that territory, political authority, people, and culture only rarely coincide" (p. 365). Third, all six of the groups treated in this book ultimately trace their status as minorities back to wars of conquest or other acts of violence: the Indians of Brazil (despite the pacific efforts of the Indian Service) and the Indians of Mexico were conquered by armed force or a show of arms; the French-Canadians were incorporated into an English colony as the result of a war; the Negroes of both the French West Indies and of the United States were brought into slavery by violence and force; and the Jews, whose origin as a minority can be traced back to military defeats occurring in Palestine some two thousand years ago, fled to the United States from Europe in order to avoid violent and intimidating acts against person and property. Violence, of course, is not a universal characteristic of the origin of minority groups, for minorities have been created by peaceful migrations, by religious conversions, and even, as we know, by well-intentioned peace treaties. Yet the presence of conquest and of violence in the process of birth of minority groups frequently provides an important key to understanding intergroup hostilities. Fourth, all the minority groups studied in this book entered the new state society as low-ranking groups—as vanquished enemies, outright slaves, or penniless immigrants. Their subsequent histories have been a struggle to overcome their initial socio-economic disadvantages. It is conceivable that there might have been minority groups who began their careers at a high point in the social and economic hierarchy of the larger society but lost status to become low-ranking depressed groups. Such might be the case of the descendants of the conquerors of Asiatic states who were subsequently overthrown, and this might even occur in certain ex-colonial countries with a minority group formed by people of the former colonial power. But as one surveys the minority groups throughout the Americas, it becomes evident that by far the greater part of our minorities has originated at a lower social level than that held by most of them today. With varying intensities and types of struggle, and with varying degrees of success and hardship, they have sought to overcome the social, economic, and political disadvantages which were imposed upon them during their formative periods.

MINORITY AND MAJORITY RELATIONS

The process by which minority groups came into existence only partly explains their depressed condition and their relations with the dominant majority of their society. It is merely the starting point in their struggle for economic and social advancement and for a fair share of wealth, power, and prestige in the larger society. It is the starting point for a dynamic relationship between the minority group and the majority as well as the other minorities and subgroups within the larger social unit. By its very nature the interaction between a minority and a majority is to a greater or lesser degree competitive and marked by conflict at many points. In this conflict, the aspirations of the minority are pitted against the vested interests and the value system of the majority group. Out of this conflict there arise, on the one hand, legal, political, economic, and social mechanisms and barriers set up by the majority to maintain its position and consolidate its advantages; and on the other, various kinds of adaptive reactions on the part of the minority aimed at minimizing or overcoming its disadvantages.

Actually, in most modern state societies, the situation is far more complex. The significant relationship is not that which exists between one minority group vis-à-vis one majority group, but the competitive interaction between several different minority groups, each with its own sub-groups, and a majority, itself composed of a variety of social segments. Relations between Negro and white in the United States for example, cannot be fully understood except in terms of the added presence of Mexican, Puerto Rican and other minority groups, and of groups such as the impoverished lower class whites of the Southern United States. We hope that the reader will bear in mind that when we speak of a minority in conflict with a majority we do not mean to imply that either group is homogeneous or that together they make up the whole society.

From even a superficial inspection, it is clear that a great variety of dynamic relationships have grown up between the majorities and minorities discussed in this book. Each majority harbors its own peculiar brand of prejudices and confronts its minorities with its own forms of discrimination; and each minority reacts in its own special way, with its own forms of resistance and particular methods for overcoming the obstacles in its path. Before proceeding with an attempt further to enlarge our understanding of the similarities encountered in the case studies, our position with respect to certain other avenues of approach ought to be stated.

Attempts have frequently been made to explain minority-majority relations in terms not of historical and socio-cultural factors, but in terms of the psychology of the prejudiced individual. From a psychological point of view, one may look for the basis of prejudice, and of the more overt phenomena of discrimination, segregation, and persecution, in the personality structure of those who manifest such attitudes and behavior. It has been suggested, for example, that the strong anti-Negro sentiment of the American South is closely related to the high level of frustration pent up inside the Southern whites of the lower and middle class because of childhood repressions, poorly paid and monotonous work, unhappy marriages, and the like. This high level of frustration finds expression in the aggressive persecution of the Negro minority (Dollard, *Caste*). Likewise, the rise of anti-Semitism in Germany has been said to derive from the many frustrations that the Germans suffered from 1914 to 1933 (Dollard, *Frustration,* pp. 43–44). Others have connected hostility and prejudice toward minority groups with a particular type of "bigoted or prejudiced" personality structure. According to one study cited by Klineberg, "Ethnocentric individuals are indiscriminately antagonistic toward Jews, Negroes, and foreigners. These individuals tend to be conservative in their social and political views, and usually support the status quo" (Klineberg, *Tensions,* p. 201).

Although these and many other psychological studies of prejudice and minority-majority relations have provided valuable insights into the reasons for which prejudices and tensions between groups are established and the nature of individual motivation, they cannot be considered substitutes for an analysis made in historical, cultural, and social terms. Anti-minority prejudices may play an important role in the economy of the individual personality. An analysis of that role must, however, presuppose an understanding of the institutions which are responsible for the molding of personalities and for sanctioning and directing the expression of personality complexes in word and deed. Or, put in another way, "bigoted or prejudiced" personality types result from certain kinds of uniform experiences to which individuals are subjected in the process of growing up and living in a society. These uniform experiences are provided by the economic, political, social, familial, and religious institutions to which the members of a society are exposed, especially during childhood and adolescence. Such institutions are the result of historical and evolutionary processes which underlie the range of phenomena usually dealt with in psychological studies. One cannot explain in psychological terms why the French Canadians rather than the English Canadians are the minority group in Canada, why the Jews have not generally become farmers in the United States, or even why lynchings were more frequent at the turn of the century in the United States than they are today. Nor can we explain by psychological studies why a person who is stable and has strikingly little hostility exhibits in specific terms prejudice against the Jews when he has never in his life seen a Jew. To understand these fundamental questions regarding minority and majority relations we must turn to history and to an analysis of the basic social institutions of the societies concerned.

The comparison inherent in our case studies suggests that it is most useful to think of minority-majority relations as an ongoing social conflict. As this conflict unfolds, it traces a path or trajectory characterized by the kinds of repressive measures, by the varying degrees of overt and covert hostility, and by the relative positions in the socio-economic hierarchy of the groups concerned at successive moments through time. To arrive at an understanding of why there should be such a conflict, and why the particular expressions of intergroup hostility are similar in some respects and different in others, a number of socio-cultural factors must be considered in addition to those already discussed. These factors fall into two categories, one of which we shall call the *structural components* of minority-majority relations, and the other, the *historical-cultural components.*

By the structural components, we mean those aspects of minority-majority relations which derive from the nature of minorities and majorities as distinctive kinds of social groups. It seems to us that intergroup hostility in all of our cases rests upon certain features of these groups which are independent of time and place, but stem rather from the way in which minorities and majorities are themselves structured and how they are "built into" the societies of which they are a part.

By the historical-cultural components we mean those aspects of minority-majority relations which derive from the special historical and cultural circumstances and which provide the specific setting and the specific motives for intergroup conflict. The historical-cultural component consists of the raw materials out of which the shape and substance of the conflict is hammered; it consists of the possibilities offered by the dominant group's ideology and total socio-cultural system for deriving advantages from the presence of the minority; and it consists of the degree of culturally induced preparedness of the minority for protecting and advancing itself against the exploitation and hostility to which it may become subject.

THE STRUCTURAL COMPONENTS

In the view of many social theorists, hostility and conflict are universal aspects of intergroup relations. We are not referring here to the aggressive behavior which is to some extent a part of all normal human personalities, but rather to institutionalized and traditional forms of conflicts between groups. Between societies which are in contact with each other, some form of hostility and conflict seems inevitable. Autonomous primitive societies as well as modern state societies seem to live in constant conflict with their neighbors, although such conflict varies from outright war to relatively peaceful forms of competition. Conflict, however, also seems to be universally present within societies as well as between them. Even within primitive societies various kinds of groups such as age clusters, moieties, and clubs compete and therefore conflict with each other. Aggressive behavior in the form of intergroup conflict seems to arise from competition for scarce resources and limited valuables both within and between societies. By this we do not mean only competition for material valuables such as lands, game, mineral wealth, money, and the like, but also competition for power and prestige. Many societies may guarantee their various groups relatively equal access to material resources, but simultaneously stress competition for power or for prestige positions. This was the case of the Tapirape Indians of central Brazil, who permitted free access to individual and cooperatively planted gardens and who widely distributed the results of the hunt, but among whom competition for shamanistic power and for prestige derived from being the head of a large household caused much conflict.

It is obvious that a high degree of hostility and conflict within a society can be disruptive to the society and costly to individuals, groups, and to the society at large. We are apt, therefore, to view intergroup conflict when it occurs within a society as always pathological. But conflict may have creative or positive functions. It is often an important mechanism in provoking social and cultural changes which eventually benefit the entire society. In fact, it might almost be said that all social changes are accompanied by some degree of conflict. It must be understood, however, that we do not mean that man in society is by nature hostile and always in conflict with his fellows. Hostility and conflict are no more "normal" than are their opposites—peaceful relations, cooperation, and cohesion. If any society is to meet the minimum requirements for survival, there must be cooperation and peaceful relations between individuals and groups. Fortunately, as Robin Williams observes: "The amount of hostility [he might have added 'and conflict'] at any given time varies greatly among individuals, among specific groups, and among social systems" (p. 51). Hostility and conflict within societies and between societies are always in some form of balance with forces leading to cohesion and peaceful relations. Yet it must not be forgotten that some degree of hostility and conflict may normally be expected in intergroup relations.

These general observations apply with particular force to relations between minorities and majorities. The tendency for hostility and conflict to be present in minority-majority relations is greatly heightened by some of the distinctive features of minorities as social groups. Minorities and majorities are, as we have seen, units of a larger society whose special characteristic is some form of state apparatus. Although minorities and majorities are bound within the larger social unit by social and economic institutions as well as by political ones, it is the state organization which accounts for the appearance of these groups in human history. As we are well aware, unity of purpose and identity of interest on the part of all the multitudinous groups (such as classes and regional groups, to mention only two) of a modern state society has never been achieved. But among the great varieties of groups found in modern societies, minority groups tend to share least in the unity of purpose and identity of interest with the larger society. This is so because the relations between minority and majority and the internal structure of these groups correspond in several important respects to the relations and structures which characteristically exist between completely autonomous societies. These features are *ethnocentrism* and *endogamy*.

ETHNOCENTRISM   The belief that one's own customs, language, religion, and physical characteristics are better or more "natural" than those of others is termed ethnocentrism. These sentiments are characteristic of all autonomous human societies. As Ruth Benedict has pointed out, the very name for many primitive tribes is simply "human beings" or "men"; thus, by default, all outsiders are only quasi-human (Benedict, p. 100). At the heart of all ethnocentric concepts, whether it be that others are quasi-human or merely that their customs are ridiculous or disgusting, is the fact that such evaluations are generally subjective rather than objective. Thus, ethnocentric biases are not exact reflections of sharp differences among societies. Minor and minute cultural and physical differences may often be given exclusive attention to prove the inferiority of another people. Cases of autonomous societies whose members are not ethnocentric are hard to find; in fact, it might even be said that some degree of ethnocentrism is necessary for the survival of a society. Without a certain belief in the special fitness of its culture, a society could hardly perform the tasks necessary for survival or train the next generation in its way of life.

Although ethnocentrism is a universal feature of the relations between separate societies, it is by no means a universal feature of the relations between groups which are members of the same society. Primitive societies, as we have seen, tend to be physically and culturally homogeneous. It is only with the development of the state form of organization that it became possible for a number of groups possessing different religions, languages, and values to be bound together into a single social unit. Similarly, it is only state societies whose populations often consist of markedly contrasting racial types. Thus, with the growth of state organization, the universal tendency to regard one's own culture and racial type as superior led to the appearance of different forms of ethnocentrism within a society. Minorities and majorities as groups which are invariably associated with some measure of racial or cultural difference may just as invariably be expected to harbor some degree of ethnocentric bias. We do not mean to imply that man instinctively dislikes or fears those who are physically or culturally different from him, but merely that groups which present cultural or physical contrasts tend, as a matter of observation, to be ethnocentric. Minorities and majorities are precisely those groups within our modern societies which present the greatest amount of physical or cultural differences and are therefore most likely to harbor some form of ethnocentric bias. All majorities possess such biases in the form of the national ideals of culture and physical type which we have previously discussed. The same cannot be said of all minorities since some minorities may actually desire to rid themselves of their special cultural and physical characteristics. But a minority which is not ethnocentric will shortly be assimilated unless, as is the case of the Negroes in the United States, they are prevented from doing so by the laws and customs of the majority.

ENDOGAMY The second feature of minorities and majorities which is typical of autonomous societies is endogamy. It is closely associated with some form of intergroup conflict. This may best be explained by stating that the opposite marriage rule, namely, exogamy, is perhaps one of the oldest mechanisms for promoting friendly relations among the groups within a society. As stated earlier, among primitive peoples personal relations are maintained to a large extent through kinship or pseudo-kinship ties. Even in the simplest societies we know, such as bands of hunters and gatherers, there are rules that marriage partners must be sought outside the group. By this means, the separate bands build up a network of kinship relations and enlarge the sphere of social order. Among tribally organized societies, such widespread and important kin groups as clans are typically exogamous. The regular exchange of wives between clans and the resulting kinsmen in other clans seems to provide a basis for peaceful relations, in that one should not fight with one's mother's clan, or the clan into which one's sister married. Since among primitives marriage is usually a contract between kin groups as well as between a husband and wife, exogamous unions tend to be accompanied by a reciprocal flow of goods and services between the kin groups concerned. Exogamy is therefore a leveling influence which promotes the wider distribution of a group's wealth, prestige, and power. Thus, exogamy, either as a rule or merely as a frequent occurrence, results in the reduction of conflict between groups.

On the other hand, although endogamy has the effect of strengthening the unity and *esprit de corps* of the members of a group, it isolates them from the rest of the society. If there are inequalities between groups, such as differentials in the control of vital resources or even in the possession of honorific titles, endogamy tends to perpetuate these inequalities. Endogamy is therefore an almost certain sign of hostility and conflict between groups. As Claude Lévi-Strauss has observed: "It is only in highly stratified societies that endogamy can be expressed in a positive fashion, namely, as a calculated attempt to confine certain social or economic privileges within a group" (p. 59). Except for state or proto-state societies, this "positive" kind of endogamy never occurs within groups belonging to the same society, but only at the boundary between separate societies.

Endogamy is one of the most distinctive characteristics of minority groups. It must be remembered however, that as a norm or rule it may arise from different sources and have different functions. Endogamy may be a rule or norm of the minority group itself, as is clearly the situation among the French Canadians and the Jews in the United States. Although there are some barriers to intermarriage presented by the dominant groups in Canada and the United States, these two minorities themselves have traditionally presented their own resistance to intermarriage. In both of these cases the minorities have strong, overt pluralistic aims. On the other hand, endogamy among both the Negroes of the United States and the people of color in the French West Indies serves a different social function and arises from another source. In both instances, endogamy is mainly imposed upon the minority by the dominant group. Among the Negroes in the United States there does seem to be growing resistance to intermarriage with whites, but this is certainly a reaction to the intense prohibition against intermarriage—which is legally sanctioned in many parts of the country. In the French West Indies, intermarriage between people of color and whites has been much more frequent than in the United States, but the elite white group has consistently imposed strong rules against it. In these two instances, endogamy serves not to strengthen and consolidate the respective minorities but rather to maintain them in their low social and economic status. Among the Indian groups of Mexico and Brazil, endogamy seems to be a result of rules which are maintained by both the minority and the majority and which have the double function of maintaining the solidarity of the Indian communities and of perpetuating their low status. There is much less uniformity among these two groups than is the case with the others, since some of the Indian communities, especially in Brazil, tend to develop assimilationist objectives after they are "pacified."

In speaking of endogamy, we must bear in mind the distinction between marriage and mating. While all the minorities studied in this book are endogamous either as a result of their own norms or of norms imposed upon them by their respective dominant groups, a large amount of intermating has gone on between some of them and their respective majorities. The Indians of Brazil and of Mexico and the people of color in Martinique and the Negroes of the United States have frequently mated with outsiders in the form of illicit unions or concubinage. These extramarital or "nonmarital" relations have produced a great deal of race mixture in all the societies concerned, but with different consequences in some of them. In Brazil and Mexico the descendants of mixed matings have entered the ranks of the majority, especially of the lower class, on a large scale; but in the United States, and to a lesser extent in Martinique the descendants of mixed matings have been confined by law or custom to the ranks of the minority.

Whatever the source of the rule of endogamy, or whatever specific functions it may serve, it is obviously a key process in minority-majority relations. A high rate of intermarriage between a minority and the dominant group would rapidly wipe out any distinctive cultural or physical differences that set them off from one another. In fact, there would shortly be no minority group. Only the imposition of a special rule of descent might prevent the disintegrating effects of a high frequency of "mixed" marriages. Thus, some minority groups attempt to preserve themselves, in cases of marriage with an outsider, by either obliging or urging the "outlander" spouse to affiliate himself with the group and by raising the offspring as group members. On the other hand, some dominant groups not only impose endogamy on a minority but also make the offspring of any mixed marriages minority members, as in the case of the offspring of mixed Negro-white marriages in the United States who are considered Negroes. Sometimes— as in Brazil and in Mexico—there is a special rule of descent that acts to create and enlarge an intermediate group such as the Mexican mestizos and the Brazilian *caboclos*.

The two structural features of minority-majority relations, "intra-societal" ethnocentrism and endogamy, are basic to the understanding of intergroup hostility in any minority situation. Yet a high degree of ethnocentrism in both the minority and majority groups and a rigid rule of endogamy do not themselves produce hostility and conflict in minority-majority relations. These features are functionally related to conflict, but are not the cause of conflict. Theoretically at least, one might postulate that a highly ethnocentric minority and majority, following a strict rule of endogamy might live together in harmony; but in fact this seldom occurs.[3] The presence of some degree of conflict in minority and majority relations seems to be guaranteed by the fact that such groups are generally in competition for what we shall call the resources and the limited valuables of the larger society of which they are a part. These objects of competition between a minority and the majority (or other minorities) may range from such vital resources as land and employment to political power and educational opportunity—or merely to prestige symbols, such as membership in clubs and honorific titles. It is important to know the objects of competition, for it would seem that the more vital or valuable the resource over which there is competition, the more intense is the conflict between the groups. In other words, competition for land or for employment should produce more intense conflict than competition for prestige symbols. Yet one must also consider the terms of competition—i.e., whether or not a minority has the instruments and the opportunity to compete with the majority in the same arena. A dominant group may by superior force of arms prevent any competition on the part of a minority for the most vital resources; this results

[3] E. J. Lindgren reports that two groups in western Manchuria—the Tungus (a nomadic group) and a group of farming Cossacks—lived in essentially peaceful and harmonious relations despite the fact that they were endogamous and ethnocentric. There was, it seems, a mutual economic dependence upon one another, without competition between the groups for land and resources. (pp. 605–21)

in at least overt peace. But a minority well-organized and vested with some legal rights is able to compete aggressively, and conflict between the groups will be intense and overt. Thus, both the objects of competition and the conditions of competition are important factors in determining the overt intensity of minority-majority conflict at any given time.

THE HISTORICAL–CULTURAL COMPONENTS

The terms and conditions of competition between a minority and a majority constitute the historical-cultural components of minority-majority relations. The structural features we have been discussing provide an adequate explanation of why all the minority situations studied in this book evidence some form of intergroup hostility. But they do not explain the specific differences and similarities among our cases. We hope by a comparison of the historical-cultural components to be able to shed some light on this aspect of minority-majority relations.

For convenience, we shall treat the historical-cultural components as if they consisted of two sets of conditions. The first is what we shall call the *adaptive capacity* of the minority—i.e., those elements of a minority's cultural heritage which provide it with a basis for competing more or less effectively with the dominant group, which afford protection against exploitation, which stimulate or retard its adaptation to the total social environment, and which facilitate or hinder its upward advance through the socio-economic hierarchy. The second is what we shall call the *arena of competition*—i.e., the resources and valuables for which the minority and majority compete, the advantages which the majority seeks to derive from the presence of the minority and the perpetuation of its subordinate status, the general opportunities or barriers to upward mobility inherent in the larger society's economy, social organization, and ideological setting. We are aware however, that the separation of these two aspects of the historical-cultural relations between minority and majority is somewhat artificial. It is clear that one cannot speak of the adaptive capacity of a minority group unless the conditions to which it must adapt are specified. On the other hand, the arena of competition is at least partially determined by the opportunities contingent upon the presence of the minority. The two sets of conditions are part of an intricate developmental process resulting partially at least from the interaction of the minority with the majority. Nonetheless, for the purposes of analysis, it is necessary that we break the continuity of the process at some convenient point in order to establish hypotheses about the nature of the actions and reactions which are involved. Let us turn first to an examination of the different adaptive capacities of the six minority groups studied in this book.

THE ADAPTIVE CAPACITY OF THE MINORITY We have seen that all the minorities discussed in this book began their careers as low-ranking groups—either as vanquished enemies, as outright slaves, or as poor immigrants. Their histories since the moment of their incorporation into the larger societies to which they now belong conform to a common pattern in so far as they all have attempted to improve their social and economic standing or at least to avoid the worst aspects of their minority status. It is clear that all six of our cases owe their present subordinate positions at least in part to competitive disadvantages stemming from their own cultural traditions and from other characteristics of their ways of life at the moment they were incorporated into their respective state societies. It is also clear that each of the groups studied owes its respective status at successive intervals throughout its career in part to its differential ability to defend itself and to achieve its own betterment. In new social settings, each of the minorities has had to discard some of its old cultural equipment in favor of adaptive patterns better suited to the new life it has had to lead. In the absence of these cultural changes, some of the minorities studied in this book suffer from disabilities which are an integral part of their own cultural traditions. Let us look at our cases from this point of view.

Of all the groups studied, the Brazilian Indian minorities began their career especially handicapped by their own cultural heritage. Their culture prior to minority status contained no knowledge of writing, metal tools, money, markets, domesticated animals (except perhaps dogs), plows, wheeled vehicles, guns, law courts, jails, cities, and numerous other elements of European civilization with which they were suddenly faced. They had no previous experience which would tell them what it meant to "buy and sell," to honor a peace treaty, to hold titles for lands, or to honor formal and written codes of law. Furthermore, there was a wide gap between their kinship type of social organization and the politically organized national state of Brazil. It is obvious why minority status has so often been disastrous to these primitive groups. They have little or no basis in their cultural heritage for adaptation to the new social environment. This initial disadvantage was well illustrated by the Tapirape Indian who in 1957 had learned to request "money" for his products but who accepted twenty *cruzeiro* notes as easily as he did fifty *cruzeiro* notes. The reluctance of the Kaingang to change their marriage rules in the face of severe depopulation well illustrates how the barriers to successful adaptation may originate in the cultural traditions of the minority rather than those of the majority.

Among the Indian tribes of Brazil, as long as they were aware of only a fragment of the dynamic civilization surrounding them, ethnocentrism remained strong and served to unite the tribe against encroachers. But, as the example of the Kaingang tribe illustrates, as such groups came to realize the infinite material and numerical superiority of the surrounding civilization, they often suffered a "shock" —a loss of the security provided by their tribal ethnocentrism. The result is often an attitude of deprecation of their own way of life and an eagerness to adopt the culture of the dominant group. It is strange that such groups did not become acculturated or totally assimilated more rapidly. The fact that they have not can only be explained in terms of the barriers presented by the highly ethnocentric Brazilian frontiersmen with whom they are in contact and the tremendous gap between their primitive cultures and modern Brazilian civilization.

Other primitive societies have been more malleable to incorporation into state societies and to contact with complex cultures. In *New Lives for Old* (1956), Margaret Mead tells the story of the remarkably drastic but successful adaptation which the Manus of the

Admiralty Islands in the Pacific achieved in a relatively short period, under the impact of troops stationed in the area during the Second World War. Other instances might be cited but, on the whole, groups who are heirs to such primitive cultural systems enter into minority status with great disadvantages, and the result is often as disastrous as it has been to the Brazilian Indians.

The cultural equipment of the Indians of Mexico at the time of their conquest provided a much more satisfactory basis for adaptive response to their minority status. Although there were marked differences between Aztec civilization (as an example from aboriginal Mexico) and Spanish civilization of the sixteenth century, many students have pointed out the analogies and structural similarities between the two civilizations. Like the Europeans, the Aztecs had a knowledge of metallurgy, masonry construction, calendric systems, money (or at least units of value), markets, and a primitive form of writing. Furthermore, both societies had social and economic classes, both emphasized the local community as a landholding unit (the Aztec *calpulli* and the Spanish *cabildo*), both had state religions administered by a priesthood and a formal system of education, as well as other parallel and analogous institutions. Despite the linguistic differences and the differences in the content of their cultures, there was a basis of understanding between the Mexicans and their conquerors. But the absence of the horse, gunpowder, iron tools, and wheeled vehicles cost the Mexican civilizations dearly in their struggle with the conquistadors. The subsequent destruction of the native priesthood in turn put an abrupt end to much native art, architecture, and science. The deposition of the native governing elite meant a loss of the traditions associated with government on a state level. Yet for the people of the countryside, in their freshly created Spanish-type villages, it was not difficult to become peasants in the new society. In the village and in the family much of the aboriginal culture survived; aboriginal gardening techniques, crops, and foods, in addition to European crops and foods, provided an adequate basis of subsistence. The landholding Spanish-Indian community came to be the basic social unit and a new Spanish-Indian culture took form as an adaptive result of the colonial situation. Superimposed, so to speak, upon these localized community societies were the successive colonial and republican governments of Mexico. Unlike the Brazilian Indian groups, the Indian communities of Mexico were able successfully to adapt to the initial period of their minority status.

Yet, with the formation of modern Mexico, the adaptation of the Indian communities to the colonial situation has become increasingly difficult to reconcile with the emergent national ideals. It is true that most of the descendants of the colonial Indian population have become indistinguishably merged within the large Mexican rural lower class. But many of the remaining Indian groups now show a lack of adaptability to modern conditions. These groups are in a sense imposing hardships upon themselves by insisting on their isolation and by resisting the introduction of schools, modern hygiene, and progressive forms of agriculture. In Mexico, as in Brazil, the state, and to a large extent the majority group which controls the state, is actually striving to remove barriers to upward mobility against the resistance of the Indians themselves. We have seen the tenacity with which the remaining Mexican Indian communities have clung to their minority cultures. The most benevolent governmental programs have sometimes been thwarted by the Indians themselves in their resistance to cultural changes which would do away with their minority disabilities. Perhaps because there was initially much less of a contrast between the level of their civilization and that of the Spanish, the Indians of Mexico have preserved strong ethnocentric attitudes down through the centuries. As long as their community organization continues to function, they have faith in the superiority of their own way of life, despite the obvious technological superiority and greater power of the Mexicans. In the security of their ethnocentrism they resist change and assimilation. Their ethnocentrism, however, largely revolves around the ways and traditions of their own isolated communities, and thus, instead of helping them to resist the attempt of the larger society to exploit them it reduces their opportunities for united action.

Both the minority groups of African origin studied in this book emerged from slave status with little of their original African heritage left intact. The very great cultural endowments of the West African kingdoms were largely obliterated by the crushing experience of slavery. It might be argued that the individual African transferred to the New World had a basis in his own cultural traditions for the understanding of markets, money, politically organized societies, courts, and even slavery itself. All of these elements in one form or another were found in West African culture. But the cultural elements of African origin which survived in the New World during slavery and afterwards, such as African dances, music, and folklore, as well as African religious cults, did not influence the course of events in any substantial way or determine the relations between Negroes and whites. Instead, as stated above, it was the institution of slavery that was crucial in determining these relations. One might even say that the Negroes began their minority-group career throughout the Americas equipped with only a "slave culture." When Negroes finally did emerge from slave status in both the French West Indies and the United States, this "slave culture" provided them with little preparation for engaging in the competitive struggle demanded by the free-market economic system. As slaves on the sugar plantations of the French West Indies or on the cotton plantations of the southern United States, most Negroes had no experience at all with commercial, professional, and skilled industrial occupations. The one-crop plantation systems had not prepared them to be successful farmers. They had little or no experience in political affairs, and they were mainly illiterate. They were thus unable to cope with this new social environment. In both the French West Indies and the United States (and in other American nations), the Negro groups went from slavery to the status of impoverished, debt-ridden agricultural wage earners, peasants, and share-croppers. The "culture of slavery" prepared them to enter national life only as humble laborers or servants at the bottom of the social hierarchy.

With but few living traditions of their own, both of these minorities came to accept the values and the culture of the dominant groups—even to the point of placing a greater aesthetic value on Caucasoid physical features among themselves. It is only since emancipation that these groups have begun to acquire a set of symbols and traditions around which ethnocentric sentiments have begun to form. The weak ethnocentrism characteristic of Negroes in the United States and to a lesser extent of the Negroes in Martinique has proved a considerable handicap in the attempt of these groups to find social justice. Without a common rallying point, except their color (about which they have tended to have mixed feelings if not open regret), they have found it difficult to unite their members against exploitation by the larger society.

The two minorities of European descent among our case studies, the French Canadians and the Jews in the United States, began their careers on a much better adaptive footing than the groups of American Indian or African origin. Their essentially European cultural traditions provided them with a basis for understanding their new social environment. Furthermore, among the Jews in the United States, a high degree of ethnocentrism is part of the apparatus developed over centuries of minority status to insure group survival. For both the French Canadians and the Jews, ethnocentrism has provided a basis for unity of action in their struggle with the dominant group, and it has been an important contributing factor to their relatively favorable status in their respective state societies.

The French Canadians successfully transplanted much of their European tradition of farming combined with animal husbandry to the New World. They also continued the European tradition of trading and engaging in small-scale entrepreneurial activities. Although their language differed from that of their conquerors, it was the vernacular of statesmen, philosophers, and scientists, and it had a great literary history. Although illiteracy ran high among the rural masses, a tradition of superior, if somewhat scholastic and theological, education was kept alive and even made to flourish by the Catholic Church. The presence of the organized Roman Catholic Church in the culture of the French Canadians has contributed greatly to their adaptive potential. All observers of the French-Canadian communities have stressed that the leadership of the *curé,* especially in earlier days, played an important role in maintaining the group's feeling of solidarity. Through its control over education, the Church has strongly defended the minority language and culture and has nurtured and stimulated French-Canadian leadership. Unlike the situation in Mexico where the Church was a powerful factor in the acculturation and subordination of the Indian (although it often acted to protect the Indians against the colonists), the Church in French Canada has provided form, substance, and coordination to the French-Canadian struggle for equality.

Of all the minorities studied in this book, the Jews in the United States seem to have begun their new life with a minimum number of handicaps deriving from their previous culture. It is true that they arrived in America with a linguistic handicap; and many of their customs associated with their religion, such as the dietary rules and the Orthodox Sabbath, were both strange to the dominant majority and ill-adapted to the American scene. Yet, as emphasized earlier, their cultural heritage contained patterns specifically adapted to centuries of minority status. Prohibited to engage in agriculture and even to own land in many European nations in which they had lived, they had already found a position in European society as traders, independent artisans, and moneylenders. Even when they lived in rural zones, they followed essentially urban occupations. They were thus comparatively well-equipped by tradition to make their way in the rapidly growing urban centers of the United States. This is especially striking in view of the fact that a large proportion of the immigrants from Europe came with essentially peasant and rural traditions (see Handlin, *Uprooted,* pp. 7 ff.). In fact, what had limited their participation in economic life in Europe became advantageous to them in the New World. As one writer has put it: "It may sound paradoxical, but it is nevertheless correct to say that the occupational structure of the whole modern world is moving in the direction of Jewish occupational structure, i.e., in the direction of urbanization and professionalization and not in the direction of agrarianization and industrial proletarianization."

Furthermore, the Jews who came to the United States, like the

French Canadians, had the advantage of possessing an ancient religious tradition with its priesthood and church organization. It is true, as we have seen in our description of the Jews as a minority group in the United States, that Judaism is not organized in the monolithic fashion of the Catholic Church and that there were schisms deriving both from the Old World and from their experience in America. Yet the various religious groupings of Jews in America, with their leaders, have contributed to efficient programs of social welfare and to the support of organizations devoted to securing equal opportunity for minority groups. Out of the ideology of Judaism as a religion were derived values that aided the Jews in their adaptation to American life. The great stress placed upon the value of learning, on the role of the scholar, and upon literacy stimulated many Jews in America to seek the advantages of higher education, often in face of great hardship. Compared to other minorities, the Jews seemed to have some advantage by virtue of their European experience and cultural traditions, yet one must not lose sight of the fact that the overwhelming mass of Jewish immigrants also suffered many grave disabilities, including culturally derived anti-Semitism, which had preceded most of them to America.

From our brief analysis of the previous cultural heritages, and the degree of adaptability to the new social scene, of the six minority groups under scrutiny, it seems fairly obvious that many of the factors determining a minority group's status derive from its cultural preparedness. In fact, one might be tempted to state the general proposition that minority groups with the greater measure of cultural preparedness have been the ones least subject to extreme forms of hostility and exploitation. This would certainly seem to hold true when one contrasts the relatively high socio-economic status of the two European minority groups with the relatively low socio-economic status of those of American Indian and African origin. But it must be remembered that the minority's adaptive capacity is only one of the historical-cultural factors influencing the trajectory of minority-majority relations. As we all know, the excellent adaptation of the Jews in Germany was of small consequence when Adolf Hitler assumed control of the German state. It is obvious that there are many historical-cultural conditions which influence a minority's fate but for which it can have no remedy. A large part of these additional historical-cultural conditions are supplied by the culture patterns and institutions of the society into which the minority has been incorporated. Let us turn next to an examination of some of these conditions as they relate to the sources and mechanisms of conflict between minority and majority.

THE ARENA OF COMPETITION   We cannot describe in any detail the cultures of the complex societies into which our six minority groups have been incorporated. Such a task would take many years of study and far more space than is available in this book. It would involve an analysis of the various dominant social, economic, political, and religious institutions of the six state societies in question not only at the time each minority was incorporated, but also throughout its development under the impact of technological change, wars, revolutions, and global trends. To a large extent these institutions and their historical development, in interaction with the adaptive capacity of the minorities, furnish the sources of conflict and motivations which animate a majority group in its relations with a minority; they also provide the mechanism for translating motive into result. The total socio-cultural system at any moment in time determines whether the minority will be crushed and exploited, left alone to pursue its own course, or helped in its attempt to advance upwards through the social hierarchy. Despite the vast network of institutionalized motivations suggested even in the brevity of our case studies, certain general aspects of the respective arenas of conflict seem to be fairly clear.

The principal source of conflict between the Brazilian Indian tribes and Brazilians seems generally to have been land. After the sixteenth century, the Indians of Brazil no longer provided a source of cheap labor; they were too few in number and did not adapt well to plantation life. The plantation owners turned, therefore, to African slaves for labor. Those tribal groups which survived decimation from disease and wars, had no point of conflict as long as they remained isolated.

From time to time as Brazil has expanded toward the interior, the Indian tribes have again become barriers to occupation of the land. This was true, as we have seen, of the Kaingang tribe, which occupied the potentially rich coffee lands of São Paulo; and this is true of some of the remaining tribes of central Brazil. The clashes between rubber gatherers in the Amazon Valley, in which both Indians and Brazilians were killed, arose from a question of occupancy of the land. And there were massacres of Indian groups in northeastern Brazil not many years ago because the Indians, almost starved for lack of game, were forced to steal cattle. Although there have been armed clashes between frontiersmen and Indian groups, the degree of hostility and conflict between the Indians and Brazilians in modern times has not been intense. This is surely related to the fact that the remaining Indian groups no longer occupy lands which are considered to be of immediate commercial value. Brazil is an enormous country and occupation of the vast interior has been slow. Although the Indian Service is to some extent able to control conflicts when they arise, it is probably the isolation of the remaining Indian groups which above all accounts for their relative security at the moment. It must also be remembered that the vast gulf in technology and social organization between the Indian tribal groups and modern Brazilians has meant that the Indians have lacked the instruments and training for competition with Brazilians in the major sectors of the society's economy. Thus the relatively poor adaptive capacity of the tribal groups alternately exposes them to and protects them from the worst forms of conflict and hostility.

In Mexico, conflict between the Indian minorities and the dominant group has also centered upon land occupancy, but more important has been the labor demand made upon the Indians. The Indian communities have attempted to maintain their communal lands against the encroaching haciendas; this was an important point of conflict between the two groups. But of greater significance was the fact that the large Indian population of Mexico was, in the past, perhaps the greatest "natural resource" of the country, and many of the laws and administrative procedures of colonial times and of the early Republic were aimed at securing the labor of the Indians. In addition, the pressure to break down Indian community landholdings seems often to have been a way of creating a labor supply. By depriving the Indians of their basis of subsistence, they were forced to seek a livelihood as wage earners on haciendas and in factories. But mainly since 1910, a non-Indian peasantry has become more numerous than the Indian groups and they now satisfy the labor requirements of many regions of the country. Thus, the need for labor, which was once the most important source of conflict between Indians and non-Indians, now provokes a similar conflict between socio-economic classes. Only when the Indian no longer provided the main source of labor supply did the highly idealistic and energetic programs and policies of the *Indígenistas* gain real support. Even today in regions such as Chiapas, which has a large Indian population and where the coffee *fincas* still depend upon Indians to a large extent for labor, is the conflict between Indian groups and non-Indians intense. Although there have been strong individual efforts and even laws in favor of the Indians since the sixteenth century, only since the agrarian revolution of 1910 have Mexican Indian communities been equipped with instruments and means for competition, in the form of laws and various governmental agencies which can protect their interests and furnish them with some educational facilities.

In the French West Indies, the source of conflict between the slaves and the masters was originally slavery itself. To a certain extent, the conditions of employment and rights to participate more fully in the economic system continues to be the main point of conflict between the white elite and the descendants of slaves. Following abolition, the endogamous white elite maintained a virtual monopoly over land and commercial life. It was able to exploit the labor of the ex-slaves cheaply. But by the time of abolition, as we have seen, a "mixed" group of mulattoes had already emerged to occupy the economic and social area between the Negroes and whites. Repressive measures were for a time established to prevent the economic competition of this intermediate group. But as that group grew in numbers and as its members acquired legal rights, they were able to

compete with the white elite for land, for participation in new occupations, for educational facilities, and for political power. Thus, the
sector of most intense hostility in the French West Indies is not between the very depressed Negro peasants or plantation laborers and
the white elite, but between this middle group and the whites. The
depressed peasants and plantation laborers are without any means or
instruments of competition with the white elite. It is only between the
highest levels of the socio-economic hierarchy and the intermediate
group—between the white elite and the "people of color"—that a
sharp break occurs, and that overt but relatively mild forms of racial
discrimination are encountered. As in Mexico a relatively numerous,
racially mixed, socio-economic middle group has been able to instigate a series of policies designed to overcome the handicaps which
the mass of people of the French West Indies inherited from slavery.

The centers of conflict between Negroes and whites in the United
States are more difficult to isolate, precisely because the Negroes
now compete with the whites on many different fronts and because
the Negroes are now armed with so many instruments and means of
competition. The situation has been further complicated by the presence in the United States of a great mass of European immigrants
who themselves were competing for economic improvement and who
occupied the middle positions which in Mexico and the French West
Indies were occupied by indigenous and racially mixed populations.
Certainly, during slavery it was the labor of the Negro which was the
point of conflict. And there is ample evidence to say that, even today,
the heart of Negro and white conflict is the effort to exclude the
Negro from full and equal participation in the American economy.

In the United States, discrimination and repression followed a
trajectory which sharply diverged from that just described for the
other three non-European minorities. It was only after the Negro in
the United States ceased to be used in a regimen of forced labor that
the highest point in majority hostility and brutality was reached. And
unlike the other three groups, the Negro in the United States is still
the object of numerous severe discriminatory practices.

In the United States, abolition occurred at a lucrative phase in the plantation system. Due to the expansion of the textile industry, cotton had replaced sugar as the world's richest crop. Abolition was accomplished by means of a violent war which shattered the economy and social order of the South. Unlike the minorities of Martinique and Mexico, the Negroes in the United States had passed through no gradual transition from slave to free labor. Above all, there had been no gradual filling of the social space between the slave group and the white elite by an intermediate half-caste group as had occurred in Mexico, Martinique, Brazil, and many other parts of the New World. This position was occupied instead by a large white mass whose ranks were rapidly expanding as a result of immigration. The whites, themselves engaged in an intense struggle to achieve middle-class standing, closed ranks and formed a solid phalanx against the sudden deluge of millions of ex-slaves upon the free labor market. In the prolonged "race riot" which ensued the whites emerged victorious, and by the beginning of the century had established "Jim Crow" on a legal basis. In recent years, progress has once again been made toward the destruction of some of the many barriers which were thrown up around the Negro in the United States to nullify his competitive ability in relation to the European groups. But the obstacles with which the Negro in the United States is daily confronted are among the harshest to be found anywhere in the New World.

Paradoxically, the Negro in the United States also enjoys the highest standards of health and material consumption of any Negro group in the world today. This fact throws additional light on the extreme measures employed by the majority in the United States to keep the Negro "in his place." In our other non-European cases, the relatively slow rate of economic development in post-slavery times is associated with an agrarian economy, a low rate of social mobility, and a stunted middle class. Under these circumstances, the continued subordination of the ex-slave groups has been achieved as a natural consequence of a stagnant social order. With competition for status kept to a minimum by the lack of economic opportunity, little in the way of special repressive measures are necessary in order to maintain the minority-majority status quo. In the United States, on the

other hand, the post-slavery period coincides with a period of explosive economic developments. Indeed, the Civil War which freed
the slaves also greatly stimulated the growth of Northern industry.
The middle class in the United States has expanded to unprecedented
proportions; and the entire social order is still characterized by a
degree of social mobility unusual in the history of the world.

As we have already indicated, the two minorities of European
descent—the French Canadians and the Jews in the United States—
have been able to avoid the most extreme forms of repression and
exploitation. We can say this with some confidence because of the
simple fact that neither of the two European groups were used to
furnish slave or semi-slave labor. A vast gulf separates the treatment
of the French Canadians and the Jews from the appalling restrictions
of life and liberty that were the daily routines of slavery and peonage.
It is clear that in the case of these European groups, the respective
majorities lacked the power, the institutional motivations, and the
economic opportunities for using either of them as slaves or as other
kinds of forced laborers. Moreover, the lands of the French Canadians at the time of their conquest by the English were unsuited for
the plantation crops which elsewhere provided the motivation for
severe forms of conflict. For a number of years, the economy of the
New World required both free and slave labor. In the Jewish case, as
for all other New World minority groups which owe their origin to
voluntary migration, it was precisely the promise of greater economic
freedom and civil liberties which induced their migration. Without
such an inducement they would scarcely have bothered to migrate to
the New World. The sources of conflict between Jews and "native"
Americans, and between the French and English Canadians, have
therefore never been as critical for life and dignity as they have for
the other minority groups studied in this book. For the Jews or for
the French Canadians the issue has never been whether they would be
allowed to work as free men rather than as slaves or peons, but rather
whether they would be allowed to enter certain occupations, professions, and commercial areas. Neither has the issue been, for these
two minority groups, whether they be deprived of their lands and

isolated on an Indian reservation or be forced into debt peonage. Nor has it been their experience that they are crowded into Harlems and forbidden equal use of public transportation. Their right to send their children to existing public schools has not been disputed. Instead, the Jews in the United States have disputed the right to enter universities on an equal basis, and the French Canadians have struggled to maintain their right to their own educational system.

Nevertheless, the relatively successful adaptations of the French Canadians and the Jews in the United States were achieved only after they had passed through periods of more severe and more overt forms of conflict. The period of greatest conflict between English and French Canadians was the first half of the nineteenth century, during which there was an actual French Canadian rebellion and even an attempt on their part to secure annexation by the United States. By 1867, when Canada became a Dominion, the peak of conflict had passed. Uniquely among our cases, both the minority and the dominant group had, in a sense, won out. The French Canadians gained in the new constitution considerable provincial autonomy and formal recognition of the bilingual and bicultural composition of Canadian society.

The high point of conflict between the Jews and the dominant group in the United States came only after the mass of immigrants who arrived between 1880 and 1914 had begun to climb toward middle-class standing. To a greater extent than even the French Canadians, the Jews have been successful in raising their socio-economic status. Aided by their own prior adaptation to the urbanism of the United States, and by a phenomenal growth in the sectors of the American economy and social system for which they were well equipped, the Jewish group has been able to flourish and prosper despite a consistent undercurrent of hostility and resentment among both the "Old" and "New Immigrants." It should not be taken for granted, however, that the present position of the Jews in the United States represents a secure or stable adjustment. During a period of economic expansion, the middle-class position of a minority can be of considerable use in controlling and deflecting the hostility directed against its members. During a political or economic crisis however, such a position in the social hierarchy may actually increase the danger to the lives and welfare of the entire minority group. Despite (or even because of) their middle-class affiliation in Germany, the Nazis found the Jews to be convenient scapegoats for the seething discontent of the German masses. With the democratic basis of German society destroyed, and with all power concentrated in the hands of a rabid anti-Semite, the Jews derived no advantages from their relatively high position within the old socio-economic hierarchy. Perhaps it is for this reason that the Jews in the United States, despite their current relative material prosperity and their civil and political freedoms, tend to feel insecure and to be extremely sensitive to even purely verbal expressions of hostility.

THE IDEOLOGICAL SETTING   All of the American republics and the nations with territories within the New World share what has been called a "creed" of equality of access to justice, freedom, and opportunity for all people.[4] These creeds are often written into our constitutions and embodied in our laws, and they are manifest in a complex of national traditions and cultural values. Yet in all of the nations these creeds are contradicted by at least a portion of the population in word and deed, and in some nations they are contradicted by law and by official policy. In fact, the majority in a nation cannot fully hold to a national creed of full opportunity for a minority without some degree of ambivalence, for such a policy works directly against the material and nonmaterial advantages accruing from the majority's superordinate status. Only those nations which would frankly advocate in their national creeds the exclusion, the outright continued subjugation, or the extermination of minorities escape this dilemma. This is not so of any nation in the Americas. Thus, all of the minorities discussed in this book share, in a greater or lesser degree, a

[4] "Viewed sociologically," states Merton in regard to the United States, "the creed is a set of values in American culture, to which Americans are expected to conform. It is a complex of affirmations, rooted in the historical past and ceremonially celebrated in the present, partly enacted in laws of the land and partly not. Like all creeds it is a profession of faith, a part of a cultural tradition sanctified by the larger traditions of which it is a part." (p. 99)

similar dilemma to that which Gunnar Myrdal called the "American dilemma" in his monumental study of the Negro in the United States.

The "creeds of equality," if we may call these official policies and traditional values by this term, have taken form at different times in the various American states discussed in this book. These creeds have changed over time not only in content but also in degree of application to a particular minority. Such changes in the creed are the result of changes in the total socio-cultural system of a nation, but it must also be said that the creed may dynamically promote changes in the socio-cultural system. The effect of the creed upon the socio-cultural system may be seen in the influence upon our society of the process of desegregation of schools as the result of the decisions by the United States Supreme Court. From a comparative point of view and in the perspective of time, it would seem that the width of the gap between the national creed and the reality of conduct reflects the intensity of conflict between a minority and the majority at any given time and at any given place. Since a creed of equality is so much a part of the ideology of all American democracies, it is important that we examine briefly the relationship between creed and conduct as it effects the minorities studied in this book.

Brazil is known throughout the world for its insistence upon racial equality. Brazilians have made this creed a point of national pride and a symbol in art, literature, and popular thought. It is embodied in Brazilian laws. This creed has in theory been applied to the Indians as far back as the colonial period when the Portuguese Crown urged marriages with native women. But this Brazilian creed has not, either in the past or in the present, been extended to the frontiers where there has been face-to-face contact and competition for land between Indians and Brazilians. On the frontiers, in the past and now, the Indians have been despised for their miserable standard of living and their strange and "repulsive" customs. This has provided justification for evasion of the national creed—for acts of violence against Indians and even extermination of whole groups. Yet, equally, it is the Brazilian creed that provides the basis for the idealistic policies and efforts of the Brazilian Indian Service.

In Mexico there has been a creed of equality for the Indians since the days of padres Vasco de Quiroga and Bartolomeu de las Casas, who spoke strongly in favor of the rights of the Indians. But as long as the Indian provided the largest reservoir of labor, the gap between the creed and the reality of conduct was great. Evasion of the creed took the form of "protective laws" and of outright exploitation which ignored the law. However, especially since the revolution of 1910, the Mexican creed of equality has been applied with increasing vigor. The Indian past of Mexico has become a national symbol as a reaction against the foreign orientation of the old ruling class. But, as we have indicated earlier, by this time it was the mestizos, and not the Indians, who were the largest labor force in the country. Yet even today the Mexican creed is evaded in those regions of the country where Indians are most numerous and are depended upon for their labor. In such regions, the dominant group disagrees with the Mexican creed and finds justification again in the old stereotypes of the Indian as an uncouth savage. The dynamic force of the creed to promote change is felt in these same regions of Mexico in the idealistic programs of the National Indian Institute.

During the early colonial period in the French West Indies, the Negro slaves were brought into the Catholic Church. There was an obvious contradiction between the status of being a Christian and a slave, for the Church insists that all men are equal in the sight of God. But this did not seem to pose any great moral problem for the planters, who were enriched by the sale of sugar. There was an attempt to give the slave legal protection (beginning with the Code Noir of 1685) but these same laws gave legal sanction to sometimes brutal repression of slaves. It was not until the idealistic concepts of the French Revolution reached the West Indies that the French creed of equality took explicit form and the "French dilemma" came into focus. The continuation of slavery and the legal limitation of the participation of the free *mulâtre* class in colonial society were obvious evasions of the creed of *liberté, égalité, fraternité*. Gradually, as the arena of competition changed—as sugar became less lucrative, as the planters came to be dependent upon free wage labor, and as the people of color became more numerous and powerful—the gap between the French creed and practice has been narrowed. Slavery was abolished peacefully and all legal restrictions on people of color were removed. Only local color prejudice, the distance of the islands from metropolitan France, and poor economic resources remain today as barriers which prevent the people of color of the French West Indies from participating fully as citizens in French society.

The Canadian creed was clearly manifest in the official organization of the Canadian state, which is bilingual and bicultural. Canadians are proud of this creed of linguistic, religious, and cultural tolerance; as one English Canadian expressed it, "a sense of common Canadianism does not depend for its strength on a concept of national uniformity." Yet, as we have seen in our discussion of the French Canadians, this Canadian creed has often been in the past, and to some degree still is, contradicted by both English and French Canadians. Especially outside the French-Canadian homeland of Quebec, people have suffered economically and socially because they speak French—one of Canada's official languages. English Canadians have in the past considered the French-Canadian tradition as a drag upon the development of the nation. Contrary to the official creed, they have urged assimilation of French Canadians. At times of crisis, such as the period during the two world wars, linguistic and cultural differences provoked overt hostility between the two groups. Furthermore, the evasion of the Canadian creed has not been entirely one-sided; many French Canadians have looked down upon *les anglais* as cultural barbarians and as people of divided loyalties. In recent years there seems to be a spirit of *bonne entente* and good will between the English and French Canadians, and the gap between the Canadian creed and the reality of conflict between the two groups seems to have narrowed. One suspects that this has been more the result of general prosperity and of the political power and improved economic position of the French Canadians than of more general acceptance of the Canadian creed by both groups. Yet there is no

doubt that the official Canadian creed has provided a legal basis for
equality of English and French Canadians and has been an important
factor in diminishing conflict.

The gap between the creed of equality of the United States which
is stated in the Declaration of Independence, in the preamble of its
Constitution, and in the Bill of Rights, and the conduct of the dominant white group toward the Negro minority is so well known that we
need not discuss it here. As Myrdal has shown so well, this creed is
contradicted by law and by the beliefs, attitudes, and practices of a
large segment of the American population. In addition, it should be
pointed out that this "American dilemma," resulting from the gap
between creed and conduct, has in the past extended—in perhaps a
less intense and less dramatic form—to almost all other minorities
in the United States. This has been true whenever and wherever conflict has been intense between a particular minority and the dominant
majority. The American creed was evaded in many ways in relation
to the Jews, especially in the early decades of this century when they
began competing in large numbers in middle-class spheres. In recent
years, the Puerto Rican migrants to New York have become victims
of this same "dilemma." It continues most strikingly, however, in the
case of the Negroes in the United States because of their greater
visibility, because of their numerical strength, and because they are
in conflict with whites on many different fronts. Yet the very presence
of the American creed has had a profound influence on the arena of
competition for Negroes and whites in the United States by providing
a legal and moral basis for the Negroes' struggle.

It is clear that many specific differences and similarities among the
minorities studied in this book can be explained by the relation of
the sources of conflict and the terms of competition in the larger
society to the adaptive capacity of the minority groups. At least in
the Americas, "the terms of competition of the larger society" have
included a traditional and often official creed advocating equality of
justice, freedom, and opportunity for all people. These idealistic
creeds have clashed with the realities of competition for the resources

and limited valuables of the larger society between minority and majority. Although it is often honored only in the breach, an idealistic
creed favorable to minorities has been a common factor present in
all of the minority-majority situations studied in this book.

We do not believe that all the features of minority-majority relationships can be explained in terms of the sources of conflict, the
terms of competition, the adaptive capacity of the minority, or in the
presence or absence of an idealistic creed favorable to the minority.
Each minority-majority situation undoubtedly contains unique historical features which cannot be subsumed under any general state-
ment. Certainly there are many more factors in the arena of competition for any particular minority than we have been able to identify.
Our purpose has not been to be exhaustive but rather to emphasize
the value of a long-range, historical, and comparative view for the
understanding of the minority phenomena.

PLURALISM OR ASSIMILATION

The future prospects for any minority group depend to a large
extent upon the ultimate aims and goals which it holds for itself.
Some time ago Louis Wirth proposed a classification of minority
groups in terms of their ultimate objectives (pp. 354–63). Following Wirth, there are four main aims which a minority may seek. First,
a minority may have *pluralistic* aims—it may seek to preserve its own
identity and culture upon a basis of tolerance of differences and
equality of opportunity. Second, a minority may have as its goal
assimilation—it may seek ultimately to lose its identity as a discrete
group and to merge with the dominant group. Third, a minority may
have *secessionist* aims, to achieve political as well as cultural independence from the dominant group (Wirth, p. 361). Finally, the
aims of a minority may be *militant*—it may not be interested in mere
toleration, assimilation, or secession, but may set as its goal political
domination over the majority and the other minorities of the society.
It would be difficult to find minorities in the New World whose ultimate aims might be classified as either secessionist or militant. At

one time there was a secessionist movement for a separate nation among the French Canadians and among American Negroes,[5] Zionism among some Jews in the United States might be considered secessionistic in its aims. But in the main, minorities with secessionistic or militant aims are characteristic of Europe and of colonial areas. Secession has been the aim of many so-called "national minorities" of Europe—the Sudeten Germans, to cite one example, certainly had militant aims in Czechoslovakia. But broadly speaking, only two alternatives seem to have been left open to minority groups in the New World, namely some form of pluralism or of assimilation.

It is, of course, very difficult to classify any specific minority by its major goals or aims. First, as Wirth points out, the members of a minority group seldom if ever have unanimous aims and goals. Disagreement or even bitter partisanship is often prevalent between factions of a minority group. There is hardly agreement, for example, among the various factions of Jews in the United States as to their ultimate objectives; some are pluralistic, some are assimilationist, and even a few might be said to be secessionist. Second, one must take into account the commonplace principle of cultural analysis that men frequently say one thing and do another. A minority group may have a traditional aim or goal, yet the trends deriving from their actions indicate another. It might be argued, for example, that the traditional stated goal of the Jews in the United States has been pluralism, yet there is a marked trend toward assimilation in their actions.

Despite these difficulties, it will be useful in our analysis to look upon the aims of pluralism on the one hand, and of assimilation on the other, as abstract and opposite poles toward which our minorities in the New World strive, but about which they are never fully in agreement. Looked at this way, these concepts provide us with a useful tool for considering the future prospects of the minority groups

[5] This was the Garveyite movement, which began in 1918 and reached its peak in 1920–21. Led by Marcus Garvey, a West Indian Negro, the movement claimed six million members but its enemies state that it never exceeded one million. Its aims were to flee the United States and return to Africa. (see Myrdal, pp. 746–49)

included among our case studies. There are different consequences which may arise from the respective attempts to reach each of these goals. Different strategies are called for in order to work toward assimilation on the one hand, or a satisfactory state of pluralism on the other. Unfortunately, many programs concerned with the problems of minority groups avoid a commitment to either of these abstract but opposite poles—pluralism or assimilation. They concern themselves solely with the problem of reducing intergroup tensions—or, in the terms of Talcott Parsons, "the indiscriminate attack on every form of existing discrimination"—without considering the ultimate consequences or working out long-term strategies for either peaceful and egalitarian pluralism or complete assimilation.

What are these consequences and long-term strategies? First, let us consider what the achievement of peaceful and egalitarian pluralism might involve and what processes are most likely to bring this about. Pluralism means a continuation of the minority as a distinct unit within the larger society. This necessarily means that either endogamy or a rule of descent (or both) will continue to function. Pluralism probably also means that ethnocentrism in at least some degree continues to play a part in minority and majority relations. There must be some acculturation in the minority group culture, but of a highly selective sort. The minority must adopt certain aspects of the culture of the dominant group and of the society at large, for some acceptance of common institutions and expected behavioral responses is necessary if the larger society is to function. On the other hand, the dominant group must recognize the distinctive cultural traits of the minority as acceptable "specialties" (i.e., behavior expected of certain groups) or "alternatives" (i.e., various responses to a given situation open to all members of the society), to use Ralph Linton's terms (pp. 272–73). In fact, some of the distinctive cultural equipment of the minority will probably need to be given new emphasis if it is to serve as a rallying point for sentiments of group solidarity. Religious traditions may, as we have seen from our case studies, be especially effective as a means of organizing and developing unity of purpose in a minority.

A satisfactory pluralistic adjustment implies not only that the dominant group will accept a minority's distinctive traits without prejudice, but also that the minority will have a more equal share in the material and nonmaterial wealth of the nation. This means that the minority must improve its power position, which may be done by legal, political, and economic means, or by strengthening the unity of the group. In the effort of a minority to achieve a satisfactory pluralistic status there is always a chance that their efforts will "backfire," and achieve only reprisals in the form of greater hostility and repression from the dominant group. This is why so many leaders of minority groups have advocated a policy of slow and cautious pressure rather than an aggressive fight against discrimination. Certainly, as we have seen, the presence of semi-autonomous, endogamous, and ethnocentric groups which are in competition for the resources or limited valuables of a society is a predisposition for conflict. It must be said that pluralism will always be fraught with danger and that the probable consequence of pluralistic aims is perpetuation of some degree of conflict between minority and majority.

On the other hand, what are the consequences and the long-term strategies involved in making assimilation the goal? Assimilation is premised upon a decline in the sentiment of attachment to the group, upon the willingness on the part of the groups' members to ignore the rules of descent and endogamy and to abandon the special cultural traits which set them off from the majority. Obviously, as we have seen from the case of the Negro in the United States, acculturation does not inevitably lead to assimilation. Still, acculturation is undoubtedly a necessary precondition for assimilation. Furthermore, those groups which are distinguished from the majority by physical traits must in time become absorbed into the larger population by miscegenation, if they are to be assimilated. Assimilation means, in the long run, that descendants of the former minority group will be allowed full and free access to all positions for which they have the personal prerequisites in the economic, social, and power hierarchies of the society. Complete assimilation implies essentially the absorption of one group by another. It is therefore often rejected with some emotional and moral indignation as "undemocratic," as denying "self-determination," and as tending toward impoverishment of human culture. Yet it must be remembered that in assimilation cultures are not obliterated, for acculturation is a two-way process and many of the values and institutions of assimilated groups become part of the emergent dominant culture. Human culture is not impoverished, for new cultures emerge. Furthermore, assimilation need not deny "self-determination," for it may be the aim of the minority itself and it may take place peacefully and without recourse to force.

These considerations of pluralism and assimilation do not constitute a special plea for either alternative, except insofar as each seems to imply opposite strategies and consequences. Each is a legitimate aim but, in fact, seldom is either fully achieved. One of the reasons why minorities always seem to fall short of their aims, aside from the fact that these aims are rarely agreed upon by the minority itself, is that minorities are subordinate to a dominant group and minority-majority relations involve two groups. As Simpson and Yinger have so ably pointed out, it is generally the interacting aims of the dominant and minority groups that determines the direction of the integration of a minority into the larger society (p. 14).[6]

How does this interaction of minority-group aims and dominant-group policy affect the minority groups in our study? Of the six minorities studied earlier, four might be classified as basically pluralistic in their aims—namely, the Indians of Brazil (with many exceptions), the Indians of Mexico, the Jews in the United States, and the French Canadians. The other two—the Negroes in the United States, and the people of color in the French West Indies—seem to have assimilation as their ultimate goal. But among the pluralistic minorities studied, at least one—the Indians of Mexico—seems to be headed for ultimate assimilation. As we have seen, the Indians of Mexico tend to resist assimilation, and many communities have been suc-

[6] Simpson and Yinger describe six major types of dominant group policy "sometimes paralleling, sometimes opposing the aims of minorities"—namely, assimilation, pluralism, legal protection, population transfer, continued subjugation, and extermination. The terms give us the key to what these policies consist of. (pp. 25–32)

cessful in doing so for over four hundred years. The process has therefore been slow. However, faced with the essentially assimilationist policy of the dominant group of Mexico and the rapid expansion of moden technology and national institutions, assimilation of the remaining Indian groups seems inevitable. The assimilation of a pluralistic minority by an assimilationist dominant group is not an easy and rapid process, as the many enclaves of American Indians in the United States illustrates.

On the other hand, the Jews in the United States and the French Canadians will probably be able to maintain—even to improve—their present relatively favorable pluralistic positions unless there is a decided reversal of trends in their respective societies. Both are faced with a dominant group which advocates, but does not aggressively instigate, assimilation; and both are subject to strong forces for acculturation to the general Canadian and American culture patterns. But a large number of Jews and French Canadians have been able to resist assimilation, and they have maintained the minority patterns and institutions necessary to do so. Both groups, on the whole, have been able to maintain endogamy as by far the most usual practice for group members. Both have kept alive a strong sense of ethnocentrism and have maintained institutions and symbols of group unity. For both, religion has been an important aspect of group unity providing a basis for group organization. But the French Canadians, and more especially the Jews, because of their pluralistic position and aims in their respective societies, are vulnerable to shifts in the aims of the dominant group toward them. It is possible to imagine, but it is hardly probable, that Canada might suddenly decide to make English the only language to be used in parliament and in schools and to do away with the local autonomy of the provinces. But as we have seen, anti-Semitism could very well flare up again in the United States. At present, however, both Canada and the United States seem to be eminently successful in regulating and reducing the tensions and conflict which might derive from the presence of these pluralistic minorities. Among the minority groups in our case studies, the Jews in the United States and the French Canadians have been the most successful in terms of their struggle for some measure of equality in the economic, political, and social life of their respective societies. In some measure, as discussed earlier, this is a result of their greater cultural preparedness for their roles but it is also in part a result of their greater unity of action in seeking a peaceful and egalitarian pluralistic adjustment.

At least one of the minorities we have classed as assimilationist in their ultimate goals, the Negroes in the United States, seems fated for at best a more satisfactory pluralistic adjustment within the larger society. Faced by the strong pluralistic policy of the dominant whites this would seem their only alternative, at least within the near future. The rule of descent imposed by the dominant group says, in effect: "Anyone with a Negro ancestor is a Negro." Thus, not even miscegenation on a wide scale would lead to assimilation. No matter how closely a Negro responds to the behavior patterns of his socio-economic class, his physical appearance (or sometimes just his ancestry) remains to place him in the minority group. Still, faced with only the alternative of a pluralistic adjustment, the Negroes in the United States have often seemed to follow a strategy (if a strategy might be said to have existed in the past) aimed at assimilation. Slavery left the Negro minority group without a distinctive living cultural tradition to serve as a basis for group unity. Divided into numerous sects, religion never provided a basis for unity of action. Acculturated to the dominant culture of the United States, the Negro has even learned to value the physical characteristics of the Caucasoid, and color prejudices among Negroes themselves have worked against group unity. In the past Negro leaders, fearful of attracting additional repression that might offset their small advances, have often advocated conciliation, patience, and even humility. Only in recent years, with the new policies and program of the National Association for the Advancement of Colored People, has a new and more realistic strategy been adopted and has a serious attempt to marshal the massive force of the large and now better educated Negro population into unity of action been made. The Negroes in the United States seem to have realized that pluralism does not necessarily mean segregation and that "separate but equal" never means "equal." They have realized that the struggle for satisfactory pluralistic adjustment necessarily involves conflict.

The prospects of coming nearer to achieving their assimilationist aims is much better for Negroes and the people of color in the French West Indies. Like the Negroes in the United States, they carry the stigma of physical traits that are symbols of ex-slave status, but they are not faced by a dominant group which has adamantly stressed color as a criterion to implement its pluralistic policy. Although the white elite of the French West Indies attempts to maintain endogamy for itself, miscegenation between whites and people of color and between people of color and Negroes has been, and continues to be, frequent. By far the largest number of people of the French West Indies are at least partly of Negroid ancestry. As people of color take over higher positions in government and industry, even the small endogamous white elite may disappear through intermarriage. All of French West Indian society would then be composed of people of color, except for the metropolitan French who might be present. Yet assimilation would not be complete, for color—or the degree of African or Caucasoid ancestry indicated by color—will continue for a long time to serve as an indication of rank. But if the process of miscegenation continues apace, and social and economic mobility can be stimulated, a time should come when color no longer is a sufficient criterion to set off one group from another in the French West Indies.

The prospects for the Brazilian Indian minority actually depend upon the aims of neither the minority or the dominant group. As indicated by the idealistic policies of the Brazilian Indian Service, the dominant Brazilian group maintains an assimilationist goal for the Indians. We have seen that, faced with the obvious technical and numerical superiority of the Brazilian civilization, many tribal groups lose faith in their own way of life and are anxious to become Brazilians. Thus, it might seem that an assimilationist minority and an assimilationist dominant group would produce a situation with a high proclivity for assimilation, but such is not always the case. Acculturation, as we have said, does not necessarily lead to assimilation, but it seems to be necessary for assimilation. The gap between the simple tribal cultures and Brazilian civilization is great, and the process of acculturation among most Brazilian tribes is slow although time is short. Many small tribal groups have disappeared—decimated by disease, alcohol, warfare, and social disorganization—before they are sufficiently acculturated to enter Brazilian society. The process is still taking place among tribes which have been "pacified" in the last twenty years. Unless the protective devices of the Indian Service are more effective in the future than in the past, the fate of most of the remaining Indians may well be decimation rather than assimilation. In fact, the few tribes that have resisted the impact of Brazilian civilization have done so by following a pluralistic, not an assimilationist, strategy. Like so many North Indian tribes, although they have acquired much of the dominant culture, they have maintained tribal endogamy and a sense of tribal unity and have retained (or were granted new) lands in the form of a reservation. Often their language and many of their old rituals serve as symbols of their distinctive group.

Neither pluralism nor assimilation can be offered as a panacea or a solution for a particular minority group. In fact, as Donald Young has pointed out:

Solutions . . . have been offered freely but not by scholars. Deportation of minorities back to Africa, the Orient, Mexico, and Europe, the exclusion of minority immigrants, extinction through 'racial degeneracy,' geographic, residential, and economic and social segregation, biological amalgamation, cultural assimilation and a 'true brotherhood of man' are among the more common panacea urged upon communities suffering from complaints as serious as race riots or as trivial as social snobbishness. (p. 578)

Yet pluralism and assimilation, although not panaceas, do offer two possible but alternate roads to the integration of a minority group into the larger society. They involve different consequences and different strategies. This fact must be kept in mind by any agency or organization devoted to the problems of minority and majority relations, and any specific program of action should be aimed at the objective it hopes to achieve. Between the two alternatives, assimilation should in the long run provide a sounder basis for a truly democratic society, for the presence of pluralistic minority groups in a society seems always to harbor the danger of conflict and of the subordination of one group by another.

The fundamental motivation of anyone interested in reading about, writing about, or studying minority groups is ultimately the practical application of this knowledge to alleviate the plight of those who suffer disadvantages of one kind or another as members of minority groups. It would be presumptuous of the present authors to set forth a specific program of action. There are literally hundreds of agencies and organizations devoted to promoting, in one way or another, intergroup harmony. Many specialists have evaluated the great variety of techniques and devices used by such agencies and organizations, and have attempted to measure their effectiveness in action (see Williams.) As social anthropologists, it is simply our hope that we may have placed the phenomena of minority-majority relations in the historical and comparative perspective offered by our discipline.

Out of our study there seems to emerge some very simple, but perhaps somewhat unpalatable, facts about minority groups. It should be kept in mind that the presence of minority groups has been a normal condition of our complex civilizations for over five thousand years. In the Americas, the incorporation of minorities has been a basic process as our societies were formed. As older minorities have become assimilated, or have reached a relatively satisfactory pluralistic adjustment, new ones have come to take their place. In all of our nations there are today minorities anxious to assimilate, while there are others eager to maintain their separateness. The presence, whether temporary or relatively permanent, of these discrete social and cultural groups within our societies poses problems for which there are no simple solutions. Pluralistic minority groups engender hostility and conflict, yet assimilation may sometimes run counter to the vested interest of the dominant group, which often has something to gain by maintaining a minority as a discrete and subordinate group. Conflict must be recognized as an inevitable and often necessary aspect of our social life. Only through some measure of conflict will the disabilities of minority groups be removed. Minorities will find no rewards, nor will our nations extend democratic rights to all citizens, without conflict in the process. Yet conflict may be regulated within the institutional framework of our societies. In a world able to harness atomic energy and even to propose voyages into space, it is hardly asking too much that we learn how to regulate the conflict arising out of different social and cultural groups in our societies, while allowing them the freedom to struggle for a more equal share in our democratic systems.

RECOMMENDED ADDITIONAL READINGS

As stated in the preface to this book, publications on ethnic and minority groups and their relations with the dominant groups of their societies are so numerous that it is next to impossible to "keep up with" the literature on the subject. Hardly a week goes by without a new publication, often significant, on some aspect of the general subject or on a particular minority group. In fact, the importance of minority groups to our societies is indicated by the vast and evergrowing literature on the subject. We do not pretend to provide a highly selected bibliography, but the following are a few general studies on minority groups which we found useful and readable. There are, of course, many others.

Baron, Milton, ed. American Minorities. New York: Knopf, 1957.
Frazer, Franklin E. Race and Culture Contacts in the Modern World. New York: Knopf, 1957.
Hughes, Everett C., and H. MacGill Hughes. Where Peoples Meet, Racial and Ethnic Frontiers. Glencoe, Ill.: Free Press, 1952.
Lind, Andrew W. Race Relations in World Perspective, Conference on Race Relations in World Perspective. Honolulu: University of Hawaii Press, 1955.
Locke, Alain, and B. J. Stern. When Peoples Meet. Rev. ed. New York: Hinds, Hayden, and Eldredge, 1946.
Park, Robert. Race and Culture. Glencoe, Ill.: Free Press, 1950.
Rose, Arnold, ed. Race Prejudice and Discrimination. New York: Knopf, 1951.
Rose, Arnold and C. B. Rose. America Divided, Minority Group Relations in the United States. New York: Knopf, 1948.

Schermerhorn, R. A. These Our People, Minorities in American Culture. Boston: D. C. Heath, 1949.

Simpson, George Eaton, and Milton Yinger. Racial and Cultural Minorities. New York: Harper, 1953.

Williams, Robin M., Jr. The Reduction of Intergroup Tensions. Bulletin 57, Social Science Research Council. New York, 1947.

Wirth, Louis, "The Problem of Minority Groups," in Ralph Linton, ed., The Science of Man in the World Crisis. New York: Columbia University Press, 1949.

Bibliography

Acción Indígenista, Boletín mensual del Instituto Nacional Indígenista (January, 1954).

Aguirre Beltrán, Gonzalo. Teoría y Práctica de la Educación Indígena. Mexico: Instituto Nacional Indígenista, 1954.

Aguirre Beltrán, Gonzalo, and A. Ricardo Pozas, "Instituciones Indígenas en el México Actual," in Alfonso Caso *et al.*, Métodos y Resultados de la Política Indígenista en México. Mexico, 1954, pp. 171–269.

American Jewish Yearbook, 1954, 1955, 1956. New York and Philadelphia: American Jewish Committee.

Aptheker, Herbert. American Negro Slave Revolts. New York: Columbia University Press, 1943.

Ashmore, H. S. The Negro and the Schools. Chapel Hill, N.C.: University of North Carolina Press, 1954.

Azevedo, Thales. Les Elites de couleur dans une ville brésilienne. Paris: UNESCO, 1953.

Baldus, Herbert, "O Professor Tiago Marquês, e O Caçador Aipobureau" Ensaios de Etnologia Brasiliera. São Paulo: 1937, pp. 163–86.

Barbosa, L. B. Horta, "Relatorio dos trabalhos realizados pelo Inspetoria do SPI durante o Ano 1916," *Revista do Museu Paulista,* VIII (1954), 59–78.

Baron, Salo. A Social and Religious History of the Jews. 1st. ed., Vols. I, II, III, New York: Columbia University Press, 1937.

Beals, Ralph. Cherán, A Sierra Tarascan Village. Washington, D.C.: Smithsonian Institute of Social Anthropology, 1946.

Beausoleil, Giles. Salaires du Quebec et de l'Ontario, Edition conjointe de la confédération des travailleurs Catholiques du Canada et du congrès canadien du travail (n.d.).

Benedict, Ruth. Race, Science and Politics. New York: Viking, 1945.

Berger, Morroe. Racial Equality and the Law. Paris: UNESCO, 1955.

Bernard, Jessie. American Community Behavior. New York: Dryden, 1949.

Boyer de Peyreleau, Eugène-Edouard. Les Antilles Françaises. Paris, 1823.

Brown, George W., ed. Canada. Berkeley: University of California Press, 1950.

Brunet, Machel, "Premieres réactiones des vaincus de 1760 devant leur vainqueurs," Revue d'histoire de l'Amérique française, VI (No. 4, 1953), 489–505.

Burt, A. L., "The British North American Colonies," in George Brown, ed., Canada. Berkeley: University of California Press, 1950, pp. 78–98.

Cash, W. J. The Mind of the South. New York: Knopf, 1941.

Caso, Alfonso, and others. Métodos y Resultados de la Política Indígenista en México. Memórias del Instituto Nacional Indígenista, Vol. VI. Mexico, 1954.

Chapin, Miriam. Quebec Now. New York: Oxford University Press, 1955.

Childe, V. Gordon. What Happened in History. London: Penguin Books, 1942.

Cline, Howard F. The United States and Mexico. Cambridge, Mass.: Harvard University Press, 1953.

Cook, Sherburne, and L. B. Simpson. The Population of Central Mexico in the Sixteenth Century. Berkeley: University of California Press, 1948.

Costa Pinto, L. A. O Negro em Rio de Janeiro, Rio de Janeiro, 1953.

Davie, Maurice R. Negroes in American Society. New York: McGraw-Hill, 1949.

Diário de Notícias (July 27, 1955), Rio de Janeiro.

Dollard, John. Caste and Class in a Southern Town. New Haven, Conn.: Yale University Press, 1937.

Dollard, John, and others. Frustration and Aggression. New Haven, Conn.: Yale University Press, 1939.

Drake, St. Clair, and Horace Cayton. Black Metropolis. New York: Harcourt Brace, 1945.

Dunn, L. C. Race and Biology. Paris: UNESCO, 1951.

Ellis, Alfred Jr. Meio Seculo de Bandeirismo. São Paulo, 1948.

Fairchild, Henry P., ed. Dictionary of Sociology. New York: McLeod, 1944.

Falardeau, Jean C., "The Changing Social Structures," in Jean C. Falardeau, ed., Essais sur le Québec Contemporain. Québec, 1953, pp. 101–122.

Faucher, Albert and Maurice Lamontagne, "History of Industrial Development," in Jean C. Falardeau, Essais sur le Québec Contemporain. Québec, 1953, pp. 145–65.

Fernandes, Florestan, and Roger Bastide, eds. Relaçoes Raciaes entre Pretos e Brancos em São Paulo, São Paulo, 1955.

Fortune, Editors of. The Jews in America. New York: Random House, 1936.

Fraser, Blair, "The Grave Inequalities of our Separate Schools," Mac-Lean's, LXVIII (May 28, 1955), pp. 9 ff.

Frazier, Edward Franklin. The Negro in the United States. New York: Macmillan, 1949.

Freyre, Gilberto. The Masters and the Slaves. New York: Knopf, 1946.

Fuente, Julio de la, "Ethnic and Communal Relations," in Sol Tax and others, Heritage of Conquest. Glencoe, Ill.: Free Press, 1952, pp. 76–96.

——, "Cambios Socio-Culturales en México," Acta-Anthropologica, III (December, 1948).

Gans, Herbert, "The Future of the American Jewry," Commentary, XXI (June, 1956), 555–63.

Garigue, Philip, "French Canadian Kinship and Urban Life," American Anthropologist, LVIII (December, 1956), 1090–1101.

Gerin, Léon. Le Type Economique et Social des Canadiens. Montreal, 1938.

Gordon, Albert I. Jews in Transition. Minneapolis: University of Minnesota Press, 1949.

Grant, Madison. The Passing of the Great Race. New York: Scribner, 1918.

Groulx, Lionel. Notre Maître, le passé. Montreal, 1937.

Handlin, Oscar. Adventure in Freedom, Three Hundred Years of Jewish Life in America. New York: McGraw-Hill, 1954.

——. The Uprooted. Boston: Little Brown, 1951.

Hearn, Lafcadio. Two Years in the French West Indies. New York: Harper, 1890.

Henriques, Fernando. Family and Colour in Jamaica. London, 1953.

Herberg, Will. Protestant—Catholic—Jew. New York: Doubleday, 1955.
Herskovits, Melville. The Myth of the Negro Past. New York: Harper, 1941.
Hohenthal, W. D., and Thomas McCorkle, "The Problem of Aboriginal Persistence," *Southwestern Journal of Anthropology,* XI (Autumn, 1955), 288–300.
Hope, John. Negro Employment in Three Southern Plants of the International Harvester Company. Washington, D.C.: National Planning Association, 1954.
Horowitz, Eugene L., " 'Race' Attitudes," in Otto Klineberg, ed., Characteristics of the American Negro. New York: Harper, 1944, pp. 141–247.
Hughes, Everett C. French Canada in Transition. Chicago: University of Chicago Press, 1943.
Hughes, Everett C., and H. MacGill Hughes. Where Peoples Meet. Glencoe, Ill.: Free Press, 1952.
Innis, H. A., "Fundamental and Historic Elements," in George Brown, ed., Canada. Berkeley: University of California Press, 1950, pp. 155–64.
Johnson, Charles S. Patterns of Negro Segregation. New York: Harper, 1943.
Kennedy, Raymond, "The Colonial Crisis and the Future," in Ralph Linton, ed., The Science of Man in the World Crisis. New York: Columbia University Press, 1945, pp. 307–46.
Klineberg, Otto. Characteristics of the American Negro. New York: Harper, 1944.
———. *Tensions Affecting International Understanding.* Bulletin 62, Social Science Research Council. New York, 1950.
Kubler, George, "The Quechua in the Colonial World," in Julian Steward, ed., Handbook of South American Indians, II, 334–38. Washington, D.C.: Bureau of American Ethnology, 1946.
Labat, Jean Baptiste. Voyages aux isles de l'Amérique, (Antilles), 1693–1705. Vols. I, II, Paris, 1931.
La Hontan, Armand Louis. New Voyages to North-America. Ed. by Reuben Gold Thwaites. Chicago, 1905.
Lanctot, Gustave. Les Canadiens français et leurs voisin du sud. Montreal, 1941.
La Porte, Pierre, "Le Scandale de Pontiac," *Le Devoir, supplément du dimanche* (July 23, 1955), Montreal.
———, "Pontiac, terre abondonnée," *Le Devoir, supplément du dimanche* (July 11, 12, and 13, 1955), Montreal.

Learsi, Rufus [Israel Goldberg]. The Jews in America, a History. Cleveland: World Publishing Co., 1954.

Leiris, Michel. Contacts de Civilisations en Martinique et en Guadeloupe, Paris: UNESCO, 1955.

——. Race and Culture. Paris: UNESCO, 1951.

Leite, Serafin. História de Companhia de Jesuitas no Brasil, Vol. II. Lisbon, 1939.

Lestchinsky, Jacob, "Economic and Social Development of American Jewry," *The Jewish People, Past and Present,* Jewish Encyclopedic Handbooks, IV, 1–77. New York: Marstin Press, 1955.

Lévi-Strauss, Claude. Les Structures élémentaires de la parenté. Paris, 1949.

Lewis, Oscar, "Social Change in Mexico Since 1940" (unpublished paper).

Lindgren, E. J., "An Example of Culture Contact without Conflict," *American Anthropologist,* XV (1938), 605–21.

Linton, Ralph. The Study of Man. New York: Appleton-Century, 1936.

Lortie, Léon, "Le Système Scolaire," in Jean C. Falardeau, ed., Essais sur le Québec Contemporain. Québec, 1953, pp. 170–86.

Lower, Arthur, "Religion and Religious Institutions," in George Brown, ed., Canada. Berkeley: University of California Press, 1950, pp. 457–86.

——. Colony to Nation, A History of Canada. Toronto, London and New York: Longmans, Green, 1949.

McDonagh, Edward C., and E. S. Richards. Ethnic Relations in the United States, New York: Appleton-Century, 1953.

McWilliams, Carey. A Mask for Privilege, Anti-Semitism in America. Boston: Little Brown, 1948.

Marchant, Alexander. From Barter to Slavery. Baltimore: Johns Hopkins Press, 1942.

Marden, Charles F. Minorities in American Society. New York: American Book Co., 1952.

Mead, Margaret. New Lives for Old, Cultural Transformation—Manus, 1928–1953. New York: William Morrow, 1956.

Melo Franco, Afonso Arinos de. O Indio Brasileiro e a Revolução Francesa. Rio de Janeiro, 1937.

Merton, Robert. "Discrimination and the American Creed," in R. M. MacIver, ed., Discrimination and National Welfare, New York: Harper, 1944, pp. 99–126.

Miner, Horace. St. Denis, A French Canadian Parish. Chicago: University of Chicago Press, 1939.

Moreau de Saint-Méry. Description de la partie française de l'Isle Saint-Domingue. Philadelphia, 1797–98.

Murphy, Gardner. In the Minds of Men, The Study of Human Behavior and Social Tensions in India. New York: Basic Books, 1953.

Myrdal, Gunnar. An American Dilemma, The Negro Problem and Modern Democracy. New York: Harper, 1944.

Nash, Roy. The Conquest of Brazil. New York: Harcourt Brace, 1926.

Navarro, Moisés González, "Instituciones Indígenas en México Independiente," in Alfonso Caso *et al.*, Métodos y Resultados de la Política Indígenista en México. Mexico, 1954, pp. 113–67.

Park, Robert. Race and Culture, Glencoe, Ill.: Free Press, 1950.

Parkman, Francis. The Old Regime in Canada, Vol. II. Boston: Little Brown, 1897.

Parra, Manuel, and Alfonso Caso. Densidade de la Poblacion de Habla Indigena en la Republica Mexicana. Memórias del Instituto Nacional Indígenista, Vol. I, 1950.

Philémon, Césaire. Galeries martiniquaises, Paris, 1931.

Pierson, Donald. Negroes in Brazil. Chicago: University of Chicago Press, 1942.

Pope, Liston, "Religion and Class Structure," in Milton Baron, ed., American Minorities. New York: Knopf, 1957, pp. 353–63.

Powdermaker, Hortense. After Freedom, A Cultural Study in the Deep South. New York: Viking, 1939.

Redfield, Robert. The Primitive World and Its Transformations. Ithaca, N.Y.: Cornell University Press, 1953.

Reich, Nathan, "The Economic Structure of Modern Jewry," in Louis Finkelstein, ed., The Jews, Their History, Culture, and Religion, Vol. IV. Philadelphia: Jewish Publication Society of America, 1949, pp. 1239–66.

——, "Economic Trends," in Oscar I. Janowsky, ed., The American Jew. New York: Harper, 1942, pp. 161–82.

Revert, Eugène. La France d'Amérique, Martinique, Guadeloupe, Guyane, Saint-Pierre et Miquelon. Paris, 1949.

Ribeiro, Darcy, "Assimilação dos Indios do Brasil," MS. submitted to UNESCO. Paris.

——, "Convivio e Contaminção," *Sociologia,* XVIII (March, 1956), 3–50. São Paulo.

Rious, Marcel. Description de la Culture de l'Ile Verte. Ottawa, 1954. Bulletin No. 133 of the National Museum of Canada.

Rondon, Candido Mariano da Silva. Lectures on the Rondon-Roosevelt Scientific Expedition. Translated by R. G. Rudy and Edward Tiung. Rio de Janeiro, 1916.

Rose, Arnold, ed. Race Prejudice and Discrimination. New York: Knopf, 1951.

Rose, Arnold, and C. B. Rose. America Divided. New York: Knopf, 1948.

Rosenblat, Angel. La Población Indigena de America, desde 1492 hasta la actualidad. Buenos Aires, 1945.

Ross, Aileen D., "French and English Canadian Contacts and Institutional Change," The Canadian Journal of Economics and Political Science, XX (No. 3, 1954), pp. 281–95.

Rowe, John, "Inca Culture at the Time of the Spanish Conquest," in Julian Steward, ed., Handbook of South American Indians, Vol. II. Washington, D.C.: Bureau of American Ethnology, 1946.

Ruiz, U. Ramón Eduardo, "The Struggle for a National Culture in Education," in Estudios Antropológicas publicados en homenaje al doctor Manuel Gamio. Mexico, 1956, pp. 473–90.

Sanders, Wilfrid. Jack and Jacques, A Scientific Approach to the Study of French and Non-French Thought in Canada. Toronto, 1943.

Schaden, Egon. Aspectos Fundamentais de Cultura Guaraní. Faculdade de Filosofia, Ciencias, e Letras da Universidade de São Paulo, Bulletin No. 188. São Paulo, 1954.

Schermerhorn, Richard Alonzo. These Our People, Minorities in American Culture. Boston: D. C. Heath, 1949.

Senturia, Joseph J., "Mass Expulsion," in Encyclopedia of the Social Sciences, X, 185–89. New York, Macmillan, 1942.

Shanks, Hershel, "Jewish-Gentile Intermarriage, Facts and Trends," Commentary, XVI (October, 1953), 370–75.

Simpson, G. E., and J. Milton Yinger. Racial and Cultural Minorities. New York: Harper, 1953.

Soares de Souza, Gabriel. Notícia do Brasil, Vols. I, II. São Paulo (n.d.).

Tannenbaum, Frank. Mexico, the Struggle for Peace and Bread. New York: Knopf, 1951.

——. Slave or Citizen, The Negro in the Americas. New York: Knopf, 1947.

Tax, Sol, and others. Heritage of Conquest. Glencoe, Ill.: Free Press, 1952.

Underhill, Frank H., "Political Parties and Ideas," in George Brown, ed., Canada. Berkeley: University of California Press, 1950, pp. 331–52.

United Nations Commission on Human Rights, Subcommission on Prevention of Discrimination and Protection of Minorities. Definition and Classification of Minorities. Lake Success, New York, 1950.

Vance, Rupert, "Racial Competition for the Land," in Edgar Thompson, ed., Race Relations and the Race Problem. Durham, N.C.: Duke University Press, 1939, pp. 97–124.

Wade, Mason. The French Canadians, 1760–1945. Toronto, 1955.

Wade, Mason, "Political Trends," in Jean C. Falardeau, ed., Essais sur la Québec Contemporain. Québec, 1953.

Wagley, Charles, "The Indian Heritage of Brazil," in T. Lynn Smith and Alexander Marchant, eds., Brazil, Portrait of Half a Continent. New York: Dryden, 1951.

Wagley, Charles, ed. Race and Class in Rural Brazil. Paris: UNESCO, 1952.

Wagley, Charles, and Eduardo Galvão. The Tenetehara Indians of Brazil. New York: Columbia University Press, 1949.

Walker, H. J., "Changes in the Status of the Negro in American Society," International Social Science Bulletin, IX (No. 4, 1957), 438–74.

Wallace, Anthony, "Revitalization Movements," American Anthropologist, LVIII (No. 2, 1956), pp. 264–81.

Walter, Paul A. F. Race and Cultural Relations. New York: McGraw-Hill, 1952.

Ware, Caroline, "Ethnic Communities," Encyclopedia of Social Sciences, V, 613–14. New York: Macmillan, 1942.

Warner, W. Lloyd, and Leo Srole. The Social Systems of American Ethnic Groups. New Haven, Conn.: Yale University Press, 1945.

Watson, James. Cayuá Culture Change. Memoir of the American Anthropological Association, No. 73. Menasha, Wisconsin, 1952.

Weintraub, Ruth. How Secure These Rights? Anti-Semitism in the United States in 1948. New York: Doubleday, 1949.

Whetten, Nathan. Rural Mexico. Chicago: University of Chicago Press, 1948.

Williams, Robin M. Jr. The Reduction of Intergroup Tensions, A Survey of Research on Problems of Ethnic, Racial and Religious Group Relations. Bulletin 57, Social Science Research Council. New York, 1947.

Wirth, Louis, "The Problem of Minority Groups," in Ralph Linton, ed., The Science of Man in the World Crisis. New York: Columbia University Press, 1945, pp. 347–72.

Wirth, Louis, and Herbert Goldhamer, "Negro-White Intermarriage in Recent Times," in Otto Klineberg, ed., The Characteristics of the American Negro. New York, 1944, pp. 276–300.

——, "Passing," in Otto Klineberg, ed., The Characteristics of the American Negro. New York: Harper, 1944, pp. 301–20.

Wolfe, Eric, "Aspects of Group Relations in a Complex Society, Mexico," American Anthropologist, LVIII (December, 1956), 1065–78.

Young, Donald. American Minority Groups. New York: Harper, 1932.

Zavala, Silvio, and José Miranda, "Instituciones Indígenas en la Colonia," in Alfonso Caso et al., Métodos y Resultados de La Política Indígenista en México. Mexico, 1954, pp. 29–93.

Index